IS-LM and Modern Macroeconomics

RECENT ECONOMIC THOUGHT SERIES

Other books in the series:

Well, Paul: POST-KEYNESIAN ECONOMIC THEORY
Schofield, Norman: COLLECTIVE DECISION-MAKING: SOCIAL CHOICE AND POLITICAL ECONOMY
Menchik, Paul L.: HOUSEHOLD AND FAMILY ECONOMICS
Gupta, Kanhaya L.: EXPERIENCES WITH FINANCIAL LIBERALIZATION
Cohen, Avi J.; Hagemann, Harald; and Smithin, John: MONEY, FINANCIAL INSTITUTIONS AND MACROECONOMICS
Mason, P.L. and Williams, R.M.: RACE, MARKETS AND SOCIAL OUTCOMES
Gupta, Satya Dev: THE POLITICAL ECONOMY OF GLOBALIZATION
Fisher, R.C.: INTERGOVERNMENTAL FISCAL RELATIONS
Mariussen, Å. and Wheelock, J.: HOUSEHOLDS, WORK AND ECONOMIC CHANGE: A COMPARATIVE INSTITUTIONAL PERSPECTIVE
Gupta, Satya Dev: GLOBALIZATION, GROWTH AND SUSTAINABILITY
Gupta, Satya Dev: DYNAMICS OF GLOBALIZATION AND DEVELOPMENT
Medema, Steven G.: COASEAN ECONOMICS: LAW AND ECONOMICS AND THE NEW INSTITUTIONAL ECONOMICS
Peoples, James: REGULATORY REFORM AND LABOR MARKETS
Dennis, Ken: RATIONALITY IN ECONOMICS: ALTERNATIVE PERSPECTIVES
Ahiakpor, James C.W.: KEYNES AND THE CLASSICS RECONSIDERED
Wolfson, Murray: THE POLITICAL ECONOMY OF WAR AND PEACE
Jain, A.K.: ECONOMICS OF CORRUPTION
Wheelock, J. and Vail, J.: WORK AND IDLENESS: THE POLITICAL ECONOMY OF FULL EMPLOYMENT
Dean, James M. and Waterman, A.M.C.: RELIGION AND ECONOMICS: NORMATIVE SOCIAL THEORY
Gupta, Kanhaya: FOREIGN AID: NEW PERSPECTIVES
MacDonald, R. and Stein, J.: EQUILIBIRUM EXCHANGE RATES
Chilcote, Ronald M.: THE POLITICAL ECONOMY OF IMPERIALISM: CRITICAL APPRAISALS
Silber, Jacques: HANDBOOK ON INCOME INEQUALITY MEASUREMENT
Elsner, W. and Groenewegen, J.: INDUSTRIAL POLICIES AFTER 2000

IS-LM and Modern Macroeconomics

edited by

Warren Young
Ben Zion Zilberfarb
Department of Economics
Bar Ilan University
Israel

SPRINGER SCIENCE+BUSINESS MEDIA, LLC

Library of Congress Cataloging-in-Publication Data

IS-LM and modern macroeconomics / edited by Warren Young, Ben Zion Zilberfarb.
p. cm. -- (Recent economic thought series)
Includes bibliographical references and index.
ISBN 978-0-7923-7966-9 ISBN 978-94-010-0644-6 (eBook)
DOI 10.1007/978-94-010-0644-6
1. IS-LM model (Macroeconomics) 2. Macroeconomics. I. Young, Warren, 1949- II. Zilberfarb, Benzion. III. Series.

HB172.5 .I8 2000
339--dc21 00-048786

Printed on acid-free paper.

Dedication

For our daughters:

Shani and Natalie;

Shelly, Ella Vered, Noa, and Rachel

TABLE OF CONTENTS

List of Contributors

Huw Dixon	University of York, UK
Bill Gerrard	University of Leeds, UK
David Colander	Middlebury College, USA
David Heathfield	University of Southampton, UK
Ingo Barens	Bergische Universitaet, Wuppertal, Germany
Colin Rogers	University of Adelaide, Australia
T.K. Rymes	Carleton University, USA
Bruce Littleboy	University of Queensland, Australia
Bert Hickman	Stanford University, USA
Robert Dimand	Brock University, Canada
J.W. Nevile	University of New South Wales, Australia
L.R. Klein	Nobel Laureate, University of Pennsylvania, USA

PREFACE

IS-LM is perhaps the prime example of "cognitive dissonance" in economics, and as the subject of this book, it is problematic to many economists. On the one hand, the IS-LM model is still taught by many academic economists or they use it to derive the AD-AS approach. On the other hand, the same economists realize the limitations of the basic IS-LM model and would not now use it for policy analysis, as they did in the past. The distinction between pedagogical and analytical efficacy is made by all the authors in this volume regarding the IS-LM model. Indeed, even those who would reject using the model for modern policy analysis still see the basic model as useful for teaching purposes. Moreover, in an ***augmented form***, some of the authors in this volume would even see fit to use IS-LM for modern policy analysis. As will be seen, therefore, the IS-LM model is "not yet dead". Rather, as one of the editors put it some years ago, the model's "plasticity" has enabled it to undergo a metamorphosis into ***augmented form,*** enabling its continuing utilization in economics accordingly.

At this point, we would like to thank all the authors of the papers in this volume for their support in seeing the project through. We would also like to thank Helen Ovadia for retyping the manuscripts and Kluwer Press for its patience in waiting for the final product to be produced.

Warren Young
Ben Zion Zilberfarb
Department of Economics
Bar Ilan University, Ramat Gan, Israel
June 2000

INTRODUCTION: QUO VADIS IS-LM?

IS-LM has been described in a number of ways. Dornbusch and Fischer termed it the "core of modern macroeconomics", Patinkin deemed it as the "central message" of Keynes, Solow called it "the trained intuition" of the economics profession, while one of the editors of this volume described it as a "chimera". The focus of the essays presented in this book is, in the main, on the closed-economy version of IS-LM, as against the open economy Mundell-Fleming approach. The reasons for this, in our view, are clear. Firstly, the closed economy model developed almost *two decades prior* to the Mundell-Fleming model. Indeed, the Mundell-Fleming model has its *own* history and development. Secondly, the open economy model is only one example of IS-LM's "chameleonic nature" or, as the present editors would now say, its "putty" characteristic, that is to say, its ability to be *"augmented"*. Thirdly, IS-LM is, in our view, essentially a *general equilibrium model* and therein lies its ability to serve not only as the basis of the development of more sophisticated *general equilibrium macromodels*, ranging from Patinkin through AD-AS, but *enables* its *augmentation* via rational expectations into a *long-run "full employment" model.* It is as if IS-LM did not exist, to paraphrase the old saying, "its invention" would be *"warranted"*; and this, due to its *androgynous* nature, combining the "Classics" and Keynes. There are a number of *key* issues, therefore, that must be dealt with here. Among these are:

- whether Macroeconomics will *continue to develop with* IS-LM as its "core" model;
- whether or not the IS-LM model is "dead" or still "alive", albeit in *augmented form*; and, if "dead", can be resurrected by *augmentation*;
- whether Macroeconomics *could have developed without* IS-LM and related elements, such as the Aggregate Demand and Supply Curves.

We have deliberately opened the volume with an important survey essay by Dixon and Gerrard focusing on "Old, New and Post Keynesian Perspectives", which calls into question the very efficacy of what they call "the IS-LM framework" for modern macroeconomics. Their "general conclusions", given at the beginning of their paper, are "that the IS-LM model has become a largely irrelevant framework in mainstream economics" and "to a certain extent, the IS-LM model is 'dead' as a framework for contemporary macroeconomic research". In the concluding section of their paper, they reiterate these statements, saying that "the IS-LM model has become marginalized ... [and] has gone out of fashion in modern mainstream macroeconomics". But they end their paper by saying that "An *augmented* IS-LM model [our emphasis], based on the microeconomics of intertemporal optimization and allowing for the supply of output to be directly affected by labor-supply adjustments in response to changes in the rate of interest, may feature more prominently in the near future, in the textbooks at least". In this essay, Dixon and Gerrard do not discuss in detail the Monetarist and New Classical models, even though as they note, these approaches initially utilized an IS-LM framework in their debate with the Keynesian approach. What Dixon and Gerrard do stress, however, is that IS-LM has been "augmented" in the past, and –in its augmented form—will remain an important part of the analytical toolkit of economists, at least at the pedagogical level.

The essay following Dixon and Gerrard, by Colander, actually *complements,* rather than contradicts their final conclusion regarding the pedagogical efficacy of the augmented form of IS-LM. In his essay, Colander tries to outline the relationship between his vision of "Post Walrasian Macroeconomics" and IS-LM from the perspective of "the pedagogical use of the IS-LM framework". What Colander attempts to do in his paper is to synthesize, as he puts it "the vision of traditional macroeconomists such as Tobin, Friedman, Keynes, Hayek, and Lerner" with the IS-LM framework to develop what he calls "Post Walrasian IS/LM analysis" for pedagogical purposes. Colander's augmented IS-LM model, therefore, encompasses "complex dynamics" and its related "multiple equilibria", and is one which "can change the pedagogical use of IS/LM analysis"; something which, as we said, actually *complements* the Dixon-Gerrard approach.

The two papers that follow, by Heathfield and Barens respectively, deal with the issue of Aggregate Demand. This is an important issue, for as Dixon and Gerrard write "the IS-LM model still appears in undergraduate macroeconomic textbooks but increasingly it is used as a mere stepping stone in the construction of the aggregate demand schedule". In Heathfield's view, "supply side dominance" has resulted in the neglect of demand "policies". In his paper, he proceeds to develop a model based upon neo-classical assumptions with fully flexible prices and wages, perfect competition, profit maximization, full information, an auctioneer and a "well behaved" aggregate production function. And this, as he writes in his conclusion, in order to "focus attention on what might be meant by a Keynesian aggregate demand curve and to demonstrate its use in explaining persistent, involuntary unemployment in…flexible price models which obey all the usual assumptions of the neo-classical model".

In his paper, Barens takes the position that the "Aggregate Demand Curve" does not necessarily follow from the IS-LM model of *"Hicksian"* vintage. Rather, in Baren's view, its introduction "to augment the fix price IS-LM analysis of macroeconomics textbooks to allow" the discussion of "the endogenous determination of the price level" has, in his opinion, raised more "problems" than it has solved, especially on the pedagogical level. Barens attempts to show that "if one adheres to the modeling approach" as it appears in the *original Hicksian model* , not only is the "textbook" Aggregate Demand Curve "not needed for the determination of the price level", but that it "cannot even be constructed". In other words, as Barens notes, if IS represents goods market equilibrium "the textbook AD cannot be constructed". If, on the other hand, "the IS curve is *not* constructed to be the goods market equilibrium curve—as is the case in many textbooks—one may derive the textbook AD curve". This raises the question, as Barens puts it "What is this textbook AD curve?" and Barens attempts not only to provide the answer but to show that there is a basic disjunction between "the dis-equilibrium story" extant in AD-AS augmented IS-LM, and "the underlying [Hicksian] equilibrium model, as he sees it.

In their paper "On 'Money' in IS-LM and AD-AS Models", Rymes and Rogers argue that, in effect, "the 'money' in the IS-LM and AD-AS model no longer exists...There are no longer any nominal anchors, rather they have been replaced by discretionary policy". The "major point" of their paper "is that the stock of nominal fiat high powered money has vanished in modern monetary economics". By "reconstruction of IS-LM and AD-AS analysis" without a "nominal anchor", they present a simple model where there are no "real balance" effects and where there are "no price level forces re-equilibrating the economy". On this basis, they conclude that "the LM portion of IS-LM has vanished". Within the assumptions of their model, Rymes and Rogers have, in fact, created a *new* augmented form of IS-LM. In their model, AD augmentation emanated *not* from the LM curve and real balance effects—as in New Classical and New Keynesian economics, in their view—but from the institutional structure and the provision of services by the Central Bank. The central message of their approach, that is "that central banks are fundamentals", has implications which call into question the premises underlying Keynesian and New Classical approaches alike.

The next two papers, by Littleboy and Hickman respectively, deal with the re-appraisal of IS-LM as Keynes' "central message" on the one hand, and its application as the "core" of Keynesian-based macroeconometric models on the other. These themes characterized the period up to what can be called the "Rational Expectations Revolution in Macroeconomics", although the use of IS-LM as a "core model" in macroeconometrics is still justified, at least in Hickman's view. Littleboy's paper "argues that Leijonhufvud's critique of textbook Keynesianism [IS-LM] is even more valid now than it was" when it was published over three decades ago. Littleboy examines the debate between Leijonhufvud and Samuelson regarding IS-LM as the "core model" of the Keynesian approach, and brings in Solow's arguments to show that, as he puts it "in careful hands, IS-LM still has some value as an instrument of analysis".

In his paper, Hickman takes a position opposite to that of Littleboy, when he says that after six decades, Hicks' "mathematical formulation of the core" of Keynes' approach "remains solidly lodged in macroeconomics textbooks as the basic theoretical paradigm", going on to say that the "principal theme" of his paper "is that the IS-LM apparatus"—when *augmented* by AD-AS—"provides a fruitful approach to the analysis of the structures of mainstream macroeconometric models and their forecasting and simulation properties". Hickman maintains that "most structural econometric models are disaggregated IS-LM systems...so that it is natural to interpret their properties in terms of the IS-LM, AD-AS model". He concludes that the method he proposes, that is "IS-LM and AD-AS decomposition" can "accommodate a wide range of model specifications", including "rational expectations in financial markets" and "instantaneous market clearing", and "can be applied even to avowedly nonstructural VAR models which incorporate prices and interest rates along with real variables". In other words, with regard to macroeconometric models, in Hickman's view, at least, the IS-LM approach provides what we would call a "*portmanteau*" framework.

The next set of papers, by Dimand and Neville respectively, deal with two ostensibly distinct—albeit upon reflection interconnected—questions: whether macroeconomics could have developed without IS-LM; and what Keynes would have thought about IS-LM. In what he calls "a counterfactual", Dimand sets out "other paths" in the development of macroeconomics if the early algebraic representations of Keynes's system—including that of Keynes himself in his 1934 lectures—had not become "the trained intuition of macroeconomists", that is, as he puts it, "in the absence of IS-LM". Among these were the "Z-D diagram", that is the Aggregate Supply(Z) and Aggregate Demand (D) functions as they appear in Chapter 3 of Keynes's *General Theory*, although Keynes himself "did not illustrate this by a diagram", as Dimand duly notes. He continues on to say, however, that "in the absence of IS-LM, the vast controversial literature about Keynes's *General Theory* would very likely have used Keynes's own Z and D notation, and drawn the diagram implied by his remark about the intersection of the function" as "the only readily apparent Keynesian alternative to IS-LM was the Z-D framework". However, as Dimand then shows, there were other alternatives to the Keynesian approach to macroeconomics. These included the multiplier-accelerator models of Samuelson and Tinbergen, the mathematical models of business cycles of Frisch, Tinbergen, and Kalecki, and the monetary models of Fisher. According to Dimand, Fisher "far more" than either Pigou or Hayek "provided an available non-Keynesian source for macroeconomics in a counterfactual world lacking IS-LM". Dimand concludes that the three possible alternatives to IS-LM: the Z-D approach; business-cycle theory; and the monetary theory of fluctuations "would have been considerably more prominent in the postwar era had the conveniently teachable IS-LM framework not swept the discipline", and thus it was IS-LM, as he puts it, the "tractable, teachable apparatus" that "became the trained intuition" that Solow and Tobin earlier described.

Nevile's paper tries to answer the question "what Keynes would have thought of the development of ISLM? ". In his view, "while Keynes may not have gone as far as some of his disciples in rejecting IS-LM in the way it was used in the 1950s and 1960s—the way ISLM has been used in the last decade or so would have been rejected outright by Keynes as completely against the central message of the *General Theory*". Nevile goes on to outline his view of "what Keynes was saying in the *General Theory*" with an emphasis on his theory of employment and output on the one hand, and his liquidity preference theory of interest on the other. He then deals with how Keynes would have reacted to the development of ISLM in the 1950s through the 1990s. Nevile duly notes that "there is no difference between the neo-Keynesians and the neo-Classical economists in their use of ISLM", and concludes that "Keynes' way of doing economics was fundamentally Marshallian. ISLM is not. Like most modern economic theory it is fundamentally Walrasian". Again, it is not surprising, therefore, that as a *model* it came to dominate modern macroeconomic theory.

The penultimate contribution to this volume is by Klein, one of the fathers of modern macroeconometrics and one of the earliest chroniclers of the "Keynesian Revolution" . In his seminal paper "The IS-LM Model: its Role in Macroeconomics", Klein notes that in the period after the publication of Keynes' *General Theory*, "a clear understanding" of its "theory and message was provided through the medium of compact mathematical models that were capable of being solved for major macroeconomic magnitudes". Klein describes the model of Hicksian vintage—comprising the IS-LM equations and diagram—stressing that "the diagram is the pair of *implicit* relations between interest and income" and also that the position of the two curves "depends on monetary and fiscal policy". He goes on to say, however, that the model of Hicksian vintage also has, as he puts it, "a deficiency", in that "it makes sense in nominal terms" only, that is to say "the interest rate is the nominal rate if the whole analysis is in nominal terms". This, of course, follows from the fact that Hicks' original approach *was* in nominal terms.

Klein therefore suggests taking "another route", that is to "think of the ISLM equations as a *real* system". But if this is done, then it is also necessary to either assume a fixed price or to add another pair of equations—real Aggregate Demand and Supply, each depending upon "the general price level"—to provide a solution for the price level *itself.* Klein goes on to say that in this case "the elegant simplicity" of the *original* model of Hicksian vintage "is lost", and in addition, "there is a problem in justifying" such an approach. For, as he puts it "one would be very hard put to derive these two functions explicitly from macroeconomic principles and straightforward aggregation". Klein therefore suggests another alternative to deal "explicitly with the price-level problem", that is, an *augmented "stylized* system" with what he calls a "realistic ISLM core". Klein makes the convincing argument that it has more pedagogical and analytical efficacy than the "three-equation log-linear model", as Hahn once put it, advocated by some proponents of the Rational Expectations approach to Macroeconomics. And, in concise and lucid terms, Klein proceeds to outline his suggested "small system" approach, concluding that it is not only a "good teaching device" at *all* levels, but also a system "capable of generating realistic values" for "quick" research purposes.

But perhaps the most important point that Klein makes in his paper involves his "stress on realism". For, as he says "the ISLM construct is enduring and very useful, especially as a pedagogical device...originally, the concept was introduced...without numerical parameter values and without regard to the correspondence between observation and theory". Such an *application* of the ISLM model can only proceed, however, as Klein shows, if we "enhance" it, as he puts it, that is, *if it is augmented.*

Thus, we have indeed come full circle, from Dixon and Gerrard, who doubt whether a *pure Walrasian-based general equilibrium approach to macroeconomics* such as IS-LM can be utilized for modern macrotheory, advocating—albeit in different terms—a "post-Walrasian" framework; via the debate between Heathfield and Barens as to the efficacy of the Aggregate Demand curve as a means by which to augment IS, to the critiques of Rymes and Rogers, who question the "existence" of LM, and that of Littleboy, who reinterprets Leijonhufvud's criticism of the model as a whole; and then on to Hickman, who sees efficacy in its macroeconometric application, to the contributions of Dimand, who maintains that macroeconomics could have proceeded without it, and that of Nevile, who asserts that Keynes would not have accepted it in its *augmented form*; and finally to Klein, who *shows that only in its augmented form does the model and its core have a future*. In this context, therefore, let us leave the last word to Fischer, who agrees with Klein, and who wrote, over a decade ago (1987, p247 n.6)

The versatility of the model is responsible for its survival; it can be used to analyze both monetary and fiscal policy in both full employment and unemployment modes; it can generate quantity theory or pure Keynesian results with only minor modifications. The model is capable of accommodating monetarist and Keynesian views, as Friedman's (1970) theoretical framework shows. In my view it can also accommodate a basic rational expectations-market clearing view, although I am not sure adherents of that approach would agree.

REFERENCES

Fischer, Stanley, 1987. "1944,1963 and 1985" in *Macroeconomics and Finance: Essays in Honor of Franco Modigliani*, edited by R. Dornbusch, S. Fischer and J. Bossons, Cambridge: MIT Press.

1

OLD, NEW AND POST KEYNESIAN PERSPECTIVES ON THE IS-LM FRAMEWORK: A CONTRAST AND EVALUATION

Huw Dixon and Bill Gerrard

1.1 INTRODUCTION

The IS-LM framework has been the standard model used for understanding and teaching Keynesian macroeconomics since 1960. Indeed, even a monetarist such as Friedman could subscribe to a modified version of the IS-LM model (1970); Sargent and Wallace (1975) formulated the first New Classical neutrality proposition with an IS-LM model of aggregate demand. The main decisive break from this tradition was Barro's textbook, *Macroeconomics*, whose first edition was 1984. This relegated the IS-LM analysis to an afterthought at the end of the book; the bulk of the textbook was devoted to the market clearing intertemporal equilibrium approach to macroeconomics, which had its origins in the work of Lucas and Rapping (1969). In this paper we trace a brief history of the IS-LM framework, and how it has been reinterpreted over the last few decades by economists of an essentially "Keynesian" viewpoint.

The IS-LM model was developed as a way of understanding Keynes's General Theory. What defines the IS-LM approach? There are two crucial factors:

1. Output is an endogenous variable which is demand-determined.
2. The rate of interest is an endogenous variable, and affects both the demand for goods (investment and possibly consumption) and the demand for money.

The IS-LM model can be viewed either as merely a model of aggregate demand (as in the AD-AS model), in which case (1) becomes the demand for output. Alternatively, the IS-LM model can be viewed as a model of the output determination (implicitly including the supply side).

The main driving force behind the reinterpretations of the IS-LM model has been an attempt to provide it with some sort of microfoundations. When Keynes formulated the General Theory and related writings, the relationship between the new macroeconomic approach that he pioneered and traditional microeconomics (price theory or general equilibrium analysis) was unclear. The whole thrust of research in macroeconomics since the Second World War has been to try to integrate our understanding of macroeconomic systems with our understanding of microeconomics.

This paper examines several successive waves in this enterprise: from Hick's original formulation of the IS-LM model, through the work of Hansen and Patinkin to the 1960's textbook (exemplified by Ackley), to the Keynesian reappraisal of the 1960's and the resultant fix-price approach of the 1970's, to New Keynesian economics of the 1980s. Of course, the division of time and people into these compartments is a little false; for example, part of the Keynesian reappraisal was presaged by Patinkin's analysis of quantity constraints in the 1950's. We will not be paying much attention to Monetarist and New Classical thought in all of this. This is not because it is unimportant. Clearly "classical" thought had reemerged by 1980 as the dominant school of macroeconomics in the US. The IS-LM model was always an essentially Keynesian framework, and even when Monetarist or New Classical economists did use it, they did so in the context of a vertical aggregate supply curve so that the classical dichotomy held.

What are our general conclusions? We believe that the IS-LM model has become a largely irrelevant framework in mainstream macroeconomics. Modern reinterpretations of the theory of effective demand have tended to concentrate on quantity constraints of one kind or another: either in the output market (menu costs), the labor market (involuntary unemployment and efficiency wages), or the credit market (liquidity constraints). The role of the interest rate has become very unimportant in these treatments. One could argue that the case of the completely interest-inelastic (i.e. vertical) IS curve was always part of the extreme Keynesian character in textbooks. Thus, to a certain extent, the IS-LM model is "dead" as a framework for contemporary macroeconomic research.

1.2 THE ORIGINS OF THE IS-LM MODEL

The IS-LM model emerged out Hicks's paper, 'Mr. Keynes and the "Classics": a suggested interpretation', published in Econometrica in April 1937.[1] Hicks's paper had originally been presented at a symposium on Keynes's General Theory held at the Sixth European meeting of the Econometric Society in Oxford in September 1936. The symposium consisted of three papers by Harrod (1937), Meade (1937) and Hicks. All three papers sought to clarify Keynes's departure from prevailing classical theory. The three papers presented broadly similar algebraic expositions of Keynes's theory but only Hicks illustrated his arguments with a set of diagrams. These diagrams were eventually developed into the IS-LM model.

Hicks's paper was motivated by a concern to overcome the bewilderment of many readers of Keynes's General Theory caused in part by Keynes's use of Pigou's *The Theory of Unemployment* as typical of classical theory. Hicks considered Pigou's book to be 'fairly new' and 'exceedingly difficult'. Thus Hicks presented a simpler form of classical theory which was more typical and directly comparable with Keynes's own theory.

Hicks set up a common framework within which to compare different variants of both classical theory and Keynes's theory. This common framework consisted of four simplifying assumptions, a model of the supply-side and the demand-side equilibrium condition. Hicks's four simplifying assumptions are: (i) fixed capital stock; (ii) homogeneous labor; (iii) no depreciation; and (iv) fixed money-wage rate. The model of the supply-side is a conventional profit-maximizing model in which price is equated to marginal cost in both the consumption-goods industry and the investment-goods industry. It follows that, given the money-wage rate, the level of output and employment is determined by demand-side conditions. Assuming that the money supply is fixed, the determination of the demand-side equilibrium depends on the form of the three aggregate demand-side functions: the demand-for-money function, the investment function and the saving function. Thus, from Hicks's perspective, Keynes and the "Classics" differed crucially in their analyses of the form of these three aggregate demand-side functions. Hicks examined these differences by means of five models of the demand-side presented in Table 1 below.

Model 1 is Hicks's representation of the typical classical theory. The Cambridge quantity equation, $M = kY$, implies that the quantity of money determines money income. As Hicks noted, it follows that cyclical fluctuations in money income can only be explained by changes in the money supply and/or changes in k. Given that the quantity of money determines money income, the rate of interest becomes a purely goods-market phenomenon, ensuring that investment and saving are brought into equilibrium. This is the loanable funds theory of the rate of interest.

Model 2 is a variant of the classical theory, which Hicks termed the Treasury View. The Treasury View includes one element of Keynes's theory, namely, that saving is perfectly interest-inelastic. When combined with the Cambridge quantity equation, it follows that the quantity of money determines saving and, hence, investment. The rate of interest acts as the rationing device reconciling the level of

Table 1: Hicks's five models of the demand-side.

Model	Demand for Money	Investment	Saving
1. Classical Theory	$M = kY$	$I = I(r)$	$S = S(r, Y)$
2. Treasury View	$M = kY$	$I = I(r)$	$S = S(Y)$
3. Keynes's Special Theory	$M = L(r)$	$I = I(r)$	$S = S(Y)$
4. Keynes's General Theory	$M = L(r, Y)$	$I = I(r)$	$S = S(Y)$
5. Generalised General Theory	$M = L(r, Y)$	$I = I(r, Y)$	$S = S(r, Y)$

where $M \equiv$ money supply, $L(.) \equiv$ demand-for-money function, $k \equiv$ constant (the so-called Cambridge 'k'), $I \equiv$ investment, $S \equiv$ saving, $r \equiv$ rate of interest and $Y \equiv$ money income.

investment with the pre-determined level of saving. This theory underpinned the Treasury View that crowding-out is complete; deficit-financed public works programs would displace an equal amount of private investment given the available fixed amount of saving.

Model 3 is Keynes's special theory. As with the Treasury View, saving is perfectly interest-inelastic. However, unlike the two classical models, the Cambridge quantity equation is dropped. Instead liquidity preference is introduced such that the demand for money depends only on the rate of interest. In this restricted version of Keynes's theory, the rate of interest becomes a purely money-market phenomenon, ensuring equilibrium between money demand and supply. The rate of interest is no longer affected by either investment or saving. Given the equilibrium rate of interest, investment is determined by the marginal-efficiency-of-capital (MEC) schedule and, in turn, money income is determined by the multiplier (i.e. the saving function). Thus it is the introduction of liquidity preference in place of the Cambridge quantity equation, which is the key innovation of Keynes since this is the necessary condition for income to be determined by goods-market conditions via the multiplier process. However, as Hicks pointed out, liquidity preference was not Keynes's innovation. Both Lavington and Pigou had conceived of the demand for money depending on the rate of interest. Rather Keynes's contribution was to be the first to recognize the important macroeconomic implications of liquidity preference.

Model 4 is the more general form of Keynes's theory in which the demand for money depends on both money income and the rate of interest. The implication is that money income and the rate of interest are determined simultaneously by both goods-market and money-market conditions. It is at this point that Hicks had recourse to a diagram (see Figure 1). He represented the goods-market equilibrium condition, $I(r) = S(Y)$, by a downward-sloping IS curve. The money-market equilibrium condition, $M = L(r,Y)$, is represented by an upward-sloping LM curve (denote as the LL curve in Hicks's original paper). Together these two curves determine the equilibrium level of money income, Y^*, and the equilibrium rate of interest, r^*.

Hicks viewed Keynes as having taken 'a big step back to Marshallian orthodoxy' by incorporating traditional classical elements (i.e. the quantity theory and the loanable funds theory) within his new theory of liquidity preference and the multiplier. Ultimately Hicks considered the crucial difference between Keynes and the "Classics" as their respective views on the slope of the LM curve. Indeed, as Hicks illustrated diagrammatically, Keynes and the "Classics" could be seen as analyzing the opposite extremes of the same LM curve. Keynes's General Theory is the 'Economics of Depression' appropriate at low levels of income when liquidity preference dominates the determination of the rate of interest and the multiplier dominates the determination of money income (i.e. the LM curve is relatively flat). Classical theory, on the other hand, is appropriate at high levels of income when the quantity of money dominates the determination of money income and goods-market conditions dominate the determination of the rate of interest (i.e. the LM curve is relatively steep).

Hicks's argument that Keynes and the "Classics" provide complementary analyses appropriate under different phases of the cycle is reinforced by Model 5, the Generalized General Theory. In this model Hicks considered the possibility that all

Figure 1. The IS-LM model.

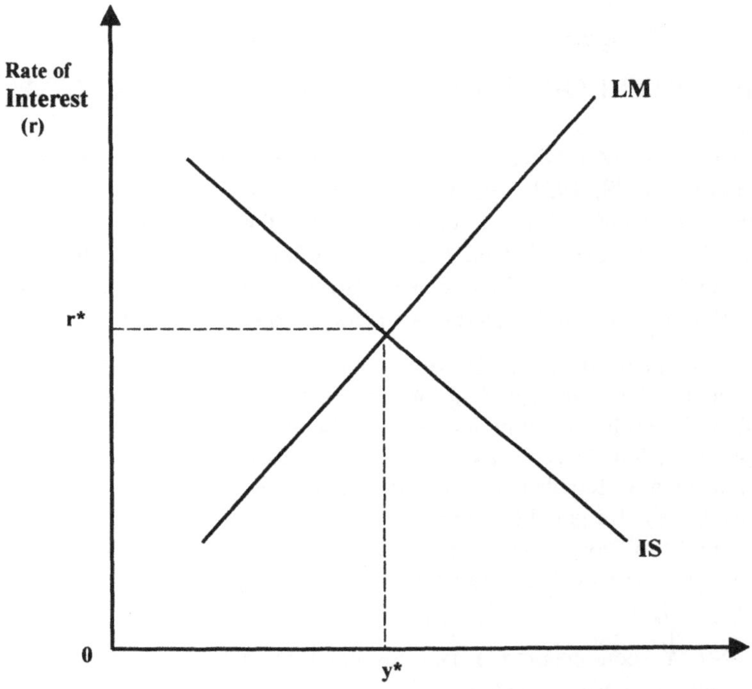

three aggregate demand-side functions could be determined by both the rate of interest and money income. The two classical models and Keynes's two models are all restricted cases nested within this more general model. In the context of this more general model Hicks considers various other special cases including the Wicksellian case of a horizontal IS curve at the natural rate of interest, the possibility of an upward-sloping IS curve due to the effects of inflationary expectations on investment, and extending the LM curve to allow for changes in the money supply if the monetary authorities target the rate of interest.

Overall, a re-examination of Hicks's original 1937 paper from which the IS-LM model emerged suggests the following observations. First, Hicks was well aware of the importance of specifying supply-side microfoundations and, indeed, did so before commencing on his IS-LM analysis of the demand-side. Second, Hicks considered the key difference between Keynes and the "Classics" to be liquidity preference, a necessary condition for the multiplier process to determine money income. Third, Hicks viewed Keynes and the "Classics" as complementary analyses, restricted versions of a more general model with the empirical relevance of the different restrictions depending on the phase of the business cycle. Finally, Hicks considered the IS-LM analysis to be limited. It was a 'skeleton apparatus', 'a rough and ready sort of affair'. He acknowledged difficulties in specifying the concept of income as well as the need to introduce the distribution of income in order to render the curves determinate. He also flagged the importance of the timing of the various processes, concluding that the '... *General Theory* is a useful book; but it is neither the beginning nor the end of Dynamic Economics.' (p. 159).

1.3 THE DEVELOPMENT OF IS-LM KEYNESIANISM

Hicks's exposition of Keynes's theory was first formulated as the IS-LM model by Alvin Hansen (1949, 1951, 1953). It was largely due to Hansen that the IS-LM model became established in the postwar period as the principal model of the macro economy. Hansen acknowledged Hicks's contribution in integrating the classical loanable funds theory (the IS curve) and Keynes's liquidity preference theory (the LM curve) to provide a fully determinate theory of the rate of interest:

> '... a determinate theory of interest is based on: (1) the investment demand function, (2) the saving-function (or conversely the consumption function), (3) the liquidity preference function, and (4) the quantity of money. The Keynesian analysis, looked at as a whole, involved all of these. But Keynes never brought them all together in a comprehensive way to formulate an integrated interest theory. He failed to point out specifically that liquidity preference plus the quantity of money can give us not the rate of interest, but only an LM-curve. It was left for Hicks to supply us with the tools needed for a comprehensive analysis.' (Hansen, 1951, pp. 431-2)

The IS-LM soon become a familiar element in macroeconomics textbooks. Gardner Ackley's, *Macroeconomic Theory* (1961), provides a representative treatment of the IS-LM model. Ackley designated the IS-LM model as the Hicks-Hansen analysis. The algebraic formulation adopted is that of Hicks's Generalized General Theory (Model 5) but the explanation of the causal processes reverts to the standard Keynesian presentation (Model 3) with the effects of the rate on interest on saving and income on investment treated as secondary influences which can be neglected. Unlike Hicks, Ackley assumes that prices are fixed, determined autonomously. Ackley considers fixed prices as part of the standard Keynesian system but recognizes that this an exaggeration given Keynes's own lengthy discussions of prices and wages. Ackley constructs the IS and LM curves from the underlying functions both algebraically and diagrammatically. He also supplements the standard IS-LM diagram with three-dimensional diagrams and numerical examples. He then uses the IS-LM model to examine the comparative statics of changes in the money supply and the marginal propensity to save. In addition Ackley follows Hicks in considering the classical special case of a vertical LM curve and the Keynesian special case of a horizontal LM curve. Ackley discusses the limitations of the IS-LM model: too aggregative and too static. He is also concerned that its 'elegant simplicity' means that 'most of the "works" are out of sight' (p. 372). Thus Ackley complements the IS-LM model with an alternative four-quadrant diagram of the underlying aggregate behavioral functions.

The IS-LM model provided a focus for the Keynesian-neoclassical debate. Much of the debate can be seen as following from Hicks's contention that the main differences between Keynes and the "Classics" concerns the slopes of the IS and LM curves. The Keynesians tended to believe that the IS curve is relatively steep (i.e. interest-inelastic) but the LM curve is relatively flat (i.e. interest-elastic). The Keynesians denied that the rate of interest has a significant impact on investment, stressing instead the capacity-adjustment role of investment in the accelerator theory in which investment depends on changes in output (Chenery, 1952). The Keynesians also argued that the demand for money is highly interest-elastic. The Baumol-Tobin inventory model showed how the rate of interest influences the transactions demand for money as rational agents minimize the opportunity cost of holding non-interest-bearing money balances (Baumol, 1952; Tobin, 1956). In contrast the neoclassical view was that the IS curve is relatively flat but the LM curve is relatively steep. Jorgenson's cost-of-capital model highlighted the role of the rate of interest in determining investment (Jorgenson, 1967). The intertemporal theories of consumption, namely, the permanent income hypothesis (Friedman, 1957) and the life cycle hypothesis (Ando and Modigliani, 1963), downplayed the role of current income in determining current consumption while emphasizing the importance of expected future income, the stock of wealth and the rate of interest. In addition the revival of the quantity theory of money (Friedman, 1956) in which the demand for money is treated as a portfolio allocation process involving a wide range of financial and real assets suggested that the demand for money is not highly interest-elastic.

Taken together the Keynesian arguments suggest that the Hicksian mechanism (Modigliani, 1977), whereby demand shocks are automatically partially offset by the money-market feedback effects via the rate of interest, is weak. There is, therefore, a need for active stabilization policies. Fiscal policy is relatively effective. The neoclassical view, on the other hand, is that the Hicksian mechanism is strong, implying that stabilization policies are unnecessary and fiscal policy is relatively ineffective due to the crowding-out effect.

The ISLM model also provided a starting point for the development of various extensions of Keynes's analysis. The IS-LM model was extended to deal with the open economy by Mundell (1960, 1963) and Fleming (1962). The Mundell-Fleming model, sometimes referred to as the IS-LM-BP model, introduced a third equilibrium condition, the balance of payments equilibrium, represented by the BP (or foreign-exchange, FE,) curve. There were also attempts to introduce dynamic adjustment into the IS-LM model. The "discovery" of the Phillips-curve relationship between unemployment and the rate of change of money-wages (Phillips, 1958) was seen as providing the supply-side price dynamics to complement the static demand-side ISLM model. A more sophisticated dynamic analysis was developed by Smyth (1963) who integrated the Keynesian trade cycle theory based on the multiplier-accelerator interaction due to Samuelson (1939) and Hicks (1949, 1950) within the IS-LM framework to produce a dynamic IS-LM model in which the IS and LM curves are recast as second-order difference equations. Smyth's model allowed for cyclical adjustments and suggested the possibility that active monetary policies may be destabilizing.

The IS-LM model focused on the demand-side of the macro economy. As a result the implicit supply-side microfoundations were not given sufficient attention. Modigliani (1944) gave the definitive statement of the 'neoclassical synthesis', highlighting the importance of the Keynesian assumption of rigid wages:

> It is usually considered as one of the most important achievements of the Keynesian theory that it explains the consistency of economic equilibrium with the presence of involuntary unemployment. It is, however, not sufficiently recognized that, except in a limiting case ..., this result is due entirely to the assumption of 'rigid wages' and not to the Keynesian liquidity preference. (Modigliani, 1944, p. 65)

However there was little attempt to justify the assumption of rigid wages in choice-theoretic terms. It became conventional wisdom that the Keynesian analysis rested on the assumption of rigid wages. This was made explicit in the aggregate demand and supply (AD-AS) model in which the price level is determined endogenously. The Keynesian analysis is characterized by an upward-sloping AS schedule due to rigid money-wages. The AD schedule, representing the real balance effect, is derived from the IS-LM model. Again, however, the main focus was the demand-side. Patinkin (1956, 1959) and Hicks (1957) debated the size of the real balance effect. Patinkin criticized Hicks for only allowing for the Keynes effect (represented by shifts in the LM curve) and ignoring the more direct Pigou effect (represented by shifts in the IS curve).

In summary, the IS-LM model provided a simple and very effective framework for the exposition and extension of Keynesian analysis. It embodied the twin characteristic features of the early Keynesian research program: an emphasis on the determination of aggregate demand but with little attention given to the supply-side microfoundations. The latter was a significant contributory factor to the decline of Keynesian economics from the mid-1960s onwards. It became the task of subsequent new Keynesian theorists to re-establish the mainstream Keynesian research program as progressive by providing the missing choice-theoretic explanations of price and/or wage rigidity.

1.4 FIX-PRICE MODELS

Traditional textbook IS-LM models had always talked about the assumption of constant prices underlying the IS-LM approach. However, this was merely a device to ensure that changes in nominal income were translated directly into changes in real output. There was no direct thought given to the microeconomic foundations of consumer and producer behavior when prices were fixed. In textbook microeconomic theory, at least of the perfectly competitive variety, agents act as price-takers and choose quantities. An assumption of this approach is that agents can make unlimited trades at the prices they face (firms of course are limited to technical feasibility). But this assumption only makes sense if there is a Walrasian price ruling: one that clears the market, so that supply is equal to demand. If the price is not the Walrasian price, then there will be excess demand/supply: agents desired actions are inconsistent, and hence someone will be disappointed. Hence price-taking with no restrictions on trade only makes sense if it goes along with instantaneous market clearing, so that Walrasian prices are always maintained.

The textbook IS-LM model of course still stayed with Keynes in treating consumption as a function not of prices, but of a quantity, namely income. This was one of the major innovations of the *General Theory*. There was a tension between the generally accepted macroeconomic theory of the consumption function, and the way economists thought about most other things. The "reappraisal of Keynes" movement which gathered momentum in the 1960s was an attempt to resolve this tension (Clower, 1965; Leijonhufvud, 1967, 1968), building on the insights of the "neoclassical synthesis" of Patinkin (1956) and Hansen (1953).[2] The culmination of this was the work on fix-price temporary equilibria in the 1970's by, amongst others, Barro and Grossman (1971), Benassy (1975, 1976, 1978) and popularized by Malinvaud (1977). It is perhaps appropriate that the most comprehensive work in this research program was undertaken by Jean-Pascal Benassy in his Ph.D thesis at Berkeley under the supervision of Gerard Debreu (Benassy, 1973).

The research program aimed to keep the price-taking assumption of Walrasian microeconomics, but drop the assumption that prices equate demand with supply. Rather, prices were to be assumed to be fixed exogenously. This was of course a weakness of the theory. However, it must be remembered that the assumption of fixed prices was quite common at the time in this context, and, furthermore, that this was seen as the only alternative to the assumption of perfectly flexible prices. Thus the theory of the firm and the consumer had to be extended to allow for quantity constraints and rationing if agents could not sell or buy all that they wanted in one market, then this would affect their demands in other markets. For example, if households were unable to supply as much labor as they wanted to at the prevailing prices,[3] then this may affect their consumption decision. If firms are unable to sell all that they want in the output market, this may affect their employment decisions. Thus, in addition to the budget constraint, there were quantity constraints that the firm or household needed to take into consideration. This was seen as the microfoundation for the concept of effective demand, which Keynes had introduced. The distinction was made between a notional demand (supply), which was the demand (supply) derived in the traditional manner without any attention to limits to trade, and the effective demand (supply) which took these into account.

There are many themes here that we could pursue, but since this chapter is focusing on the IS-LM framework rather than more general theory of macroeconomic equilibrium, we will examine the model of Rankin (1986,1987) which interpreted the IS-LM framework in terms of a fix-price model (henceforth the "Rankin" model). In the Rankin model there is an overlapping generation's framework: households demand assets in order to save for old age. In a world of certainty, bonds dominate money (since they earn a positive return): hence in order to have money and bonds coexisting, the Rankin model introduces real money balances into the utility function. Hence the consumers' problem is:

$$\begin{aligned}&\max\ U(c_t^y, M_t / P_t, c_{t+1}^o)\\&\text{s.t.}\, w_t L_t \geq c_t^y + M_t + B_t\\&\quad (P_{t+1}/P_t)c_{t+1}^o \leq M_t + (1+r_t)B_t\\&\quad L_t \leq L\end{aligned}$$

where c_{t+1}^o is the consumption when old in t+1, c_t^y is consumption when young in t. The solution can be written in general form as:

$$\begin{aligned}c_t^y &= c(w_t L_t, r_t, P_{t+1}/P_t)\\M_t &= M(w_t L_t, r_t, P_{t+1}/P_t)\\c_{t+1}^o &= (M_t + B_t)/P_{t+1}\end{aligned}$$

These will be effective demands if employment when young L_t is less than the endowment L. Turning to firms, the labor demand depends on the output demanded (assuming that firms are demand constrained), so that:

$$L_t = L_t(y_t, K_t)$$

We will not outline the capital accumulation side of the Rankin model, and refer interested readers to the original references for the full model. However, there will be an investment equation of the "accelerator" type if the firm is demand constrained, but the wage-rental ratio will also affect the cost-minimizing input:

$$I_t = I_t(K_{t-1}, y_t, w_t/r_t)$$

Putting together all of these equations gives us a simple IS-LM type model:

IS equation: $y_t = c(w_t L_t, r_t, P_{t+1}/P_t) + (M_{t-1} + B_{t-1})/P_t + I(K_{t-1}, y_t, w_t/r_t)$

LM equation: $\overline{M}_t = M(w_t L_t, r_t, P_{t+1}/P_t)$

The Rankin IS-LM model provides consistent microfoundation for the IS-LM model within the context of a fix-price model. However, money in this model has a double role. First, there is a direct lagged effect of money on consumption: old people spend all of the money balances that they accumulated last period in the current period. This acts in a similar way to the wealth effect in the augmented IS-LM model. Second, the young in the current period desire to hold money because it gives them utility: the trade-off between money and bonds is affected by the interest rate. Hence the LM curve is the result of a portfolio decision, and of course the lagged money holdings M_{t-1} will be linked to the money supply in period t, $\overline{M}_t$. Whilst the Rankin model provides a fully coherent IS-LM framework, it is clearly a far cry from the original spirit of Keynes's analysis.

1.5 NEW KEYNESIAN DEVELOPMENTS

The fix-price reinterpretation of the IS-LM had several features: it treated some or all wages and prices as exogenous; it was a static model; it did not have a coherent view of the monetary sector. New Keynesian developments of the 1980's were a direct response to these issues. We must stress that we use the phrase "New Keynesian" in a broad sense, not just to the narrower definition of menu-cost New-Keynesian (see, for example, Mankiw, 1992).

Turning to the first feature: wages and prices were treated as exogenous. In a Walrasian model, of course, wages and prices are "endogenous" only in the sense that they solve a set of demand/supply equations: all agents are price-takers, and the vague notion of "the market" or its embodiment as "the Auctioneer" needs to be invoked to tell a story. One natural response to the issue of having a real account of price determination is to introduce explicit price setting agents: and this is precisely what happened in the 1980's. If agents set prices, then we are in a world of imperfect competition, which may or may not have perfect competition as an interesting special or limiting case. The theories of wage and price determination were:

a) Efficiency wage theory (Salop, 1979; Shapiro and Stiglitz, 1984; Solow, 1979; Weiss, 1980),

b) Firm/union wage bargaining (Layard and Nickell, 1985, 1986),

c) Insider-outsider theory (Lindbeck and Snower, 1986),

d) Oligopolistic/monopolistic models of product markets (for example, Blanchard and Kiyotaki, 1987; Dixon, 1987; Hart, 1983; Mankiw, 1988),

e) Overlapping contracts (Fischer, 1977; Taylor, 1979).

In this brief exposition, we cannot discuss all of these, but will look briefly at the menu-cost idea.

The idea of the menu-cost literature is quite simple (see Akerlof and Yellen, 1985; Parkin, 1986; Mankiw, 1985). Suppose that a monopolist sets prices, but incurs a lump-sum (menu) cost every time it changes price. Let us first think of the "hypothetical optimum" being the optimal price in the absence of menu costs. The optimal pricing rule with menu costs is of the (S, s) type: the firm will set a price, and only change it when the actual price is far enough away from the hypothetical optimum. Thus there is at any instant a "band of inertia" within which the firm will not choose to vary its price. The reason for this band of inertia is that at the hypothetical optimum the derivative of profit with respect to price is zero: hence there is no first-order loss to small deviations of price from the hypothetical optimum. Even small second-order menu costs can cause significant first-order effects. The main problem of this account is how a result for an individual firm aggregates to the economy Caplin and Leahy (1991) show how individual rigidities of this kind generated by menu costs are perfectly consistent with aggregate price flexibility.

Now, in addition to this nominal inertia, monopolistic pricing adds a crucial second ingredient. A monopolist will want to set price in excess of marginal cost: in effect it will want to equate marginal cost with marginal revenue, and hence a markup of price over marginal cost which is related to the elasticity of demand. This means that the firm is demand constrained, in the sense that it can increase its profits if demand is higher (the marginal profit is just the difference between price and marginal cost if prices are fixed). If there were menu costs with perfect competitors (price takers), then the firm might choose to turn away customers. If we put together the two ideas of menu costs and imperfect competition, then we get some nominal rigidity and the responsiveness of real output to changes in nominal demand.

The literature on menu costs and nominal price rigidity has always been open to the problem of translating individual rigidities into aggregate price rigidity. Caplin and Spulber (1987) have presented an example where individual price rigidities are perfectly compatible with complete aggregate flexibility. The idea is simple: suppose that firms change price once a year, with 25% of firms changing price each quarter. It is perfectly possible to have an annual aggregate growth in the money supply of 10%, and in each quarter the firms that then change price raise their price by 10%. The average inflation rate in each quarter is 10/4=2.5%, giving an annual rate of about 10%. Thus the nominal money supply and aggregate price level both rise at 10% per annum despite the fact that any individual firm only changes its price once per year. Caplin and Spulber's model is very much a special case, and as Sutherland (1995) shows, it is much more likely that micro rigidity will give rise to some degree of macro nominal rigidity (the key feature is how price changes are clustered over time).

The second important feature that New Keynesian thought has highlighted is the intertemporal nature of the decisions of households and firms. This is of course a direct response to the emphasis put on these by New Classical and Real Business Cycle analysis. The consumption function of Keynes was without microfoundations: the fix-price literature provided a coherent microfoundation in terms of the theory of effective demands and quantity constraints. This linked current rationing constraints to current demands: the relationship was conceived of in mainly static terms.[4]

The role of the intertemporal dimension was first highlighted by John Flemming (1973). In a Fisherian model of the intertemporal there is no direct link between current income and current consumption: current income only affects current consumption via lifetime income, which determines the position of the intertemporal budget constraint. Flemming argued that in practice there is a "kink" in the intertemporal budget constraint, since the borrowing rate exceeds the lending rate, as depicted in Figure 2. The one thing we know about kinks is that optima may well cluster around the kink, and that they imply the optimum may be insensitive to changes in constraints. (This occurs because the first order conditions become inequalities.) The kink in the intertemporal budget constraint occurs at the point of no borrowing or lending (i.e. consumption in each period equals income). We would expect many people to be at this kink, and hence current consumption would become very sensitive to current income (the marginal propensity to consume of people at this kink is unity). This is different to when there is a linear intertemporal budget constraint: in this case any change in income can be moved around intertemporally, and only affects current consumption insofar as it influences life-time income. Hence with a linear budget constraint, an increase in income in one period is spread out into consumption over all periods. This difference is depicted in Figure 3: in Figure 3(a) current income increases, and due to the kink all of the extra income is consumed in the current period: in Figure 3(b), with a linear constraint (no interest differential), both current and future consumption rise in response to a rise in current income.

Whilst current consumption will be very sensitive to current income in the presence of kinks, the converse is that it will be insensitive to other variables, namely the real interest rate (which determines the slopes on either side of the kink). As Mankiw argues: '...sophisticated examinations of the data usually find that the real interest rate has little effect on consumption and savings. Keynes' conjecture that consumption depends primarily on income and not on the interest rate has stood up well in the face of much empirical testing' (1992, p. 405).

An extreme form of interest rate differential is the case where no borrowing is allowed to occur at all: current consumption cannot exceed current income, or there is a fixed quantity of borrowing. There is a rich and varied New Keynesian literature on this topic (see, for example, the survey by Hillier and Worral, 1995). On the one hand it can simply be assumed that there is no borrowing. Alternatively, it can be assumed that there is some adverse selection or moral hazard problem, which means that the optimal loan contract involves rationing (i.e. limiting the amount borrowed at the equilibrium interest rate to a certain amount per borrower). This can also be applied to firm borrowing, so that investment expenditure is constrained by current profitability or cash flow. Let us take the simple case where there is no borrowing. Here we have the intertemporal budget constraint as in Figure 4(a). Let us suppose that "unconstrained" consumers have an mpc of c (that is, an increase in current income of x% will lead to an increase in current consumption of cx% through the lifetime income, as in Figure 3(b)). Those who are constrained will have an mpc of 1. The aggregate mpc will be a weighted average of the two: $c^* = h + (1\text{-}h).\ c$, where h is the proportion of households which are constrained in the current period.

Figure 2. Flemming's Model of the Kinked Intertemporal Budget Constraint.

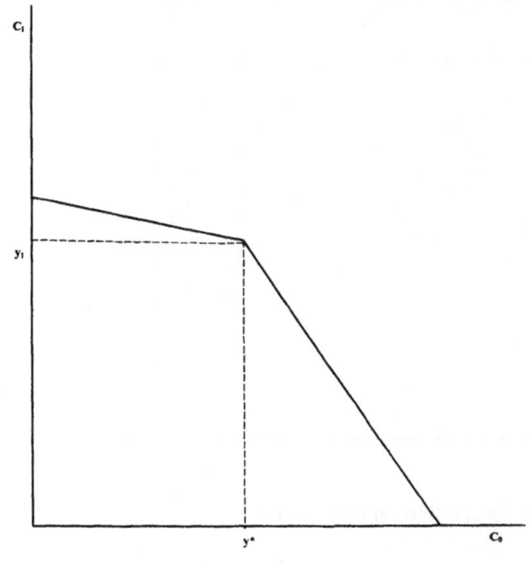

Figure 3. The Sensitivity of Current Consumption to Current Income.

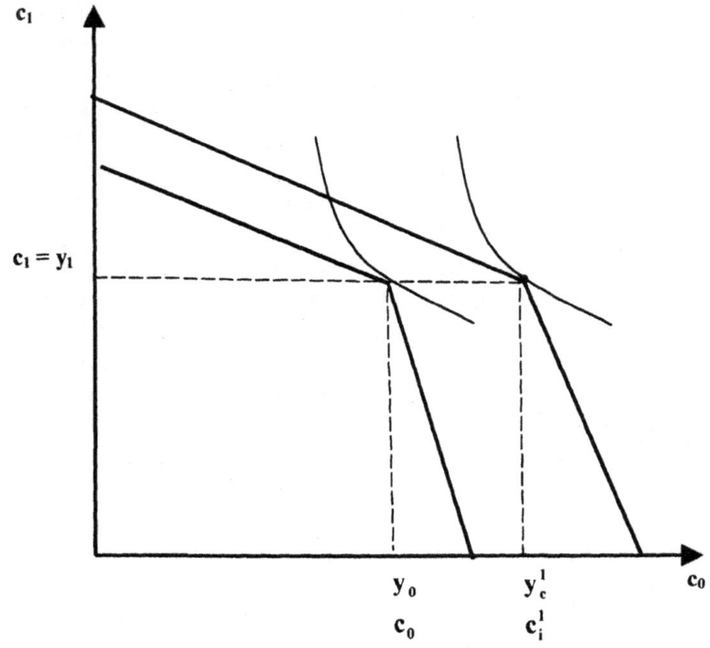

(a) Imperfect Capital Market

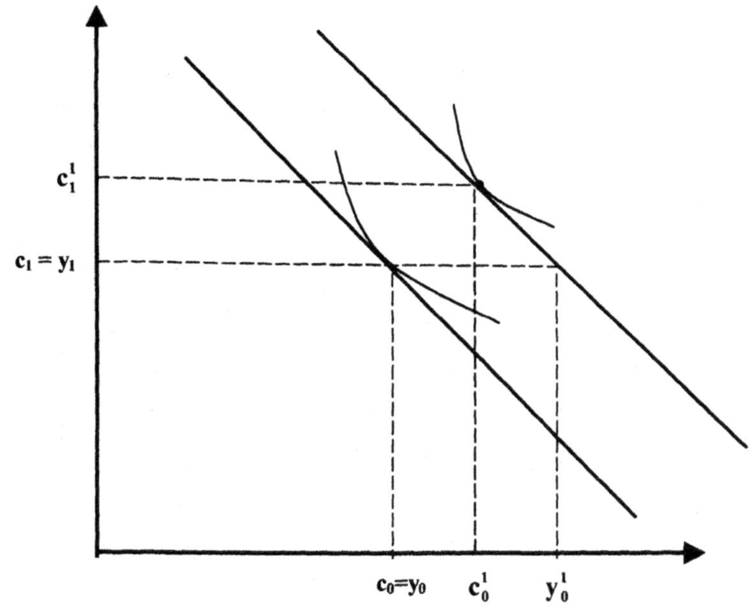

(b) Linear Budget Constraint

Figure 4. Quantity Constraints on Borrowing.

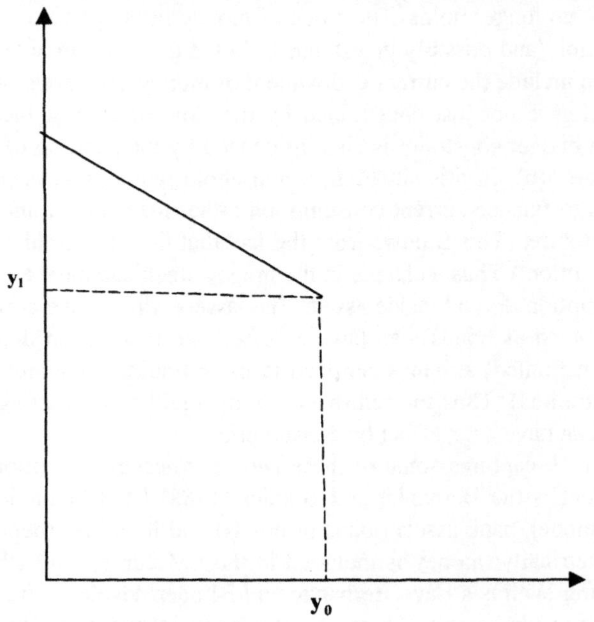

(a) No Borrowing: $c_0 \leq y^0$

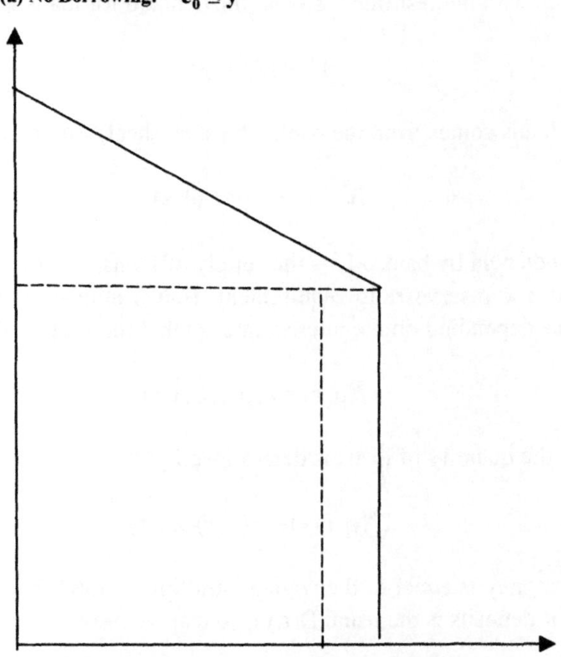

(b) No Borrowing with Assets: $c_0 \leq y^0 + A_0$

Whilst the presence of credit rationing can lead to an "effective demand" like relationship between current consumption and income, it should be clear that the IS-LM dichotomy no longer holds. The stock of money in the private sector will influence consumption (and possibly investment). To see this, we can augment the simple model above to include the current endowment of money and assets: in this case current consumption is not just constrained by the flow of current income, since the position of the budget constraint is also influenced by the position of stock of assets A_0, as in Figure 4(b). In this situation, a household would always prefer to use its stock of assets to finance current consumption rather than save it and have the extra income in the future. (This follows from the fact that the household is constrained in current consumption.) Thus a change in the money stock can have a direct impact on current consumption. Even "inside assets" (i.e. assets which have corresponding private liabilities such as bonds) can have an effect: an increase in deposits of savers (who are unconstrained) at banks can lead to more liquidity available for borrowers (who are constrained). Thus the redistribution of liquidity with an aggregate wealth effect of zero can have a net affect on consumption.

A model which captures some of these New Keynesian perceptions in a IS-LM-like environment is the Bernanke and Blinder (1988) CC-LM model. In the traditional IS-LM model, bank assets (loans or bonds) and liabilities (deposit money) are treated asymmetrically: money is included in the LM curve, whilst bonds/loans are suppressed using Walras's Law. Bernanke and Blinder develop a framework, which allows for both to play a role. There are two credit instruments: loans with interest rate ρ and bonds with interest rate r, so that the demand for loans is assumed to be

$$L^d = L(\rho\ r, y)$$

The supply of loans comes from the banks' balance sheet, which is

$$B^d + L^s + E = D(1\text{-}\tau)$$

where $B^d \equiv$ bonds held by banks, $L^s \equiv$ the supply of loans, $E \equiv$ the excess reserves, $D \equiv$ deposits and $\tau \equiv$ reserve ratio requirement. Banks allocate their assets between bonds and loans depending on the interest rate, so that the supply of loans is

$$L^s(\rho, r) = \lambda(\rho, r)D(1\text{-}\tau)$$

In equilibrium the quantity of loans is determined by

$$L^d(\rho, r, y) = \lambda(\rho, r)D(1\text{-}\tau) \tag{1}$$

The supply of money is equal to the "money multiplier" m(r) times bank reserves R. The demand for deposits is the usual D(r,y), so that we have:

$$D(r,y) = m(r)R \tag{2}$$

This is the standard LM curve. From (1) and (2) the loan interest rate ρ can be expressed as a function of r, R, and y:

$$\rho = \phi\,(r, R, y),\ \phi_r > 0 > \phi_R,\ \phi_y > 0$$

The IS curve is of the standard form:

$$y = y(r, \rho) = y(r, \phi(r, R, y)) \tag{3}$$

This is denoted the CC curve ("commodities and credit"), since it includes the goods market (commodities) and the loans interest rate (credit). If bonds and loans are perfect substitutes, then $r = \rho$, and the model is equivalent to the IS-LM model. If money and bonds are perfect substitutes (as in the liquidity trap case) so that r is fixed, then credit can play a crucial role (since ρ can still vary to influence demand for output). However, in general "credit" can play an important role here as distinct from "money". It is, Bernanke and Blinder argue, an empirical question of which is the most important explanatory variable of what happens in practice. Bernanke and Blinder argue that the instability of the money demand relationship indicates that the credit approach may be more fruitful, and present some supporting US evidence.

The New Keynesian school of macroeconomics has developed our understandings of the theory of effective demand. In particular, it has developed the theory of nominal rigidities in an imperfectly competitive environment, and in an intertemporal setting for firms and households.

1.6 POST-KEYNESIAN CRITICISMS OF THE IS-LM MODEL

The Post-Keynesian school rejects the mainstream Keynesian research program (i.e. the neoclassical synthesis; fix-price models; New Keynesian macroeconomics) as an inadequate development of Keynes's analysis. The IS-LM model has tended to be seen by Post-Keynesians as epitomizing the limitations of mainstream Keynesianism. There have been three main Post-Keynesian criticisms. First, the IS-LM model is too mechanical and fails to convey the important effects of uncertainty particularly on the investment function. In the *General Theory* Keynes devoted two chapters to investment: chapter 11 on the MEC schedule and chapter 12 on the state of long-term expectations. For Post-Keynesians the IS-LM model deals with chapter 11 only and hence understates the potential volatility of the macro economy. Indeed Keynes himself had stressed the importance of uncertainty in his QJE 1937 paper in which he drew a sharp distinction between the classical concern for probabilistic risk and his own concern with probabilistic uncertainty (Keynes, 1937). The original Post-Keynesians such as Robinson (1964, 1973) and Shackle (1967) considered uncertainty to be the very essence of Keynes's contribution. Shackle repudiated the equilibrium frame of analysis of the IS-LM model, arguing that 'the essential core of

Keynes' conception of economic activity is uncertain expectation, and uncertain expectation is wholly incompatible and in conflict with the notion of equilibrium.' (Shackle, 1982, p. 438)

A second related criticism is that the IS-LM model is a static simultaneous equilibrium analysis and, hence, inappropriate to convey Keynes's understanding of the dynamics of a macro economy. There is a need to replace the IS-LM model with a dynamic sequential analysis. This is the point of Robinson's often-repeated claim that Keynesian analysis should be set in historical, not logical, time with an irrevocable past and unknown future (Robinson, 1973, 1974). The simultaneous equilibrium analysis of the IS-LM model implies that the secondary feedback processes are treated as equally important as the initial primary processes. This may give a misleading understanding of the behavior of actual economies moving through historical time, subject to a series of shocks and structural changes, and in which the feedback processes are only partially realized. In this case it is more appropriate to analyze and use a sequential analysis. Leijonhufvud (1983) endorses this Post-Keynesian criticism, arguing that the problem with the Keynesian IS-LM analysis is that it uses a static (full information) simultaneous framework to deal with issues of dynamic adjustment under conditions of imperfect information.

A final Post-Keynesian criticism of the IS-LM model is its lack of microfoundations. Chick (1982) considers the IS-LM fix-price model as valid only in circumstances in which firms estimate aggregate demand correctly. Weintraub (1982) views the lack of microfoundations as fostering the mainstream wage-rigidity interpretation of Keynes and hence contributing to the general failure to comprehend the meaning of Keynes's analysis. Thus a major task of Post-Keynesian economics has been to provide non-neoclassical supply-side microfoundations for Keynes's analysis. Kalecki's analysis of monopolistic firms using mark-up pricing rules has been particularly influential (see, for example, Sawyer, 1985).

Interestingly Hicks himself was quite sympathetic to some of these Post-Keynesian criticisms. In a reconsideration of the IS-LM model, Hicks (1980) expressed increasing dissatisfaction with the IS-LM model. In particular, Hicks found an inconsistency between the flow equilibrium of the IS curve and the stock equilibrium of the LM curve. Hicks also recognized that the concept of stock equilibrium in the money market is problematic since it is uncertainty about the future, which creates the demand for liquidity. Hicks proposed the concept of an expectational zone in which expectations would not be revised if actual outcomes fall within a certain range. Subsequently Hicks (1988) suggested that it would be better to think of the IS and LM curves as representing the quite different modes of operation of the industrial and financial sectors, respectively.

1.7 SOME CONCLUDING THOUGHTS

In this survey we have traced the history of the IS-LM model from its origins as Hicks's attempt to expose the essential differences between Keynes and the Classics, its central role in the early Keynesian-neoclassical debates, through to its recent decline to irrelevance in both mainstream New Keynesian as well as non-mainstream Post-Keynesian approaches. The IS-LM model provides a simple framework for analyzing the interactions between the goods and money markets in the determination of aggregate demand. In particular the IS-LM focuses attention on the role of the rate of interest in providing a connecting link between the two markets. In the early Keynesian-neoclassical debate the main focus of attention was on the demand-side of the macro economy. The IS-LM model naturally became the principal point of reference. However, as we have argued, from the emergence of the neoclassical synthesis onwards, this turning point being signified by Modigliani's 1944 statement of the importance of the rigid money-wages assumption underpinning the IS-LM framework, the main focus of attention has turned more and more towards the issue of microfoundations, particularly the reconciliation of the Keynesian presumption of price and wage stickiness with the axiom of rationality. As a consequence, the IS-LM model has become marginalized. The IS-LM model still appears in undergraduate macroeconomics textbooks but increasingly it is used as a mere stepping stone in the construction of the aggregate demand schedule in the AD-AS model with the bulk of the argument being devoted to the form of the aggregate supply schedule.

Thus, to conclude, it seems clear that the IS-LM model has gone out of fashion in modern mainstream macroeconomics (and has never been in fashion in non-mainstream macroeconomics). The decline in the importance of the IS-LM model mirrors the New Keynesian emphasis on the real sector, especially the supply-side, and quantity constraints. The emphasis implies that there is little concern for the role of the nominal rate of interest as a connecting link between the real and monetary sectors, thereby invalidating the Classical Dichotomy. Not surprisingly, there is little need for a model to examine this connecting link. However, the development of Real Business Cycle theory as a paradigm in its own right in which macroeconomic behavior is derived from intertemporal optimization, is putting the role of the real rate of interest back near the top of the research agenda. From this perspective, the rate of interest not only links the money and goods markets but also links both of these markets with the labor market via the intertemporal substitution of labor supply. An augmented-IS-LM model, based on the microfoundations of intertemporal optimization and allowing for the supply of output to be directly affected by labor-supply adjustments in response to changes in the rate of interest, may feature more prominently in the near future, in the textbooks at least.

BIBLIOGRAPHY

Ackley, G. (1961), *Macroeconomic Theory*, New York: Macmillan.

Akerlof, G. A. and Yellen, J. L. (1985), 'A near rational model of the business cycle with wage and price inertia', *Quarterly Journal of Economics*, vol. 100, pp. 823-38.

Ando, A. and Modigliani, F. (1963), 'The "life-cycle" hypothesis of saving: aggregate implications and tests', *American Economic Review*, vol. 53, pp. 55-84.

Barro, R. J. (1984), *Macroeconomics*, New York: John Wiley & Sons.

Barro, R. J. and Grossman, H. I. (1971), 'A general disequilibrium model of income and employment', *American Economic Review*, vol. 61, pp. 82-93.

Baumol, W. (1952), 'The transactions demand for cash: an inventory theoretic approach', *Quarterly Journal of Economics*, vol. 66, pp. 545-556.

Benassy, J. -P. (1973), Ph.D thesis, University of California at Berkeley.

Benassy, J. -P. (1975), 'Neo-Keynesian disequilibrium theory in a monetary economy'. *Review of Economic Studies*, vol. 42, pp. 503-523.

Benassy, J. -P. (1976), 'The disequilibrium approach to monopolistic price setting and general monopolistic equilibrium', *Review of Economic Studies*, vol. 43, pp. 69-81.

Benassy, J. -P. (1978), 'A neo-Keynesian model of price and quantity determination disequilibrium' in G. Schowodiauer (ed.), *Equilibrium and Disequilibrium in Economic Theory*, Dordrecht: Reidel.

Bernanke, B. S. and Blinder, A. S. (1988), 'Credit, money, and aggregate demand', *American Economic Review Papers and Proceedings*, vol. 78, pp. 435-439.

Blanchard, O. J. and Kiyotaki, N. (1987), 'Monopolistic competition and the effects of aggregate demand', *American Economic Review*, vol. 77, pp. 647-666.

Caplin, A. S. and Leahy, J. (1991), 'State dependent pricing and the dynamics of money and output', *Quarterly Journal of Economics*, vol. 106, pp. 683-708.

Caplin, A. S. and Spulber, D. F. (1987), 'Menu costs and the neutrality of money', *Quarterly Journal of Economics*, vol. 102, pp. 703-725.

Chenery, H. B. (1952), 'Overcapacity and the acceleration principle', *Econometrica*, vol. 20, pp. 1-28.

Chick, V. (1982), 'A comment on "IS-LM: an explanation"', *Journal of Post Keynesian Economics*, vol. 4, pp. 439-444.

Clower, R. W. (1965), 'The Keynesian counter-revolution: a theoretical appraisal' in F. H. Hahn and R. Brechling (eds), *The Theory of Interest Rates*, London: Macmillan.

Darity Jr, W. and Young, W. (1995), 'IS-LM: an inquest', *History of Political Economy*, vol. 27, pp. 1-41.

Dixon, H. (1987), 'A simple model of imperfect competition with Walrasian features', *Oxford Economic Papers*, vol. 39, pp. 134-160.

Fischer, S. (1977), 'Long-term contracts, rational expectations, and the optimal money supply rule', *Journal of Political Economy*, vol. 85, pp. 191-205.

Fleming, J. M. (1962), 'Domestic financial policies under fixed and under flexible exchange rate regimes', *IMF Staff Papers*, vol. 9, pp. 369-379.

Flemming, J. (1973), 'The consumption function when capital markets are imperfect: the permanent income hypothesis reconsidered', *Oxford Economic Papers*, vol. 25, pp. 160-172.

Friedman, M. (1956), 'The quantity theory of money: a restatement' in M. Friedman (ed.), *Studies in the Quantity Theory of Money*, Chicago: University of Chicago Press.

Friedman, M. (1957), *A Theory of the Consumption Function*, Princeton: Princeton University Press.

Friedman, M. (1970), 'A theoretical framework for monetary analysis', *Journal of Political Economy*, vol. 78, pp. 193-238.

Hansen, A. H. (1949), *Monetary Theory and Fiscal Policy*, New York: McGraw-Hill.

Hansen, A. H. (1951), 'Classical, loanable funds, and Keynesian interest theories', *Quarterly Journal of Economics*, vol. 65, pp. 429-432.

Hansen, A. H. (1953), *A Guide to Keynes*, New York: McGraw-Hill.

Harrod, R. F. (1937), 'Mr Keynes and traditional theory', *Econometrica*, vol. 5, pp. 74-86.

Hart, O. (1982), 'A model of imperfect competition with Keynesian features', *Quarterly Journal of Economics*, vol. 96, pp. 109-138.

Hicks, J. R. (1937), 'Mr Keynes and the "Classics": a suggested interpretation', *Econometrica*, vol. 5, pp. 147-159.

Hicks, J. R. (1949), 'Mr Harrod's dynamic theory', *Economica*, vol. 16, pp. 106-121.

Hicks, J. R. (1950), *A Contribution to the Theory of the Trade Cycle*, Oxford: Clarendon Press.

Hicks, J. R. (1957), 'A rehabilitation of "classical" economics?', *Economic Journal*, vol. 67, pp. 278-289.

Hicks, J. R. (1980), 'IS-LM: an explanation', *Journal of Post Keynesian Economics*, vol. 3, pp. 139-154.

Hicks, J. R. (1988), 'Towards a more general theory' in M. Kohn and S. C. Tsiang (eds), *Finance Constraints, Expectations, and Macroeconomics*, Oxford: Clarendon Press.

Hillier, B. and Worral, T. (1995), 'Asymmetric information, investment, finance and real business cycles' in H. D. Dixon and N. Rankin (eds), *The New Macroeconomics*, Cambridge: Cambridge University Press.

Jorgenson, D. W. (1967), 'The theory of investment behavior' in R. Ferber (ed.), *Determinants of Investment Behavior*, New York: Columbia University Press.

Keynes, J. M. (1937), 'A general theory of employment', *Quarterly Journal of Economics*, vol. 51, pp. 209-223.

Layard, R. G. D. and Nickell, S. J. (1985), 'The causes of British unemployment', *National Institute Economic Review*, vol. 111, pp. 62-85.

Layard, R. G. D. and Nickell, S. J. (1986), 'Unemployment in the UK', *Economica*, vol. 53 (suppl.), pp. 121-166.

Leijonhufvud, A. (1967), 'Keynes and the Keynesians: a suggested interpretation', *American Economic Review*, vol. 57, pp. 401-410.

Leijonhufvud, A. (1968), *On Keynesian Economics and the Economics of Keynes*, Oxford: Oxford University Press.

Leijonhufvud, A. (1983), 'What was the matter with IS-LM?' in J. P. Fitoussi (ed.), *Modern Macroeconomic Theory*, Oxford: Basil Blackwell.

Lindbeck, A. and Snower, D. (1986), 'Wage setting, unemployment, and insider-outsider relations', *American Economic Review*, vol. 76, pp. 235-239.

Lucas Jr, R. E. and Rapping, L. A. (1969), 'Real wages, employment, and inflation', *Journal of Political Economy*, vol. 77, pp. 721-754.

Malinvaud, E. (1977), *The Theory of Unemployment Reconsidered*, Oxford: Basil Blackwell.

Mankiw, N. G. (1985), 'Small menu costs and large business cycles: a macroeconomic model of monopoly', *Quarterly Journal of Economics*, vol. 100, pp. 529-539.

Mankiw, N. G. (1988), 'Imperfect competition and the Keynesian cross', *Economic Letters*, vol. 26, pp. 7-14.

Mankiw, N. G. (1992), *Macroeconomics*, New York: Worth.

Meade, J. E. (1937), 'A simplified model of Mr Keynes' system', *Review of Economic Studies*, vol. 4, pp. 98-107.

Modigliani, F. (1944), 'Liquidity preference and the theory of interest and money', *Econometrica*, vol. 12, pp. 45-88.

Modigliani, F. (1977), 'The monetarist controversy or, should we forsake stabilization policies?', *American Economic Review*, vol. 67, pp. 1-19.

Mundell, R. A. (1960), 'The monetary dynamics of adjustment under fixed and flexible exchange rates', *Quarterly Journal of Economics*, vol. 74, pp. 227-257.

Mundell, R. A. (1963), "Capital mobility and stabilisation policy under fixed and flexible exchange rates", *Canadian Journal of Economics and Political Science*, vol. 29, pp. 475-485.

Parkin, M. (1986), 'The output-inflation trade-off when prices are costly to change', *Journal of Political Economy*, vol. 94, pp. 200-224.

Patinkin, D. (1956), *Money, Interest and Prices*, New York: Harper and Row.

Patinkin, D. (1959), 'Keynesian economics rehabilitated: a rejoinder to Professor Hicks', *Economic Journal*, vol. 69, pp. 582-587.

Phillips, A. W. (1958), 'The relation between unemployment and the rate of change of money wage rates in the United Kingdom, 1861-1957', *Economica*, vol. 25, pp. 283-299.

Rankin, N. (1986), 'Debt policy under fixed and flexible prices', *Oxford Economic Papers*, vol. 38, pp. 481-500.

Rankin, N. (1987), 'Disequilibrium and the welfare maximising levels of government spending, taxation and debt', *Economic Journal*, vol. 97, pp. 65-85.

Robinson, J. (1964), *Economic Philosophy*, Harmondsworth: Penguin.

Robinson, J. (1973), 'What has become of the Keynesian revolution?' in *After Keynes*, Oxford: Basil Blackwell.

Robinson, J. (1974), 'History versus equilibrium', *Thames Papers in Political Economy*, London: Thames Polytechnic.

Salop, S. (1979), 'A model of the natural rate of unemployment', *American Economic Review*, vol. 69, pp. 117-125.

Samuelson, P. A. (1939), 'Interaction between the multiplier analysis and the acceleration principle', *Review of Economics and Statistics*, vol. 31, pp. 75-78.

Sawyer, M. C. S. (1985), *The Economics of Michal Kalecki*, London: Macmillan.

Shackle, G. L. S. (1967), *The Years of High Theory: Invention and Tradition in Economic Thought 1926-1939*, Cambridge: Cambridge University Press.

Shackle, G. L. S. (1982), 'Sir John Hicks' "IS-LM: an explanation": a comment', *Journal of Post Keynesian Economics*, vol. 4, pp. 435-438.

Shapiro, C. and Stiglitz, J. E. (1984), 'Equilibrium unemployment as a worker discipline device', *American Economic Review*, vol. 74, pp. 433-444.

Smyth, D. J. (1963), 'Monetary factors and multiplier-accelerator interaction', *Economica*, vol. 30, pp. 400-407.

Solow, R. M. (1979), 'Another possible source of wage stickiness', *Journal of Macroeconomics*, vol. 1, pp. 79-82.

Sutherland, A. (1995), 'Menu costs and aggregate price dynamics' in H. D. Dixon and N. Rankin (eds), *The New Macroeconomics*, Cambridge: Cambridge University Press.

Taylor, J. B. (1979), 'Staggered wage setting in a macro model', *American Economic Review*, vol. 69, pp. 108-113.

Tobin, J. (1956), 'The interest elasticity of the transactions demand for cash', *Review of Economics and Statistics*, vol. 38, pp. 241-247.

Weintraub, S. (1982), 'Hicks on IS-LM: more explanation?', *Journal of Post Keynesian Economics*, vol. 4, pp. 445-452.

Weiss, A. (1980), 'Job queues and layoffs in labor markets with flexible wages', *Journal of Political Economy*, vol. 88, pp. 526-538.

Young, W. (1987), *Interpreting Mr Keynes: The IS-LM Enigma*, Cambridge: Polity Press.

ENDNOTES

[1] The origins and development of the ISLM model are detailed in Young, 1987 and Darity and Young, 1995.

[2] The feeling was that the neoclassical synthesis had achieved the synthesis at the cost of losing some of the key insights of Keynes.

[3] I will use the term "prices" in its general form, subsuming wages etc.

[4] However, note that there is nothing essentially static in the mathematical formulation. We could interpret the same good at different dates as different commodities as in an Arrow-Debreu world, and interpret all of the work of Benassy and others in this light.

2

POST WALRASIAN MACROECONOMICS AND IS/LM ANALYSIS

David Colander

2.1 INTRODUCTION

In recent work I have tried to spell out a Post Walrasian approach to macroeconomics (Colander, 1995a) and to translate that Post Walrasian vision into the aggregate supply/aggregate demand framework (Colander, 1995b). In this paper I continue that work and begin to relate the Post Walrasian vision to the standard IS/LM analysis. The paper is not about high theory; instead it is about the pedagogical use of the IS/LM framework.

I undertake this exercise because, as James Tobin (1980) has noted, the IS/LM framework is built into the way economists think about the aggregate economy and macro policy. When they talk about expansionary fiscal policy, they picture in the back of their minds an IS curve shifting out; when they talk about contractionary monetary policy, they picture in the back of their heads an LM curve shifting back. These IS/LM stories might be modified by a variety of issues, but the influence of the IS/LM framework remains.

Although IS/LM analysis has been attacked vociferously by critics, advocates of its use are unrepentant. For example, Tobin, (1980), even while acknowledging the logical problems with IS/LM analysis, writes that "I do not think the apparatus is discredited. I still believe that carefully used and taught, it is a powerful instrument for understanding our economies and the impacts of policies upon them." Certainly, IS/LM's continued use suggests that Tobin's view is not unique to him. For example, Robert Solow (1984) concurs and offers an explanation of the phenomenon of IS/LM's use, despite concern about its logical foundations. He argues that IS/LM is useful in training our intuition, to give us a handle on the facts. He says that the

IS/LM model has survived because it proves to be a marvelously simple and useful way to recognize and process some of the main macroeconomic facts.

This paper starts from the premise that Solow and Tobin are essentially correct that IS/LM analysis is useful and that it has survived because it does capture certain observed tendencies in the economy that economists should know, and that IS/LM analysis will continue to be used as a way of organizing economists' thinking about the macro economy.

The paper also starts from the premise that the critics are correct that the current textbook foundations of IS/LM analysis are suspect; they are not the foundations that most economists would accept about the way the macro economy works and that, when carried to their logical conclusions, the standard static underpinnings of IS/LM analysis fall apart.

What this paper is, then, is an attempt to rehabilitate IS/LM by giving it different underpinnings than the current texts give it. These Post Walrasian underpinnings lie in systemic institutional constraints that prevent competitive goods markets from adjusting prices instantaneously without undermining the structural integrity of those markets. Adding such structural constraints has not been part of the economists' formal approach, although it has often been part of their informal approach. Essentially what I am arguing is that the microfoundations lie in the formalization of traditional macro economists' informal approach. Until those microfoundations are formalized, my proposed solution is to be less formal in developing the microeconomic underpinnings of IS/LM models.

The ideas in this paper are not novel; as I stated above, this paper is a pedagogical, not a theoretical, paper. The ideas presented in it draw on, in varying degrees, the vision of traditional macro economists such as Tobin, Friedman, Keynes, Hayek, and Lerner. But, somehow, whenever their ideas were translated into a textbook IS/LM model, those ideas have been emasculated in an attempt to make them fit into a simple static explanation of the shapes of the IS and LM curves that are currently taught.

I begin the paper with a brief summary of the Post Walrasian vision; I then discuss how adopting that vision changes the way one thinks about modeling the aggregate economy, such as in how to interpret the short run and long run. Then I briefly discuss how that interpretation can change the pedagogical use of IS/LM analysis.

2.2 THE POST WALRASIAN VISION

The Post Walrasian framework is based on a fundamentally different vision of the economy than is the Walrasian (interpret: multiple market economy in which equilibrium is assured by a Walrasian auctioneer) framework. The Post Walrasian vision is of a functionally complex economy, by which I mean an economy that is assumed to have complex dynamics and multiple equilibria that are related to those complex dynamics. One of the implications of this assumption is that a unique rational expectation for individuals cannot be derived since such derivation is beyond the modeling capabilities of individuals.

In a functionally complex economy extra-market coordination mechanisms are necessary; some unspecified "market" cannot be assumed to fully coordinate individuals' actions. How is this extra-market coordination accomplished? In the Post Walrasian vision that coordination is accomplished via institutions that place constraints on individuals that limit their range of choice, thereby reducing the set of achievable equilibria. Given institutions, there may be a unique equilibrium, but that equilibrium can only be understood in reference to the institutions that play a central role in determining it. In order to have a full analytic model within the Post Walrasian vision, one must (1) model the institutions within which individuals interact; (2) explain how those institutions are compatible with the assumptions of individual rationality that one has made, and (3) explain how those institutions play a role in the determining the equilibrium of the economy.

Currently, economists are a long way from any such analytic model. This means that Post Walrasian IS/LM analysis cannot be a simplification of a more complex analytic model with firm microfoundations. At this point, the most we can claim for it is that it is a reduced-form description of institutionally-determined relationships without firm micro foundations. It is an empirically based, descriptive model, not a logically based, analytic model.

In formally modeling those institutions, and hence in modeling the economy, I have argued that a sequential modeling approach is necessary. All questions cannot be addressed simultaneously, and, at any moment in time, most individuals simply accept large numbers of institutions, and the constraints those institutions place on them, in order to reduce the complexity of decision making to a manageable level.

In the absence of sequentially determined decision making, and acceptance by individuals of social conventions and institutions, the complexity of interactions would lead one to expect that aggregate results would fluctuate wildly. That doesn't happen to anywhere near the degree that the complexity of the interactions would lead one to predict. Walrasians interpret that lack of fluctuation as an indication that their unique-equilibrium approach is the correct one. Post Walrasians interpret that lack of fluctuations differently; they see it as an indication of the central role of institutions limiting the interactions in the economy to manageable proportions for individuals, and thereby creating a surface stability over a core of chaos.

Thus, the Post Walrasian view is that the economy processes information in a quite different way than is assumed in the Walrasian view. In Post Walrasian economics much of the information processing is built into existing institutions, and is not fully understood by the participants. Specialists may understand parts of it and they may be working on changing institutions to take advantage of that understanding, but the complexity of the economy precludes a full understanding of, and complete reliance on the results of, their analysis. Post Walrasian rationality has local, institutionally-based, characteristics; it is bounded, not global, rationality.

2.3 INSTITUTIONS AS OPERATING SYSTEMS

An analogy to a computer may shed some light on this Post Walrasian view of the role of institutions. A computer has a general design, an operating system, software built around that operating system, and sub-software built around that software. In using the computer most individuals take the existing software for granted, much as they take institutions for granted. They operate within the limitations of that software, and their rationality is defined by that software. Thus, when someone asks, "Why hit Control Z when the computer isn't responding?" One answers, "That's what one does" Implicit in this response is the acceptance of a DOS environment. In a MAC environment hitting Control Z is meaningless. Other aspects of rationality carry over between two environments, double clicking with a mouse, for example, to open a file.

The same thing happens with institutions; individuals accept the constraints imposed by institutions on their actions as necessary constraints to operate in a complex environment. When asked why one drives on the right hand side of the street, one responds, "That's what one does." Similarly when asked why one displays the degree of honesty that one does, one does not respond, "I have analyzed the situation and determined that, given the costs and benefits, that is the optimal degree of honesty to reflect," as a Walrasian Homo Economus would. Instead, a Post Walrasian individual would state, "It's what is right." Now this doesn't mean that Post Walrasian Homo Economus is honest, or that he or she doesn't take costs and benefits of being honest into account. Instead it simply means that there is a large nonlinear cost to determining optimal actions, and in many areas, the rational decision is to follow rules, learn what is, and is not, institutionally acceptable, and generally follow those institutional rules[1]. Post Walrasians follow what Herbert Simon calls process rationality.

This sequential choice view of how the economy operates also dictates the modeling strategy used. To have a full model one must have a set of multiple nested systems—one explaining why institutions are adopted, and why sub-institutions are adopted. Most models will not concern such grand theories; instead they will accept existing institutions as given, and incorporate the constraints—like knowing about double clicking or Control Z—of those institutions into the analysis. One of the most important considerations for individuals will be limiting the nature of the decision they are making—efficiently reducing the amount of information processing they can do. Thus, the institutional constraints on micro behavior will be a central part of any but the grandest of models. They certainly play a central role in all short-run analysis; they place constraints on the type of behavior that can reasonably be assumed.

2.4 THE POST WALRASIAN CONCEPTION OF LONG RUN AND SHORT RUN

Adding a coordination role for institutions and a sequentially determined institutional structure has some important implications for the meaning we give to long run and short run. In Walrasian models, the difference between the long run and short run is simple: in the short run capital is fixed; in the long run capital is flexible. That distinction does not fit reality, since capital is often more easily changeable than is labor; hence the effect of the interpretation is that the applicability of results of the models to reality has been limited. Nonetheless, it has continued to be the key distinction between the long and short run. In the Post Walrasian construction, while there may be different degrees of lumpiness between labor and capital, that fixed/flexible capital difference is not the distinguishing feature between the long and short run. Indeed, in most of my initial thinking about the macro economy I find it useful to think of one composite input—an amalgam of capital and labor.

Instead, in the Post Walrasian model, the long run and short run distinctions center around what changes in coordinating institutions are allowed in the policy option you are considering. *What is fixed is not capital; what is fixed is institutional environment-social conventions that determine the habitual ways of doing things.* These habitual ways of doing things include pricing and inventory decisions and ways of approaching problems, as well as institutions such as corporate and market structure.

In the short run, the institutional environment is assumed fixed, and the primary macroeconomic coordination problems to be considered are expectational coordination problems that can occur within the existing institutional structure. For example, say everyone suddenly believes that aggregate demand is falling. That collectively-held expectation can cause suppliers to decrease production.

A specification of Post Walrasian short-run equilibrium involves specifying the way in which the economy coordinates expectations and how those expectations lead to an equilibrium in the economy within a range of possibilities set by existing institutions. Short-run analysis is the analysis of expectational coordination problems. Within the Post Walrasian view of macro, real fluctuations can be caused by changes in expectations as well as by real and nominal shocks. The short-run policy questions are: How well do existing institutions coordinate when presented with such shifts? And: What, if any, government actions can improve coordination?

The longer the run considered, the more institutions are allowed to change, and the greater the change in higher-level coordination mechanisms. The penultimate long run is that time period in which all institutions are considered changeable.[2] Thus, the long run and short run have nothing to do with an actual period of time, but instead have to do with the planning horizon individuals are using.

Which is the appropriate long run within which to model an economy? That is determined by the type of policy being analyzed, and the planning horizon that decision makers in the economy use. Returning to the computer analogy may shed some light on what I mean. Say one is initially operating in a DOS environment. One could, in a short time, change from a DOS environment to a Mac environment or a

Windows 95 environment; at any point in time, varying numbers of individuals will be using different planning horizons and dealing with such changes. (Others may be thinking about even more substantial changes, for example, using DNA computing, which involves a totally different type of information processing than that used by existing computers. For them, the long run would include switching from the existing system to a DNA system. But, generally, when most individuals think about the long run, they will not be thinking about such a substantial change). Those planning horizons used by individuals, not a set period of time, determine the long run one means in the model and determines the nature of changes in coordination that are analyzed. For example, corporations may or may not exist a century from now, but most of us will assume their existence in our planning horizon.

When most macro economists talk about the long run they are not talking about the time it takes to change my broadly defined concept of institutions and conventions. They are instead assuming a fixed institutional structure—usually a perfectly competitive institutional structure—and talking about the time it takes to change the capital within that institutional structure. From a Post Walrasian perspective, this conception has two problems. First, the assumed perfectly competitive institutional structure is different than the existing institutional structure. That means that they are modeling a problem quite different from the problem that exists in our economy. From the Post Walrasian perspective, the degree of price and wage flexibility exhibited by the economy is intricately connected to existing institutional structure, and if you assume the existing institutions, you must also assume the existing degree of wage and price level flexibility.

In the Post Walrasian view the explanation of the degree of flexibility lies in the theory of institutions, not in the theory of economics, given institutions. It follows that any unemployment that results from a combination of fixed prices and wages cannot be assumed to be solvable by wage and price level flexibility. That solution would require a breakdown of existing institutions. In terms of IS/LM analysis it means that the IS curve is the end of the road that must, in its derivation, necessarily include some assumption about the allowable degree of price level flexibility. It is not a curve from which a new model consisting of two curves: one which is incorrectly called an AD curve (but which is actually a goods market equilibrium curve), the other an AS curve (labor market equilibrium) curve derived from the standard production function.

2.5 THE IMPORTANCE OF INSTITUTIONS IN MACRO

The computer analogy discussed above also sheds light on the multiple equilibria aspect of Post Walrasian macro, how it pictures institutions leading people to choose among those equilibria, and the approach to policy it suggests. In the grandest of models, there are many operating systems, and the choice of one of them will exclude others. Most policy issues are addressed—given an operating system, and hence it is difficult to base any statements about global optimality on economic models. One can make predictions about the effect of policies, given institutions, and the standard reactions of individuals given those institutions, but those predictions are more the equivalent of engineering predictions—rules of thumb—than they are scientific predictions about the way macro economies, in some abstract sense, work.

Seeing the institutional structure in this way has a direct impact on the way in which one structures the underlying IS/LM model. Specifically, one wants that model to be descriptive of real-world institutions, because it is those institutions that are the economy's operating system. Non-contextual deductive reasoning from individual rationality will not provide insight into how the real-world economy is likely to respond to shocks.

The systemic role of institutions is relevant for IS/LM analysis and macro analysis generally, because it undermines the Walrasian approach to modeling. That approach involves assuming the price level is perfectly flexible, and the goods market is essentially an auction market. Our real world doesn't operate like that, and cannot operate like that. The degree of price level flexibility assumed by that approach (on the downward side) would undermine the structural integrity of the markets, causing the economy's operating system to crash. Thus, the degree of wage and price level flexibility assumed *is not* a modeling choice; it is a parameter that must be descriptive of the economy being described.

None of the above discussion would be novel to traditional macroeconomists, by which I mean old Keynesians or monetarists—that view of wage and price flexibility was part of their implicit understanding of the economy. But it was not part of the models, which were constructed within a Walrasian framework. Because it was not part of their formal model this traditional macro view was undermined as economists took seriously the challenge of developing a formal microfoundations.

The lack of any sense of this older view is obvious in New Classical work, but it is just as evident in much of the recent New Keynesian revolution. In this Post Walrasian view, the issue is not one of designing a model of imperfect competition that explains price and wage level inflexibility--the task New Keynesians have set for themselves. To even think in those terms presumes the meaningfulness of a "perfect competition" reference point. The Post Walrasian view is that without institutions there would be no economy as we know it; it is that market structure is part of the operating system of the economy, and that significant short-run price level flexibility is inconsistent with the functioning of markets as we know them. Perfect competition cannot serve as a benchmark by which to judge our economy. Instead, some concept of a "workably competitive" economy is the appropriate benchmark.

The New Classicals' and New Keynesians' failure to consider the role of institutions is the result of traditional macroeconomics' failure to specify the institutional limitations of macro models. It was that failure that, in many ways, led to the evolution away from traditional macro and towards New Classical macro. New Classical macroeconomics took seriously the global scientific claims of traditional macro. It then tried to rigorously set up the global foundations for macro in a perfectly competitive economy. It could not do so, so it claimed traditional macro was dead.

Once one takes a Post Walrasian view that individuals operate within constraints of an institutional structure (for which we have not yet developed a formal model) the New Classical claims disintegrate; there is no presumption that individual rationality leads to collective rationality. The goods market may be in long-run equilibrium, given institutions, at levels of output different than the economy's potential output.

2.6 PEDAGOGICALLY ALLOWING FOR THE TRADITIONAL MACROECONOMICS VIEW

As I stated above, this paper is about pedagogy, not about high theory, and the question I now turn to is how to incorporate this Post Walrasian view into the standard IS/LM model. My answer is: Be far humbler about what is being captured by IS/LM analysis than is currently the case.

Generally, IS/LM is presented in the texts with great fanfare as a simplified analysis formal model of the economy that has firm microeconomic foundations in an economy where the goods market is perfectly competitive. In the Post Walrasian institutional interpretation, IS/LM analysis isn't that, and should not be presented as that. Instead, it is a reasonable representation of the effects of shifts in the money supply, and of demand shocks in an economy with institutionally controlled prices, the analysis of the control of which we do not firmly understand. But that lack of understanding does not make the institutionally controlled prices any less real.

One way to make the limitations clearer is for economists, from the beginning, to emphasize the limited applicability of the IS/LM model. Currently, the IS/LM model is presented as a model based on a thought experiment that combines a predetermined combination of equilibrium interest rates and income levels in the money market with a predetermined combination of equilibrium interest rates and income levels in the goods market. The predetermination of these equilibria gives one an easy shorthand method of looking at the final equilibrium of many different policies. The analysis is standard, so I will not go through it here.

Such a thought experiment is far too grand for a Post Walrasian framework. In a Post Walrasian framework models of the aggregate economy have nowhere near the range of coverage that is generally claimed for the IS/LM model. Specifically, the assumptions that dynamics are complex—that the equilibrium is path dependent—makes it impossible to carry out the IS/LM thought experiment at the level of generality that is normally claimed for it. *In a path dependent economy, predetermined equilibria do not exist independent of a starting point and the dynamic adjustment properties.* Any system equilibrium is determined by the initial starting point and the dynamic path that the economy follows in response to a shift in one of the curves as it moves to a new equilibrium.

2.7 A MODEL OF FIRST ORDER CHANGES

To get around the problem, the Post Walrasian IS/LM approach uses a modified thought experiment that can be carried out under the assumption of path dependency. It is what might be called "a first order change" thought experiment. By this I mean the analysis takes as given that the starting point of the experiment is a long run equilibrium that has be arrived at through some historical process, and talks about changes from that equilibrium given the institutional assumptions that one is making.

This modified Post Walrasian thought experiment does not determine the full set of equilibria for the economy. It does not try to provide a complete model of the interest rate and income level in a timeless setting. In a path dependent system such a complete model would have to include all past history, since that history determines the current equilibrium. This thought experiment only provides a model of how the interest rate and income level will change from some starting point in response to shocks that hit the system. (Even this modified thought experiment requires the strong assumption that one begins the experiment in long-run equilibrium. In the real world one is never in long-run equilibrium. I justify such a starting point in two ways: First, it is the assumption used in the standard comparative static model; and second, as. a starting point in organizing one's thoughts about adjustment, it is a useful assumption). While this limits the generality of IS/LM analysis, it is consistent with how the model is generally used—as a way to discuss the effect of a shift in monetary policy or fiscal policy. It provides an explanation of how monetary and fiscal policy can change potential income.

2.8 A MODIFIED PRODUCTION FUNCTION

To further emphasize the fact that IS/LM analysis does not have Walrasian microfoundation, one would also emphasize the complications that can arise in trading among individuals when there are not perfectly flexible prices, and the implications for aggregating into a composite production function that that presents. Currently this is not done. The basic framework of the formal models has not taken seriously the interdependence of supply and demand decisions that must be dealt with if one is to talk reasonably about an aggregate composite of goods in a market structure which is not perfectly coordinated by price.

The standard production function precludes doing so. In the standard production function either supply or demand takes precedent. This was inherent in the specification of the aggregate supply curve, which saw the aggregate production function as an individual production function, writ large. (In the traditional Keynesian presentation, demand creates its own supply; in the tradition Classical presentation, supply creates its own demand. In the Post Walrasian presentation, aggregate supply and demand are interdependent; one cannot analyze one without the other).

What the standard specification of the production function rules out, by assumption, is any *demand constraints being institutionally built into supply decisions.* In the Keynesian interpretation of the standard model demand constraints and price inflexibility can lead to a demand-constrained economy, but there was always the implication that if only prices were flexible the economy could do better.

If one is to maintain a Post Walrasian vision, in which market structure is part of the operating system of the economy, one must directly deal with the problem of moving from an individual production function to an aggregate production function. The aggregate production function must include the possibility of strategic interdependence of the components of the aggregate; it must allow for the possibility that individual firms do not produce because they do not expect the demand for their product to exist.

To incorporate this inherent interdependence, I have argued that it is useful to think of the aggregate production function as differing from the individual firm production function by a coordination factor, C. This shift factor allows the amount producers choose to supply to the market to shift independently of changes in the level of employment, and hence independent of changes in the real wage. Even if both labor and capital were fixed in the relevant short run, output supplied could still fall if there is a fluctuation in expected demand because expectations of demand influence the coordination factor in the production function. (Notice that this specification allows for total labor productivity to fluctuate pro cyclically.)

At issue is how to interpret a demand-constrained aggregate equilibrium. In the standard production function, demand constrained equilibria are seen as representing disequilibrium points, off the desired supply curve. That is why it was seen as legitimate to add a supply curve, given by labor-market equilibrium curve, to the IS/LM-determined equilibrium points. In this standard interpretation the IS/LM equilibria were not true equilibria; they were goods market disequilibria. It is that characterization that Post Walrasians reject. What are ruled out by this view are any expectational problems or coordination failures on the part of the supply, which are inherent to the structure of the economy. The "true" supply curve is given by the production possibility curve, which is essentially the economy's potential income determined solely by technical considerations. It allows for no coordination problems that make the economy's potential income lower than the technological limit of potential income. The only way that the true potential income could be reached was by having a perfectly flexible price level. That is not the case with a coordination augmented production function. In that production function demand-constrained equilibria can be full equilibria, given the assumed institutional structure.

Adding the coordination variable does not explain any of the above issues; such explanations involve complicated mathematics and are still the subject of research. The addition simply allows for such issues to be part of the story that accompanies the pedagogical model. It allows an expanded story accompanying the simple pedagogical model that we present to students.

Probably the most important of these implications in the interpretation of the IS/LM model is the implication that the same amount of capital and labor can be associated with different amounts of aggregate output, depending on the degree of coordination imposed by existing institutions. The short-run production function is institutionally as well as technically determined. Thus, the Post Walrasian interpretation allows the analysis of aggregate production to go beyond the issue of relative prices. In doing this it changes the nature of policy discussion by allowing alternative paths for policy to influence the economy.

In my view a primary path through which policy influences the economy is through its effects on expectations, and the coordination variable in the production function allows one to incorporate such effects in the interpretation of models. For example, fiscal policy or monetary policy might influence the coordination variable and thereby change the level of output, even if they do not affect a single relative price. The Post Walrasian foundations of IS/LM analysis will be on these extra-market coordination variables, and how monetary and fiscal policy can change coordination factors to bring about standard IS/LM policy conclusions. These changes make a substantial difference in the story we tell to explain the workings of the macro economy.

2.8.1 The Post Walrasian Explanation of the Impact of a Fall in Interest Rates on Investment

The primary policy problem that monetary and fiscal policy might possibly solve in the Post Walrasian short run concerns coordination. Given a less than perfectly flexible wage and price operating system, expectations can become miscoordinated and expectations of low output can lead to low output. When people expect low demand, they produce low output, and their expectations are brought about by their own actions. Thus, there is a set of multiple equilibria that the economy can reach, any one of which could be an equilibrium depending on which expectations are chosen. The issue that IS/LM analysis needs to explain is how, and under what circumstances, does a fall in interest rates improve coordination, and hence lead to a downward sloping IS curve? With that downward sloping IS curve, an increase in the LM curve will lead the economy to a different equilibrium.

To see the argument of how this occurs, it is helpful to reconsider the disequilibrium saving/investment analysis above. Will a fall in the interest rate lead to a temporary increase in output or will savings be a binding constraint? In general, savings will not be the binding constraint. The reason is that there are two sources of savings—from existing income, and from wealth. Generally, savings from existing income is considered the only source of savings; savings coming from existing income can be a binding constraint. This follows since the source of these savings is prior to investment. However, savings can also come from someone guaranteeing a future payment from investment, say by establishing collateral based on their wealth. The people accepting this guarantee are saving, but it is not coming from prior income; it is coming from income that is being created by the investment. The investment increases income, and creates the actual savings necessary to finance it. Savings are simply financial assets that can be created whenever anyone is willing to accept a financial liability. So generally savings out of wealth can be created out of thin air simply by creating expectations of a growing economy. A fall in the interest rate, such as would be caused by expansionary monetary policy, is one way to get such savings created. This means that, except in times of financial crisis, investment, not savings, is the binding constraint, and there is an initial impact of a fall in the interest rate.

The Post Walrasian case assumes expectations can affect savings and that those expectations can drive the economy in the short run. Disequilibrium savings can be created out of thin air. When people believe the economy will do better, they are willing to make loans and accept more promises. If there were "too low" expectations before, this can improve the situation. Expectations of the state of the economy in the future, in conjunction with interest rates, are the driving force of savings. In normal times a fall in interest rates increases expectations of the future, so investment is the driving force when the savings market is in disequilibrium. A temporary fall in the interest rate brings about a rise in investment and output. That higher output creates patterns of trade coordination that did not exist previously, and in doing so, can increase the economy's potential income given the institutional structure. The savings curve shifts out and the economy arrives at a higher level of equilibrium.

It is within this context that the historical debate about whether the interest rate is determined in the money market or goods market plays a central role. That debate has relevance to the Post Walrasian interpretation of IS/LM if it concerned disequilibrium interest rates. If the goods market interest rate predominated in disequilibrium, the temporary rise in investment accompanying a monetary-policy-induced fall in the interest rate would be short lived, and unlikely to generate any additional trade patterns and thereby increase the economy's potential income.

However, if the money market interest rate predominated, the goods market disequilibrium would be far more likely to affect real patterns of trade, creating new patterns and changing the long-run equilibrium interest rate and potential income of the economy. In this view, given the coordination mechanisms in the economy there is a range of interest rates and income levels that will represent possible equilibria for the economy. There is not a point, but, rather, a vector of possible outcomes, and which outcome the economy achieves depends on what monetary and fiscal policy the government chooses.

The Post Walrasian IS curve captures these outcomes. It is defined as the combination of potential equilibrium interest rates and income levels that can exist if the interest rate starts at interest rate i* and is raised or lowered by a given amount, assuming a given disequilibrium adjustment path. In the Post Walrasian framework *potential income* depends crucially on the degree of coordination in the economy. Other things constant, coordination is constant, but many things can affect it. Now say that, suddenly, real income expands above expected income—this expansion opens up new paths of coordination in the economy that otherwise was not possible, and with that increases potential income. The IS curve captures that increase in potential income that is brought about by a decrease in the interest rate in normal times.

In the complex-dynamics literature there are many ways in which the dynamics can affect the final equilibrium. The interpretation of IS/LM I proposed above assumes one of the simplest of these ways—that the dynamic path affects the final equilibrium in a continuous, deterministic way. Depending on whether the disequilibrium price is above or below the initial equilibrium price, and whether the disequilibrium quantities are above or below the initial equilibrium quantity, the equilibrium prices and quantities change in deterministic ways. This is an enormously strong assumption about the dynamic properties of the system. My two justifications for it are that: (1) historically there is some empirical justification for this, and that empirical justification accounts for the longevity of IS/LM conclusions; and (2) the assumption, while enormously strong in reference to complex dynamics, is weaker than the standard assumption that no path dependency exists and that dynamics are not complex.

2.9 CONCLUSION

It is important to recognize what this Post Walrasian interpretation of IS/LM analysis is, and what it is not. It is not a general theory of aggregate income level in the economy, nor is it a theory of the interest rate. It is a component of both, but it is only a component. What the model says is that low income has a tendency to beget low income and high income has a tendency to beget high income. In some cases, by slightly pushing the economy with monetary and fiscal policy, we can increase its potential income by opening up individuals' eyes to trading possibilities that they did not previously recognize. This does not deny that the economy cannot be pushed too far, and can destroy existing patterns of coordination. IS/LM is not a general theory, but an organizing framework whose applicability to the real world depends on institutional judgments about what is feasible.

Such a model is, I believe, useful to teach students. It eminently fits Tobin's and Solow's view of the usefulness of IS/LM as a thought-organizing tool, and it has the advantage of directing students' analysis into dynamics, rather than into the static nature of the curves. As opposed to making Keynesian analysis something that simply dismisses the New Classical challenge to wage/price flexibility, it answers it with a multiple equilibrium model in which the IS curve reflects assumptions of rational expectations, but not a unique equilibrium. Thus, within a Post Walrasian framework the Keynesian model is logical; whether it is something upon which policy can be based is a more difficult question that I will not address here.

BIBLIOGRAPHY

Colander, David (ed.). 1996. *Beyond Microfoundations: Post Walrasian Macroeconomics.* New York: Cambridge University Press.

Colander, David. 1995. "The Stories We Tell: A Reconsideration of AS/AD Analysis." *Journal of Economic Perspectives,* 9, 3, summer.

Hicks, John (1980). "IS/LM: An Explanation", *Journal of Post Keynesian Economics,* vol. 3 Winter.

Nevile, J.W. and Rao, B. (1996). "The Use and Abuse of Aggregate Demand and Supply Functions", *Manchester School,* 64, 2, June.

Solow, Robert, (1984). "Mr. Hicks and the Classics", *Oxford Economic Papers* (vol. 36. Supplement).

Tobin, James. 1980. *Asset Accumulation and Economic Activity.* Oxford: Basil Blackwell.

Young, Warren, (1987). *Interpreting Mr. Keynes,* Westview Press, Boulder, Colorado

ENDNOTES

[1] By including a psychic cost of being dishonest one can make the cost/benefit approach tautological, but that simply translates institutions into something that affects individuals' taste and hence part of the analysis since tastes can no longer be assumed exogenous.

[2] It should be quite clear that the penultimate long run is irrelevant to everyone in the economy except philosophers.

3

IS-LM AND AGGREGATE DEMAND: A RESTATEMENT

David F. Heathfield

3.1 INTRODUCTION

There can be little doubt that the dominance of U.K. economic policy by supply side theorists has led to the neglect of aggregate demand. Policies such as cutting unemployment benefit, for example, are increasingly considered only in terms of their effects on labor supply. Any effect they may have on aggregate demand is neglected. On the other hand there is implicit recognition that demand is important. Over the cycle, we may await the return of consumer confidence and the upswing in exports to ensure that the green shoots of economic recovery grow into full bloom. The fact that they are `awaited' implies not only that aggregate demand is important but also that is not to be hurried. Policies may be (and indeed are) designed to influence supply but apparently little or nothing can be done about aggregate demand.

It is asserted here that the dismissal of Keynesian economics is a mistake and that policies concerning the manipulation of aggregate demand should be used albeit in conjunction with supply-side policies.

The re-examination of aggregate demand is based largely on Rowan (1983) who in turn refers to Davidson and Smolensky (1965), who follow Weintraub (1958) and chapter 19 of *The General Theory*. One reason for reiterating what has already been said elsewhere is that many, if not most, modern macroeconomic texts offer unhelpful and arguably misleading accounts of the relationship between aggregate demand and the general level of prices in 'Keynesian' models. This tide of confusion and misrepresentation is pervasive and shows no sign of abating indeed it is becoming commonplace to refer to Keynesian economics (sometimes qualified as New-Keynesian) as a fixed (or sluggish) priced version of the more general classical model.

Some examples might help to illustrate this tendency to massage Keynes into the classical mold.

"One consequence of the Keynesian revolution of the 1930's was the acceptance of a rigid absolute price level, as the starting point for analyzing short term economic change" (Friedman's Nobel Lecture).

"Certainly the short run sluggishness of wages and prices was the key assumption of the consensus (Keynesian) view of the 1960's. And the absence of an adequate theoretical justification for that assumption was one of the fatal flaws that undermined that consensus." (Mankiw, *J.E.L.*, 1990).

"Everyone knows that nominal price and wage rigidities are central to Keynesian theory." (Blinder, *Macroeconomics Under Debate*, Wheatsheaf, 1989).

"New Keynesian economists all agree that these imperfections exist, are important and together can account better for Macro phenomena ... than alternative perfect market models." (Stiglitz, *Alternative Approaches to Macro*. N.B.E.R., 1991).

This version of Keynesian economics is so close to the views of his more conservative contemporaries as not to admit the possibility of a Keynesian revolution. Yet, according to Leijonhufvud (Latis, 1976) there certainly was such a revolution. Its hallmarks (in line with Kuhn's definition) were the breakdown of language—witness the bitterness in Keynes' remarks on Pigou, the growth of knowledge—later to become Macroeconomics, and the Kuhnian loss—all value theory. This latter was, according to Leijonhufvud, too great a loss and was retained as Microeconomics.

It is intended here to examine the more commonly expressed versions of Keynesian economics and to compare them with what is in the *General Theory*. As is so often the case, the misrepresentation of Keynes is no well-specified, single-headed monster. However it is not intended here to dive too deeply into its many depths and folds but rather to construct a straw man—or, more accurately, matchstick man—in order to focus on a few main issues.

Many complexities are avoided by invoking the services of the auctioneer, thereby excluding any trading at false prices and removing problems of expectation formation. Furthermore all markets will be perfectly competitive, the economy is closed and there is an aggregate production function that satisfies the first and second order conditions for a maximum. These simplifications make the problems manageable—particularly on the supply side—and can hardly be said to bias things in favor of Keynesian models, on the contrary they should commend themselves to the neoclassicals.

Using this framework, section 2 of the chapter briefly rehearses what mainstream macro-economic textbooks have to say on aggregate demand curves; section 3 does the same for aggregate supply curves; section 4 offers a Keynesian aggregate demand curve with fixed money wage rates; section 5 extends this to cover flexible money wage rates; section 6 examines the effects of income redistribution; section 7 introduces the real balance effect and section 8 considers the wealth effects. Finally section 9 offers some conclusions.

3.2 SOME TEXTBOOK AGGREGATE DEMAND CURVES

One version of the Aggregate Demand curve is derived from the IS-LM diagram and is found, for example, in Parkin and Bade (1986) and Thompson et al. (1987). An IS-LM diagram is drawn up on the assumption of (among other things) a fixed price level. Redrawing the IS-LM diagram for a succession of different price levels yields the familiar result that as price level falls so interest rate falls and output rises. Output continues to fall as price increases until the liquidity trap is reached and thereafter no further change in output or interest rate occurs. (The wealth effect and the income redistribution effect will be considered later.) The downward sloping relationship between output and price level generated in this way is the most popular textbook of the aggregate demand curve.

To call this a demand curve at all is something of a misnomer—at the very least it is an unhelpful way to use language. In order to construct an IS-LM diagram it is necessary to assume that aggregate demand equals aggregate supply. That being so, the resulting relationship between price level and output is neither an aggregate demand curve nor an aggregate supply curve—it is a set of equilibrium points—a 'mongrel' curve.

A second, less popular, textbook version of an aggregate demand curve is that derived from the equation of exchange $(MV = PY)$. According to this equation, with fixed money supply and constant velocity, the relationship between level and output must describe a rectangular hyperbola. This downward sloping curve demand curve is discussed, for example, in Hall and Treadgold (1982) who refer to its use by Corden in Corden (1978). It is also referred to (and dismissed) in chapter 19 of the *General Theory*.

In this equation Y is simply the quantity of newly produced goods and services and is both the quantity supplied and the quantity demanded. Although it is usually interpreted in terms of the product market it applied equally to factor markets and hence supply, like demand, is limited by a shortage of money. Supply cannot exceed that which is produced when the factor market runs up against the exchange constraint. Like the IS-LM version (above) this aggregate demand curve also applied equally to both supply and demand and is therefore misnamed.

The objection to this second version however goes further. It is quite clear from the *General Theory* that money is held not only for transactions but also for asset and speculative motives—the liquidity preference schedule. It is therefore simply wrong to use the transactions demand alone to derive the Keynesian relationship between price level and aggregate demand.

A third version of aggregate demand derives from Say's Law and is rarely, if ever, mentioned in modern macro texts. This is a little surprising since Say's Law was the rock upon which Mathus's earlier attempt to show that output was limited by "want of vent" foundered. There seems to be some confusion about exactly what is meant by Say's Law and a number of variants have appeared (see, for example, Baumol (1977)). The account relied on here is that contained in the second essay of Mill (1874). The law holds that, in aggregate, in the absence of one-sided agents, supply creates its own demand and hence the relationship between price level and aggregate supply (the aggregate supply curve) will be that between price level and aggregate demand (the aggregate demand curve). The two curves are therefore identical and accordingly it is logically unnecessary to construct an aggregate demand curve—all that need be done is to model aggregate supply.

3.3 TESTBOOK AGGREGATE SUPPLY CURVES

The aggregate supply curve has been much discussed in the literature (see, for example, Roberts (1978)) and, like the demand curves, can be constructed in more than one way. First by assuming that money wage rate is fixed, that the factor and product markets are perfectly competitive and profits are maximized. The auctioneer calls out a sequence of price levels and the entrepreneurs decide how much output to offer, and how many man hours to employ, at each price. These offers are made as if the auctioneer will buy all the output that is offered and supply all the man hours that are demanded—i.e., neither entrepreneurs nor workers expect rationing in either market.

As price level rises, real wage rates fall and employment and output are expanded until full employment is reached. Thereafter output may remain constant (if labor does not actually leave the market but put up with lower and lower real wages) or output may fall (if the lower real wage rate causes the supply of labor to decrease along its supply curve). These curves are shown as (a) and (b) respectively in diagram 1.

This upward sloping supply curve relies on money wages responding to neither price changes nor to the level of unemployment. There are two variants of this. The first is that money wage rates remain constant up to full employment and thereafter rise *pari passsu* with price changes. This version of the curve is the same as the fixed money wage version with output remaining constant once full employment is reached (curve 'a' in diagram 1).

Diagram 1. Two aggregate supply curves.

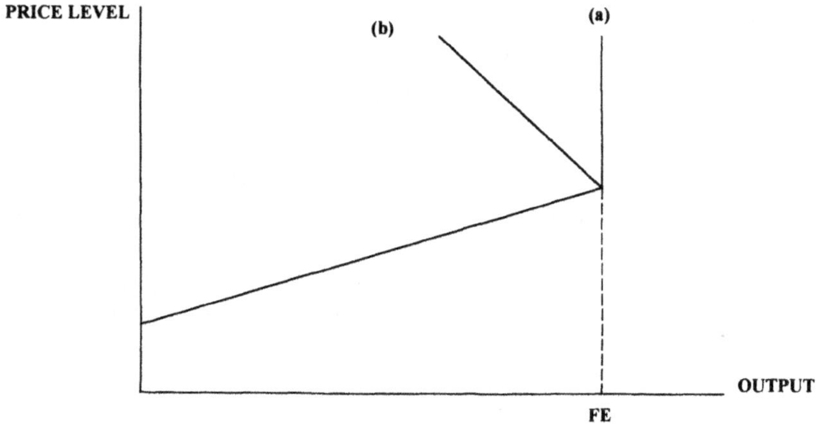

The second variant of the aggregate supply curve assumes real wage rate is held constant at that which would clear the labor market. Any increase in price precipitates an equal proportionate increase in money wage rates. The resulting version of the aggregate supply curve is referred to as either a `long run' supply curve or a neoclassical supply curve. (See, for example, Thompson et al. (1987).) It is vertical with output held constant at the level that corresponds to the `natural rate' of unemployment. There are no discussions as to how this real wage rate is actually determined. (This supply curve is shown in diagram 2.)

These three versions of the aggregate supply curve have all seen the light of day and, as far as Say's Law is concerned, each constitutes its own aggregate demand curve. Typically, however, these supply curves are used in conjunction with one of the two earlier versions of aggregate 'demand' curves to solve for price and output. This, as has been argued, can be misleading in that the 'demand' curves are, in fact, mongrel curves satisfying both supply and demand.

In what follows an alternative version of an aggregate demand is offered. It is a version which seems closest to the *General Theory* and turns out to depend upon the choice of supply curve. There will thus be one demand curve associated with each of these possible supply curves.

3.4 A KEYNESIAN AGGREGATE DEMAND CURVE

This version of an aggregate demand curve is outlined, among others, by Rowan (1983) and arguably corresponds most closely to the account given by Keynes in Chapter 19 of the *General Theory*.

In a closed economy comprising households (who consume) and firms (who invest) aggregate demand must be made up of these two components only. More gen-

Diagram 2. The classical supply curve.

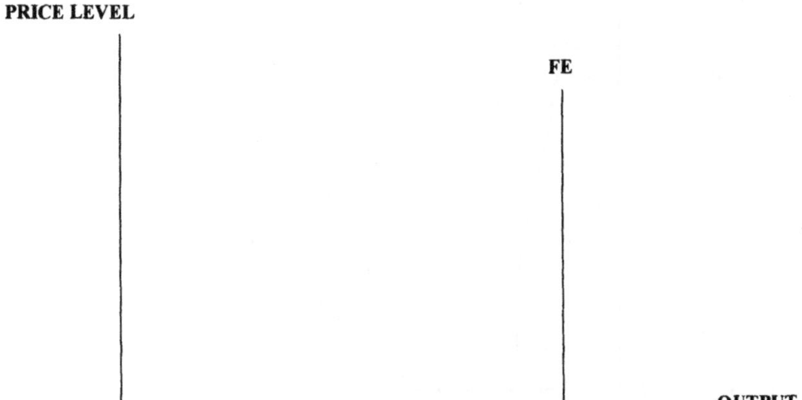

erally, the two elements of demand could be that part which is influenced by income (whether from households or firms) and that part which is influenced by interest rates (again whether by households or firms) but for simplicity the former will be referred to as consumption and the latter as investment. In order to explain what happens to aggregate demand as price level rises it is necessary to explain what happens to consumption and what happens to investment.

In this simplest of worlds, consumption depends on income in such a way that consumption exceeds income when income is low but rises by less than income so that it eventually equals and then falls below income. In order to link consumption to price level therefore, all that is necessary is to link income to price level and this is done via the supply curve. Since there is more than one version of the aggregate supply curve there will be more than one associated demand curve.

Version 1

The fixed money wage rate version of the supply curve is criticized by Rao (1986) and defended by Owen (1987a, 1987b). According to this version income rises as the price level rises and thus consumption will also rise with price level. Consumption exceeds income at low prices (low income) but rises less than income does as price level rises. This component (the consumption component) of the aggregate demand curve is therefore upward sloping and more steeply sloped than the aggregate supply curve which it therefore crosses. This is shown as curve 'a' in diagram 3.

The other component of aggregate demand is investment and, again in the simplest of models, it is determined by interest rate. The link between price level and interest rate is not straightforward. As price increases then, via the supply curve, real income increases. Since both price and real income have increased then nominal

Diagram 3. two components of aggregate demand.

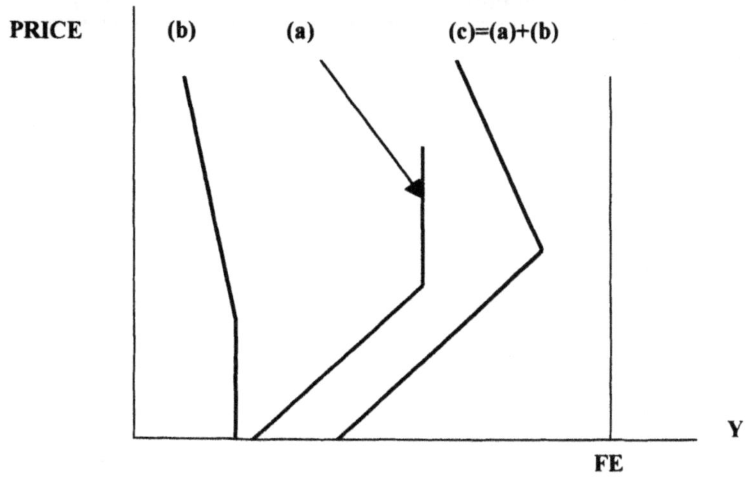

income has also increased. This will increase the demand for active balances and so reduce the level of idle balances. This, in turn, will cause interest rate to rise and investment to fall. This component of aggregate demand is therefore downward sloping. At very low prices the economy will be in the liquidity trap with minimum interest rate and maximum investment. As price level rises the economy leaves the liquidity trap and investment begins to fall. This is shown as curve 'b' in diagram 3.

Summing these two components to yield aggregate demand results in high demand at low prices (higher than supply) and then an increasing demand as price rises. The demand curve is however rising more steeply than the supply curve and eventually the two cross. Finally, as consumption reaches its maximum and investment falls the demand curve will bend back on itself and become downward sloping. This is shown as curve 'c' in diagram 3.

The Keynesian approach therefore is to neither assume nor rule out the possibility of Say's law but to explicitly model aggregate demand and see where it leads. It is conceivable that the two components of aggregate demand always sum to aggregate supply. It is also possible to work out the ways in which such equality could be maintained: this instructive exercise, however, has not, as far as I know, been attempted.

The intersection of the aggregate supply and aggregate demand curves yields equilibrium output (Keynes *effective* demand) and equilibrium price level (see diagram 4). Any increase in price level above equilibrium would cause supply to increase by more than demand would increase and hence unable to find vent—price (and therefore supply) would consequently fall back again. Any decrease in price level below equilibrium would reduce supply by more than it would reduce demand and so there would be a shortage which would induce an increase in price and return output to its equilibrium level. There may, however, be some labor seeking work at the going wage rate and unable to find it. Unemployed labor will induce the auctioneer to lower real wage by increasing price level to clear the product market. The auctioneer is therefore unable to find a price which clears both the labor market and the product market simultaneously. Persistent over-production is simply not possible

Diagram 4. The Keynesian point of effective demand.

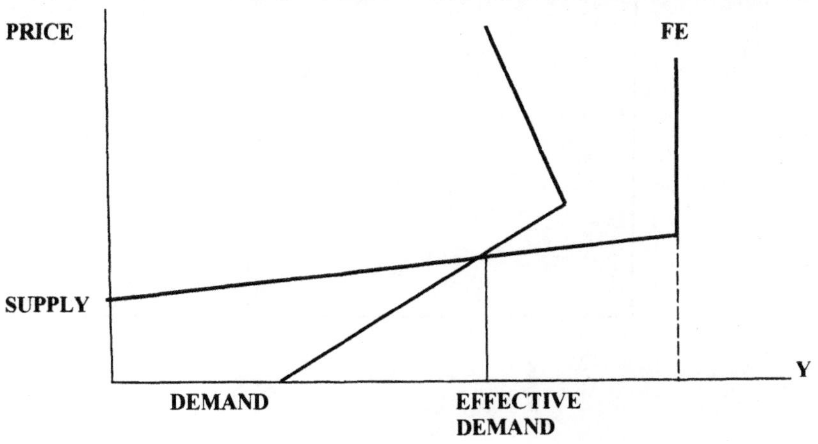

since bankruptcy lies that way and so the labor market bears all the disequilibrium. Hence Keynes' acceptance of the first classical postulate that the real wage always equals the marginal physical product of labor.

This model appears to give to the neo-classicals all they require for markets to work. Price level, real wage rate and output are all model determined and the markets are perfectly competitive and 'cleared' by the auctioneer. Even so, the model settles down at a stable, persistent equilibrium which may well occur at less than full employment.

Version 2

In the case of fixed real wage rate (fixed, by assumption, at the market clearing rate) the aggregate supply curve is vertical at the full employment level of output and hence so too will be the consumption component of aggregate demand. It will lie to the left of the supply curve since some saving is assumed to take place at the full employment level of income. The other component of aggregate demand (investment) behaves much as before—constant for low price levels when in the liquidity trap and then falling as price level and interest rate rises. This aggregate demand curve is therefore never upward sloping but may be vertical when in the liquidity trap. It may therefore never actually reach the vertical supply curve. In this case there is no equilibrium of price level and output and the auctioneer is unable to find any price which clears the goods market. This is shown in diagram 5. This outcome (and its associated aggregate supply curve) is that which would arise if the auctioneer attempted to clear the labor market and threw all the disequilibrium onto the product market, i.e., continued to buy up the excess supply.

Diagram 5. The aggregate demand associated with classical supply.

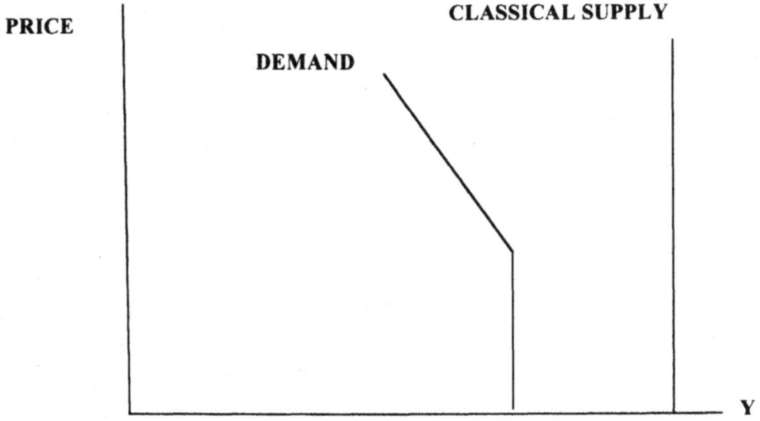

3.5 VARIABLE REAL AND VARIABLE MONEY WAGE RATES

The advantage of the fixed money wage rate supply curve (version 1) and its associated demand curve is that it yields an equilibrium in the goods market and shows how output, real wage and price level are determined once money wage rate is known. If this results in less than full employment then the model can be recast with a lower nominal wage rate to see what would happen if the labor force could be persuaded to adopt a flexible money wage policy.

If money wage rate is reduced, in the face of involuntary unemployment, then at each price level the real wage will be lower than before and hence the upward sloping part of the aggregate supply curve moves to the right. This movement alone would result in a lower equilibrium price and a lower level of output and employment. (This movement and the new equilibrium is shown as point 'a' in diagram 6). However the movement of the supply curve will induce a similar movement of the demand curve since if at each price level output will be higher than so too will consumption be higher.

The effect of a lower money wage rate on price, output and employment will depend on the relative movements of the two curves. What is certain is that as wage rate falls, price will fall. Initially, when price level is high, it will fall quicker than money wage rate so that real wages will fall and output will rise and the economy moves towards full employment. This movement continues until the liquidity trap is

Diagram 6. The locus of points of effective demand as money wages fall.

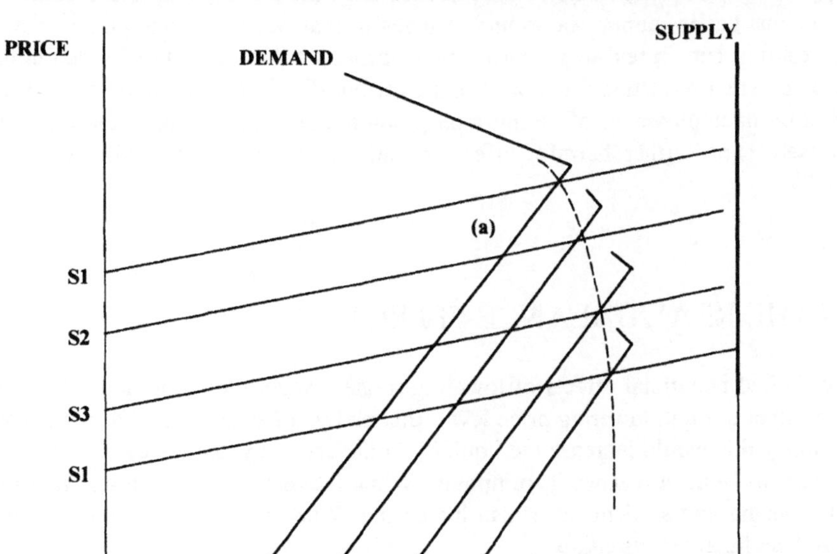

reached, therefore price falls at the same rate as wages rates and so real wage rates, output and employment remain constant. The locus of these intersections corresponds to those points traced out by the intersections of the IS-LM curves as price falls and is shown is diagram 6.

The liquidity trap prevents the economy from reaching full employment even when money wages, real wages, and prices are flexible and when perfectly competitive markets are 'cleared' by an auctioneer and with profit maximization conditions satisfied.

This endogenity of price level and its dependence on money wage rate demonstrates very clearly that labor cannot, by negotiating lower money wage rates, decrease real wage rates to market clearing levels.

3.6 INCOME DISTRIBUTION

Apart from the effects of the falling money wage rates on price level and hence on demand via the rate of interest there is also the possibility of its affecting income distribution. If falling money rates cause a redistribution of income from labor to capital then, given a lower marginal propensity to consume by capitalists, the aggregate marginal propensity to consume would fall and further depress demand, output and employment. Since the first classical postulate is met (by assumption), this supposed redistribution of income depends on the real wage rate falling as the money wage rate falls and on the aggregate production function having an elasticity of substitution between zero and unity. Were the function to take the Cobb-Douglas form, for example, then income shares would remain constant whatever happens to real wages. Tarshis (1936) offers some evidence that 'there is a positive association between changes in money wages and changes in real wages' so that cuts in nominal can result in cuts in real wage rates. The evidence on the elasticity of substitution of the aggregate production function is less clear but if it is inelastic than the corrective effect on unemployment of falling money wage rates will be moderated rather than reversed. (For further harmful effects of this 'cure' for unemployment see Dutt (1987).)

3.7 THE REAL BALANCE EFFECT

The limited beneficial effects of lowering money wage rates (outlined above) have their effect through lowering price level (though by not as much). With a fixed stock of money this would increase the liquidity in the economy and hence reduce the rate of interest—until it reaches its minimum. While interest rates are falling, investment is increasing and so demand is also increasing. When interest reaches its minimum these beneficial effects cease.

The reduction in interest rate is necessary to persuade wealthholders to accept the increased liquidity of their portfolios. In 'real balance effect' models the emphasis is on the transaction demand rather than the asset demand for money. As price level falls the money not now needed for transactions will 'burn holes in the pockets of consumers' who increase their expenditure to rid themselves of their unwanted liquidity. This increased expenditure will lead to shifts in the aggregate demand curve until full employment is reached and money wage rates no longer fall. This transmission mechanism does not act via the rate of interest and therefore continues to operate even in the liquidity trap—it has no lower bound. What is being denied is the Keynesian contention that money in circulation is endogenous and agents will absorb excess liquidity by increasing the liquidity of their portfolios rather than with increased transactions. These models also, of course, assume that all transactions are proxied by those involving currently produced goods and services. Any increase in activity in asset markets would absorb liquidity and prevent the continued movement of the demand curve.

3.8 THE WEALTH EFFECT

Like the real balance effect the wealth effect is a denial of the vertical section of the demand curve

> This revival [of monetary policy] ... pointed out a channel—namely changes in wealth—whereby changes in the real quality of money can affect aggregate demand even if they do not alter interest rates. ... fundamentally, they did undermine Keynes' key theoretical proposition, namely that even in a world of flexible prices, a position of equilibrium full employment might not exist. Henceforth, unemployment had again to be explained by rigidities or imperfections, not as the natural outcome of full operative market process. (Friedman, 1968)

Agents who hold nominal assets see the real value of this part of their wealth increase as price level falls. Insofar as these nominal assets are liabilities of other agents and insofar as the price change was not anticipated, there will be a redistribution of wealth from borrowers to lenders. Assuming a certain symmetry of agents' reactions to changes in wealth this redistribution of wealth will have no effect on aggregate demand. However, if there is 'outside' nominal wealth there will, it is claimed, be an aggregate effect. As real wealth increases the need for saving becomes less pressing and so inside agents consume more of their current incomes. This increase in consumption leads to a steadily rising level of aggregate demand as price level falls.

The existence or otherwise of 'outside' assets has come in for a great deal of questioning but it is possible to cut through much of this by following the neoclassical model itself. According to this model the wealth of the nation is the present discounted value of its future income stream. Unless that income stream changes or unless the discount rate changes there can be no change in real wealth. The proponents of the wealth effect do not argue that the discount rate has changed and, since they are seeking to show that the future income stream increases, they cannot begin by assuming it. Some support for this view is offered in Sweeney (1988).

The wealth effect does not therefore invalidate the Keynesian case and the real balance effect relies on the excess liquidity being used to buy more currently produced goods rather than to increase the exchange activity in the markets for existing goods and assets or to simply disappear into banks and idle balances.

Thus the explanations offered as to why the price mechanism continues to work, even under Keynesian assumptions, rely on a wealth effect (which is incompatible with acceptable definitions of real wealth) or on rejecting the Keynesian assumption of a liquidity trap. Furthermore, both require money to be exogenous.

For this, and other reasons, Keynes argued that flexible downward money wages is not a strategy which commends itself to the workers. The fixed money wage assumption of which Keynesian models are accused of making is, in fact, a recommendation—a conclusion of the model. Textbook accounts of 'Keynesian fixed price models' therefore put the cart before the horse. This point has been forcibly made by many writers, e.g., Patinkin (1965) and McCombie (1985-6).

The degree of aggregate price flexibility necessary to bring about full employment via the price mechanism is very high (see, for example, Pigou (1943)). The aggregate price level will move up and down by substantial amounts in response to exogenous shocks.

Diagram 7. Restoring the failure of aggregate demand by shifting supply.

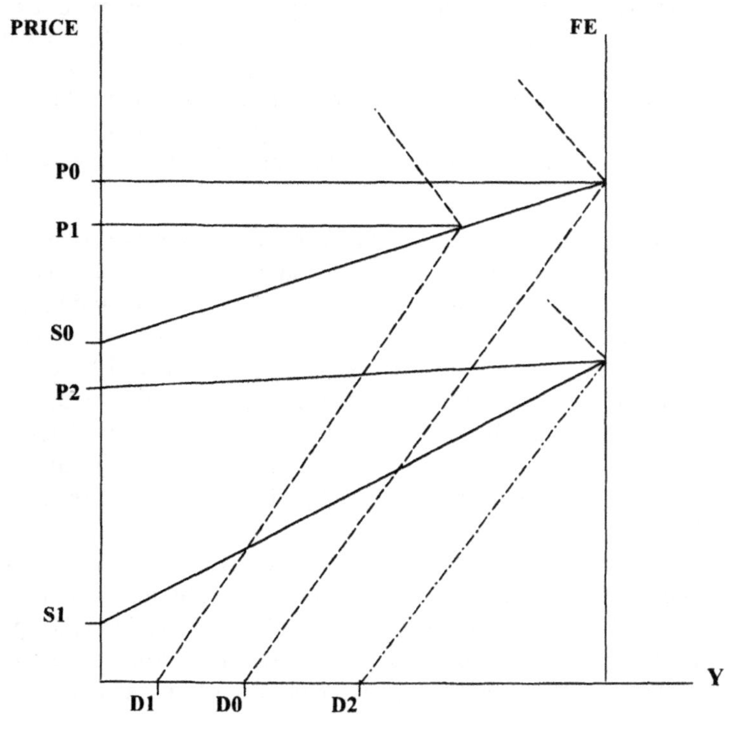

Imagine an economy at full employment equilibrium at price level *Po*. A demand side shock occurs and output falls and price level falls to *P1* (see diagram 7). According to Keynes, the preferred solution is to restore aggregate demand via fiscal expansion to bring output back to full employment and price level back to *Po*. The neo-classical solution seems to be to allow price level to continue to fall until the windfall gains perceived by certain asset holders induces them to increase their demand for currently produced goods and services. Small demand shocks thus require large price changes in order to correct them, magnified by the automatic correction mechanism. This is a somewhat strange role for aggregate price level of which, we are told, by, for example, Friedman (1968):

> Our economic system will work best when consumers, employers and employees, can proceed with full confidence that the average level of prices will behave in a known way in future—preferably that will be highly stable.

Furthermore, in an open economy with fixed exchange rates (or common currency) the task of the aggregate price level is to maintain external balance and is simply not available for the full employment duty required of it by Keynes' critics.

3.9 CONCLUSIONS

A very basic model has been constructed in order to focus attention on what might be meant by a Keynesian aggregate demand curve and to demonstrate its use in explaining persistent, involuntary unemployment in flexible nominal wage, flexible real wage, flexible price models which obey all the usual assumptions of the neo-classical model—perfect competition, profit maximization and full information.

Though conforming to most neo-classical axioms the model remains true to the *General Theory*. Aggregate demand is modeled in terms of consumption demand, via a consumption function, and investment demand which depends upon the interest rate and the marginal efficiency of capital. Interest rate is determined by the liquidity preference schedule and the supply of money. The first classical postulate is maintained: the wage is equal to the marginal product of the labor. (The second classical postulate is not satisfied. The utility of the wage is not equal to the marginal disutility of that amount of employment.)

Entrepreneurs are maximizing profits (or, more accurately, quasi-rents) by equating nominal wage rate to the marginal revenue product off labor. It is not known what the rate of profit is nor how it varies with employment unless fixed costs and the elasticity of the production function are known. The presence of excess profits may have implications for the long run but will not result in any short run improvement in employment. In the short run, whatever profits are possible at output levels below the point of effective demand, profits would fall to zero beyond the point of effective demand (if stocks are valued at cost). The demand for labor curve will therefore become vertical at the point of effective demand. Since the first classical postulate is assumed to hold then real wages are determined at the kink and hence will be held above market clearing but it is not the rigidity of money wages which brings this about. Increasing aggregate demand will reduce real wages towards the full employment wage (see Garrison (1984)).

It is possible to argue that the real balance effect will restore the case for allowing flexible money wage rates to bring about a fully employed economy. This is the best case that can be made and is extremely weak. It advocates the use of the price level to restore internal balance, ignoring the effects of redistributing income and wealth, the need to maintain external balance and monetarists claim that price level must be at least predictable and preferably constant, if the economy is to operate efficiently.

BIBLIOGRAPHY

Baumol, W.J. (1977). "Say's (at least) Eight Laws or what Say and James Mill May Really Have Meant," *Economica* XL1V, May, pp. 145-162.

Corden, W.M. (1978). "Keynes and Others: Wages and Price Rigidities in Macro-economic Models," *Oxford Economic Papers* 30, 2, July, pp. 159-180.

Davidson, P. and Smolensky, E. (1965). *Aggregate Supply and Aggregate Demand Analysis.* Harper Row.

Dutt, A.K. (1987). "Wage Rigidity and Unemployment: The Simple Diagrammatics of Two Views," *Journal of Post Keynesian Economics* 9, 2, pp. 279-290.

Friedman, M. (1968). "The Role of Monetary Policy," *The American Economic Review* LVIII, pp. 1-35.

Garrison, C.B. (1984). "Friedman versus Keynes on the Theory of Employment," *Journal of Post Keynesian Economics* 7, 1 , pp. 114-127.

Hall, P.H. and Treadgold, M.L. (1982). "Aggregate Demand Curves: A Guide to Use and Abuse," *Australian Economic Papers*, pp. 37-48.

Latsis, S.J. (1976). *Method and Appraisal in Economics.* Cambridge University Press, UK.

Mill, J.S. (1974). *Some Unsettled Questions of Political Economy.* Second Edition. Kelly, New York.

Owen, P. Dorian. (1987a). "Aggregate Demand Curves in General Equilibrium Macro Economic Models: Comparisons with Partial Equilibrium Micro Economic Demand Curves". University of Canterbury. Discussion Paper No. 8710.

Owen, P. Dorian (1987b). "Alternative Aggregate Demand Functions in Macro Economics: A Comment. University of Canterbury. Discussion Paper No. 8711.

Parkin, M. and Bade, R. (1986). *Modern Macroeconomics.* Philip Allan. Second Edition.

Patinkin, D. (1965). *Money Interest and Prices.* Harper Row. Second Edition.

Pigou, A.C. (1943). "The Classical Stationary State," *Economic Journal* LIII, 212, December, pp. 343-351.

Rao, B.B. (1986). "Alternative Aggregate Demand Functions in Macro Economics," *Australian Economic Papers*, pp. 261-264.

Rao, B.B. (1987). "What is the Matter with Aggregate Demand and Aggregate Supply?" University of New South Wales. Discussion Paper 79.

Roberts, D.L. (1978). "Patinkin, Keynes and Aggregate Supply and Demand Analysis," *History of Political Economy* 10, 4, pp. 540-576.

Rowan, D.C. (1983). *Output, Inflation and Growth.* Macmillan. Third Edition

Sweeney, R.J. (1988). *Wealth Effects and Monetary Theory.* Basil Blackwell.

Tarshis, L. (1939). "Changes in Real and Money Wage Rates," *The Economic Journal* March, pp. 150-154.

Thompson, G., Brown, V. and Levacic, R. (1987). *Managing the U.K. Economy.* Cambridge, U.K: Polity Press.

Weintraub, S. (1972). *An Approach to the Theory of Income Distribution.* Greenwood Press, Westport, CT.

4

HOW TO CONSTRUCT IS AND LM CURVES IN THE SPIRIT OF HICKS OR, WHY WE DO NOT NEED THE AGGREGATE DEMAND CURVE

Ingo Barens

4.1 INTRODUCTION

Ever since the aggregate demand curve (AD)–aggregate supply curve (AS)–framework was introduced to augment the fix price IS–LM analysis of macroeconomic textbooks in order to determine the price level, the nature of the aggregate demand curve and its relation to the IS curve has been the object of discussion.[1] Rabin and Birch (1982) pointed out that if the IS curve is interpreted as the equilibrium curve of the goods market, determining the equilibrium price level within the AD–AS diagram will lead to a logical contradiction: on the one hand, every point on the AD curve, derived by shifting the LM curve along the IS curve, will represent goods market equilibrium while, on the other hand, only the point of intersection of AD and AS curve can qualify as goods market equilibrium. Thus for every point on the AD curve except its intersection with the AS curve one has equilibrium and disequilibrium of the goods market simultaneously.

This dilemma has lead to the view that the IS curve cannot be the goods market equilibrium curve. But nevertheless, in many macroeconomic textbooks one can detect the equally widely held interpretation of the IS curve as the goods market equilibrium curve (with the precise meaning of goods market equilibrium more often than not left in the dark).[2] Thus the goods market equilibrium inconsistency pointed out by Rabin and Birch (1982) has never really been resolved.[3]

Recently, the critical interest in the exact relation of IS–LM and AD–AS diagrams has increased again.[4] Barro (1994) claims that these diagrams are incompatible or logically contradictory because the IS curve rests on the assumption of fixed price level and money wage whereas the AD–AS diagram presumes at least flexibility of the price level (on this see Barens 1997a; 1997c; 1998); Colander (1995) claims that to combine the textbook AD curve with a non-horizontal AS curve involves a logical contradiction because the Keynesian cross model and the IS-LM model rest on the assumption of a horizontal AS curve (on this see Barens 1998); Geithman (1994) stresses the didactic problem of teaching AD–AS augmented IS–LM analysis, problems which in his view reduce the teaching of macroeconomics to indoctrination by the authority of the teacher.[5]

Three variants of the IS–LM model are typically discussed in macroeconomic textbooks, each making different assumptions about the flexibility of the price level and the money wage:

- fixed price level, fixed money wage; in what follows, this variant will be called the *fixprice–fixwage model*,
- flexible price level, fixed money wage; this variant will be called the *flexprice–fixwage model*,
- flexible price level, flexible money wage; this variant will be called the *flexprice–flexwage model.*[6]

Against the background of the criticisms raised against the IS–LM/AD–AS approach, and the tendency that the use of AD and AS curve apparently begins to be severed from its IS–LM roots[7], in the present paper a fresh start to the discussion about the AD curve and its relation to the IS curve will be undertaken. A simplified version of the flexprice–fixwage IS–LM model originally introduced by Hicks (1937) will be constructed and then flexprice–flexwage and fixprice–fixwage variants of this IS–LM model will be derived as special cases of the Hicksian flexprice–fixwage model.

As will turn out, this 1937 Hicksian IS–LM model is very different from the simple fixprice–fixwage IS–LM that in macroeconomic textbooks is taken as the starting point for an exposition of Keynesian macroeconomic theory. It will be shown that these differences may contain the clue to a solution of the problems raised by the AD curve.

The paper proceeds as follows: section II points out the relevant features of the Hicksian approach to IS–LM; section III analyses the construction of IS and LM curves in a simplified Hicksian flexprice–fixwage IS–LM model; sections IV and V discuss Hicksian flexprice–flexwage and fixprice–fixwage IS–LM models respectively, while section VI summarizes the results and discusses the textbook AD curve against the background of these results.

II

In contrast to common macroeconomic textbooks, Hicks (1937) presented IS and LM curves in interest-*nominal* income (r, Y_N)-space.[8] He was forced to proceed in this manner because of the underlying macroeconomic model he used to compare "classical" theory to Keynes's theory.[9] This model assumed two sectors of production (consumption and investment good(s) sectors), a *constant* money wage and *flexible* prices (or price levels) of consumption and investment goods (equal to their respective marginal costs of production). Within this framework it is impossible to talk of "the" real income; consequently, Hicks proceeded in terms of nominal income

$$Y_N = p_C C + p_I I \tag{1}$$

and presented IS and LM curves in (r,Y_N) space. Both curves were conceived as *market equilibrium* curves, i.e. the IS curve was the equilibrium curve of the two goods markets (Hicks 1980-81, 142) and the LM curve was the equilibrium curve of the "money market".[10] The point of intersection of both market equilibrium curves not only determined the equilibrium solutions for the rate of interest and the level of nominal income but also, according to Hicks, a situation of simultaneous clearing of all three markets under consideration. The third market considered by Hicks, but not dealt with explicitly in Hicks (1937), was the market for bonds (market for loans) (Hicks 1980-81, 142). By applying Walras' Law, the market equilibrium curve for the bond market (BB) was neither constructed nor drawn in Hicks' IS–LM diagram.[11]

In principle, as Hicks emphasized[12], the equilibrium solution of his model could geometrically be represented by using either two of the three curves IS, LM and BB.[13] Hicks (1937) chose to use IS and LM curves because he wanted to analyse the validity of (what he took to be) Keynes' claim that an increase in the inducement to invest will have no effect on the rate of interest, because the latter is determined by equilibrium of demand for and and supply of money.[14]

As can be seen from equation (1), the resulting IS and LM curves in (r, Y_N) space have some interesting characteristics:

1. each point on these curves implies a specific combination of prices and relative quantities of consumption and investment goods,
2. moving along these curves implies changes in quantities *and* relative prices and
3. the point of intersection of IS and LM curves implicitly determines the equilibrium values not only of quantities (C, I) but *as well* of prices (p_C, p_I)[15] and therefore, the price level P, if one would decide on its definition in this model.

Thus Hicks (1937) had no need to construct the textbook aggregate demand curve in order to determine prices or the price level.[16]

III

In a two-sector model it is impossible to unambiguously separate price (level) effects from aggregate output effects. But if the assumption of two sectors is dropped, things become easier. Nominal income is then equal to real income (Y) multiplied by the price (level) (P), again equal to the marginal cost of production. At first sight, nothing much changes: as in Hicks' original model points on the IS and LM curves imply specific values of price (level) and quantity (real income) variables.[17]

But now price (level) and quantity effects can be separated in a straightforward manner and, as will be shown below, it becomes possible, in principle, to geometrically represent IS and LM curves in various ways: they can be drawn (i) in (r, PY) space, staying close to Hicks' original presentation of his model , (ii) in (r, Y) space and (iii) in (r, P) space.

The simplified one–sector Hicksian flexprice–fixwage IS–LM model can be summarized as follows:[18]

$$Y^S = Y^S\left(\frac{W_0}{P}\right) \text{ (AS curve), or} \tag{2}$$

$$P = P\left(Y^S; W_0\right), \text{ or}$$

$$P = \frac{W_0}{MPL},$$

$$Y^S\left(\frac{W_0}{P}\right) = Y^D\left[Y^S\left(\frac{W_0}{P}\right), r\right] \text{ goods market equilibrium (IS curve)} \tag{3}$$

$$\frac{M_0}{P} = L\left[Y^S\left(\frac{W_0}{P}\right), r\right] \text{ money market equilibrium (LM curve)} \tag{4}$$

Eq.(2) is the aggregate supply function or – in its inverse form – the price equation showing the condition that the price level is equal to the marginal cost of production, i.e. equal to the given money wage divided by the marginal productivity of labour MPL, the latter decreasing with increasing labour input (or, equivalently, output). Eqs. (3) and (4) state the goods market and the "money market" equilibrium conditions, respectively.[19] Hence we have three equations to determine the three unknowns P, r, Y^S.[20]

From the system of equations (2)–(4) the market equilibrium curves IS and LM can be constructed in the following manner:

<u>Step 1</u>: Assume an arbitrarily chosen price level P_1.

<u>Step 2</u>: At P_1 profit–maximizing firms will want to supply Y_1^S (eq. (2)).

Step 3a: Assume clearing of the goods market ($Y_1^S = Y_1^D$); what will be the resulting rate of interest?

Step 4a: With supply Y_1^S the goods market will be in equilibrium at the rate of interest r_{IS_1} (eq. (3)).

Step 3b: Assume clearing of the "money market" $\left(\frac{M_0}{P_1} = L_1\right)$; what will be the resulting rate of interest?

Step 4b: With real income Y_1^S and real quantity of money $\left(\frac{M_0}{P_1}\right)$ the "money market" will be in equilibrium at the rate of interest r_{LM_1} (eq.(4)).

Thus proceeding from step 1 to step 4 we can derive the values of the rate of interest at which the goods and the money market, each taken in isolation, may be in equilibrium if the prevailing price level is P_1. If this procedure is repeated for all P_i we arrive at the respective market clearing combinations of price level and rate of interest, i.e. (P_i, r_{IS_i}) and (P_i, r_{LM_i}) (see Table 1).

As already mentioned above, there are, in principle, three possibilities to represent the resulting IS and LM curves geometrically:

A1: we can combine step 1 with step 4a,b; this results in market equilibrium curves drawn within a *(r,P)*–diagram. This diagram is analogous to Hicks' two–dimensional representation of three–way exchange in *Value and Capital* (Hicks 1939; 1946, Chap. V) mentioned above[21],

Table 1. The Flexprice–Fixwage IS–LM Model.

Step 1	Step 2	Step 3a	Step 4a
		$Y_i^S = Y_i^D(Y_i^S, r_i)$	→ r_{IS_i}
	↗		
P_i →	$Y_i^S = Y^S\left(\frac{W_o}{P_i}\right)$		
	↘		
		$M_0/P_i = L_i(Y_i^S, r_i)$	→ r_{LM_i}
		Step 3b	**Step 4b**

A2: we can combine step 2 with Step 4a,b; this results in market equilibrium curves drawn within a *(r, Y)*–diagram. This, of course, is the common practice of macroeconomic textbooks.[22]

A3: we can first combine step 1 and step 2 and then combine the result $\left(P_i{\cdot}Y_i^S\right)$ with step 4a,b; this results in market equilibrium curves drawn within a $\left(r, Y_N\right)$–diagram. This was the procedure in Hicks (1937; 1957; 1967) and Modigliani (1944).

Although it would be natural to follow Hicks (1939; 1946, Chap. V) and represent the IS and the LM curve in *(r,P)* space, in what follows possibility A2 will be chosen in order to bring out clearly the differences of this approach compared to macroeconomic textbooks. Fig. 1a shows the goods market equilibrium curve (IS) and the "money market" equilibrium curve (LM) in *(r, Y)* space.[23]

Because by construction every value of *Y* is uniquely linked to a specific value of *P*, every point on the IS and LM curve implies a unique value of *P*. This has at least four important implications compared to the textbook analysis of IS–LM:

1. *high* values of *Y* are linked to *high* values of *P* ($P_1 < P^* < P_2$, see fig. 1a) and *vice versa,*
2. there is only a single LM curve, *not a family of LM curves* (with each LM curve only valid for a specific value of the price level),[24]
3. the point of intersection of IS and LM curve not only determines the equilibrium value of r^* and Y^* but the equilibrium price level P^* as well – even if only implicitly and
4. an aggregate demand curve is not needed for the determination of P^*.

If the IS–LM diagram is combined with a *(P, Y)* diagram showing the AS curve, the determination of P^* can be demonstrated explicitly (see Fig. 1b).[25]

As just shown, in the Hicksian IS–LM model under consideration the textbook AD curve is not needed for the determination of the equilibrium price level. Indeed, its construction is not even possible within this model! The reason for this is that the price level does not enter the "money market" equilibrium condition (4) as a shift parameter. Assuming a price level different from P^*, say $P_1 < P^*$, does not – as in textbooks – shift the LM curve to the right but instead implies moving along the LM curve from (P^*, Y^*) to (P_1, Y_1). But if the LM curve does not shift, the textbook AD curve, being the result of shifting the LM curve along the IS curve, cannot be constructed.[26]

The next two sections will discuss the flexprice–flexwage and the fixprice–fixwage variants of IS–LM.

Figure 1. Flexprice-fixwage IS-LM.

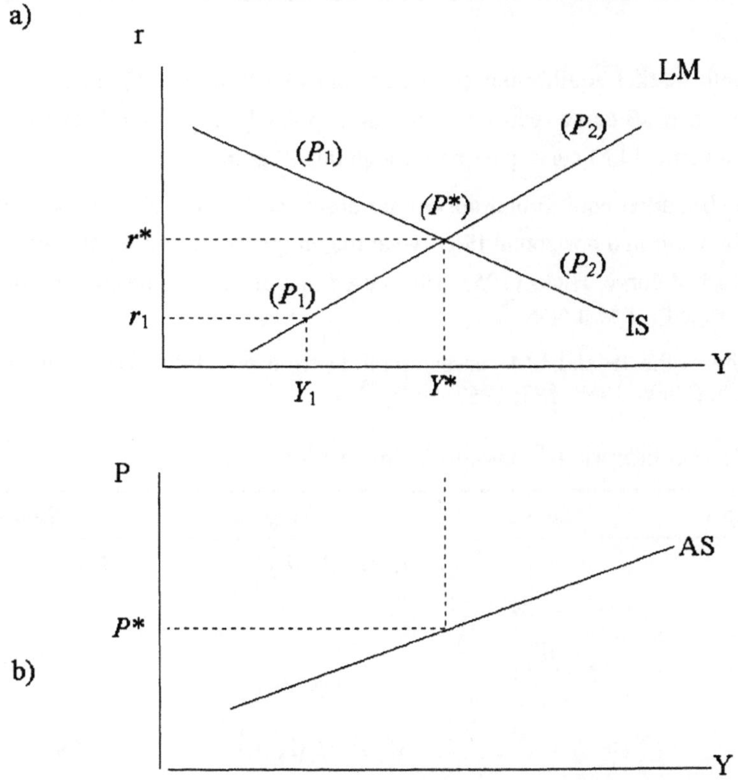

IV

If the price level and the money wage are perfectly flexible, the real wage will continually be at its labor market clearing value (w^*) and the supply of goods by profit-maximizing firms will be uniquely determined as full employment output Y_F^S.

$$Y^S = Y^S(w^*) = Y^S\left[\left(\frac{W_i}{P_i}\right)\right] = Y_F^S \qquad (5)$$

With Y^S no longer uniquely related to P, any arbitrarily chosen price level will yield the same value of aggregate supply. Table 2 incorporates the necessary changes.

How will the resulting IS and LM curves look like, if drawn in the alternative diagrams discussed above?

B1: if both market equilibrium curves are drawn within a (r,P)–diagram this will result in a horizontal IS curve at the unique equilibrium value of r_{IS}^* and a rising LM curve.[27]

B2: if both market equilibrium curves are drawn within a (r,Y)–diagram this will result in an IS curve reduced to the single point $\left(r_{IS}^*, Y_F^S\right)$ (see Hicks 1967, 149) and a vertical LM curve passing through this IS point.[28]

B3: if both market equilibrium curves are drawn within a (r, Y_N)–diagram this will again result in a horizontal IS curve at the unique equilibrium value of r_{IS}^* and a rising LM curve. Hicks (1957; 1967) used this diagram to discuss the flexprice–flexwage IS–LM model.[29]

Fig. 2 shows the IS and LM curves resulting from possibility B3 (identical to the diagram in (Hicks 1957, 283; 1967, 149)).[30]

Table 2: The flexprice-flexwage IS-lm model

Step 1	Step 2	Step 3a	Step 4a
		$Y_F^S = Y_i^D\left(Y_F^S, r_i\right)$	→ r_{IS}^*
	↗		
P_i →	$Y_F^S = Y^S\left(\dfrac{W_i}{P_i}\right)$		
	↘	$M_o/P_i = L_i\left(Y_F^S, r_i\right)$	→ r_{LM_i}
		Step 3b	**Step 4b**

Fig. 2. Flexprice-flexwage IS-LM.

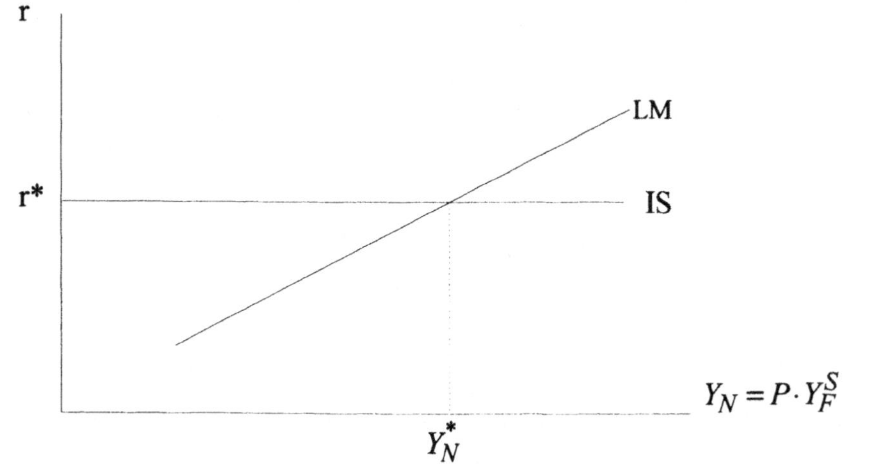

Fig.2 depicts the well known neoclassical dichotomy reproduced from the Keynesian flexprice–flexwage model. The labour market (together with production technology) determines full employment equilibrium aggregate supply, the goods market (i.e. $I=S$) determines the equilibrium rate of interest and the "money market" (the nominal quantity of money) determines the equilibrium price level.[31] Of course, this result comprises the central idea of the Neoclassical Synthesis: simply adding Keynesian concepts (consumption function, liquidity preference function) to a neoclassical model with *perfectly flexible* prices and money wages *as such* will not yield equilibrium outcomes different from the neoclassical full employment solution.

V

If both the price level and the money wage are fixed, the real wage will be fixed as well. A common textbook assumption – even if not always stated explicitly – is that aggregate supply passively adjusts to aggregate demand, i.e. aggregate supply is "... assumed to be no constraint on the level of output" (Froyen 1993, 205)(more will be said on this below).[32] This view of the behavior of aggregate supply at a given real wage has recently been dubbed "Hansen's Law" (demand creates its own supply) by Clower (1994), contrasting it with "Say's Law" (supply creates its own demand).

With P no longer uniquely related to Y, the procedure to derive IS and LM curves adopted in the present paper breaks down. Step 1 of this procedure becomes otiose and it is only possible to start from step 2. Nevertheless, in principle, it is still possible to draw the resulting IS and LM curves in the three alternative diagrams:

C1: if both market equilibrium curves are drawn within a (r,P)–diagram this will result in vertical IS and LM curves coinciding at the given price level P_{0}.[33]

Table 3: The Fixprice–Fixwage IS–LM Model

Step 1	Step 2		Step 3a	Step 4a
			$Y_F^S = Y_i^D\left(Y_i^S, r_i\right)$	→ r_{IS_i}
		↗		
P_o →	$Y_i^S = Y^S\left(\dfrac{W_o}{P_o}\right)$			
		↘	$M_o / P_o = L_i\left(Y_i^S, r_i\right)$	→ r_{LM_i}
			Step 3b	**Step 4b**

C2: if both market equilibrium curves are drawn within a (r, Y)–diagram this will result in the common textbook IS–LM diagram.

C3: if both market equilibrium curves are drawn within a (r, Y_N)–diagram this will again result in a falling IS curve and a rising LM curve.

There are two possibilities to conceive of the behaviour of aggregate supply at the constant price level P_0. On the one hand, aggregate supply may be interpreted as *notional* (planned) aggregate supply under the condition of constant costs of production, i.e. the AS curve is assumed to be horizontal. This may be caused either by constant returns to scale.[34]

$$Y^S\left(\frac{W_0}{P_0}\right) = \mathbf{R}_+ \tag{6}$$

or by constant costs of production up to full capacity utilization (Y_{MAX}),

$$0 \leq Y^S\left(\frac{W_0}{P_0}\right) \leq Y_{MAX} \tag{7}$$

i.e. the AS curve breaks off or becomes vertical at Y_{MAX}.

On the other hand, aggregate supply may be interpreted as *actual* aggregate supply Y_A^S (or realized output) with

$$0 \leq Y_A^S\left(\frac{W_0}{P_0}\right) \leq Y^S\left(\frac{W_0}{P_0}\right) \tag{8}$$

In this view, the passive adjustment of *actual* aggregate supply to the level of aggregate demand simply reflects firms adjusting the level of output to the short side of the market and the horizontal part of the aggregate supply curve refers to the behavior of *actual* aggregate supply.[35]

Thus the horizontal AS curve may either refer to *notional* (planned) aggregate supply and reflect characteristics of the underlying production technology or refer to *actual* aggregate supply and reflect the existence of quantity rationing on the goods market.[36] In the first case, the price level is *endogenous* but nevertheless constant and the IS curve is the equilibrium curve of the goods market.[37] In the second case, the price level indeed is truly exogenous and the IS curve cannot be the equilibrium curve of the goods market because now the "... `equilibrium' in the commodity market is one of *output*, not of *supply*" (Patinkin 1965, 331).

VI

It has been shown that, if one adheres to the modeling approach adopted by Hicks (1937),

1. the IS curve has to be constructed as the equilibrium curve of the goods market,
2. this results in different IS and LM curves for every variant of IS–LM (*fixprice-fixwage, flexprice-fixwage, flexprice-flexwage*)[38],
3. the textbook AD curve is not needed for the determination of the price level and
4. the textbook AD curve cannot even be constructed.

Thus the IS–LM variants resulting from Hicks' modeling approach are very different from the IS–LM and AD–AS models of macroeconomic textbooks.[39]

These results may solve the dilemma pointed out by Rabin and Birch (1982) that has been mentioned in the first section: if the IS curve is *constructed* to be the goods market equilibrium curve the textbook AD cannot be constructed. The equilibrium inconsistency turns out to be nothing but the reflection of an incorrect interpretation and/or geometrical representation of the underlying model.

This conclusion implies that if the IS curve is *not* constructed to be the goods market equilibrium curve (in the sense of equality of aggregate supply and aggregate demand) – as is the case in many textbooks[40] – one may derive the textbook AD curve. Typically, the AD curve is constructed by shifting the LM curve along an IS curve that is derived from an aggregate demand function like

$$Y^D = C(Y) + I(r), \tag{9}$$

together with the condition that *expenditure* (aggregate demand) equals current real *income* (realized output)

$$Y = Y^D, \tag{10}$$

i.e. by plotting the combinations of (r, Y) solving

$$Y = C(Y) + I(r). \tag{11}$$

What can be said about the precise nature of this textbook AD curve in the light of the reconstruction of Hicks' original IS–LM presented in this essay?

Of course, the first thing to note is that calling the AD curve an aggregate demand curve is a somewhat unfortunate use of language, because by its very nature it is not on the same footing as the partial–analytical microeconomic demand curve.[41] Instead, this AD curve is an *equilibrium locus* showing pairs of (P, Y) that are compatible with (i) equilibrium in the "money market"[42] and (ii) fulfillment of the expenditure–equals–income condition.

To shed additional light on the nature of this AD curve, consider the textbook *flexprice-flexwage* or Neoclassical Synthesis model of IS–LM. As was mentioned above, at the core of the Neoclassical Synthesis lies the notion that simply adding Keynesian concepts to a neoclassical model with *perfectly flexible* prices and money wages *as such* will not yield equilibrium outcomes different from the neoclassical solution.

In the Neoclassical Synthesis model, a vertical AS curve (price inelastic full employment aggregate supply) is confronted with a falling AD curve. The latter is constructed on the basis of IS and LM curves taken from the fixprice–fixwage model. In the fixprice–fixwage model, the IS curve is constructed on the assumption of perfectly price elastic aggregate supply. This leads to a contradiction: the AD curve rests on the assumption of *perfectly price elastic* aggregate supply but is combined with an AS curve showing *perfectly price inelastic* aggregate supply.

This is just the criticism made by Barro (1994) re–stated in terms of price elasticity of notional (planned) aggregate supply instead of in terms of flexibility of the price level. But above it has been pointed out that a horizontal AS curve may be understood as showing the behavior of *actual* aggregate supply (at a given price level above its equilibrium level). If one adopts this interpretation of aggregate supply, the contradiction, so it seems, disappears: the AS curve refers to price inelastic *notional* (planned) aggregate supply and the AD curve refers to perfectly price elastic *actual* aggregate supply (at *alternatively given* values of the price level). The IS curve, in turn, emerges as a curve showing alternative quantity–constrained "equilibria" in the goods market, i.e. $Y_A^S = Y^D$.

But this is to jump from the frying pan into the fire: the fixprice–fixwage IS–LM model reflects the assumption that in contrast to the neoclassical view quantities react infinitely faster than prices. Thus the implications of *perfectly* flexible prices and money wages are discussed only after *tacitly* reversing the relative speeds of adjustment of quantities and prices assumed by neoclassical theory. Consequently, the adjustment of the price level (and the level of real income) to its equilibrium value in fact is analyzed by means of a sequence of constant real wage fixprice–fixwage models, each one assuming a different temporarily fixed, i.e. *sticky*, price level.[43] Looked at from this perspective, the AD curve is just the locus in (P, Y) space of the alternative equilibrium solutions of this sequence of fixprice–fixwage IS–LM models—it is a trajectory showing the adjustment path to full employment.

As it turns out, the textbook Neoclassical Synthesis model does not really portray the Neoclassical Synthesis. Furthermore, the textbook model is incomplete or even mis-specified. It is mis-specified insofar as the labor demand derived from profit maximization is not really relevant for out–of–equilibrium behavior of firms in situations of excess supply of goods and it is incomplete insofar as the out–of–equilibrium labor demand of firms and the adjustment of the sticky price level are not modeled.[44] The *dis*–equilibrium story told with the help of IS–LM– and AD–AS–diagrams is incompatible with the underlying *equilibrium* model.[45]

Table 4: A Marshallesque Flexprice–Fixwage IS–LM Model.[1]

Step 1	Step 2	Step 3a	Step 4a
		$P_i^S = P_i^D(Y_i, r_i)$	→ r_{IS_i}
	↗		
Y_i →	$P_i^S = P^S(Y_i; W_0)$		
	↘		
		M_0 / P_i^S	→ r_{LM_i}
		Step 3b	**Step 4b**

Thus, at least for teaching purposes, it seems we have to choose between the textbook fixprice–fixwage IS–LM models pretending (after being augmented by AS-AD) to analyze flexible prices and being marred by serious insufficiencies and IS–LM models built along the lines of Hicks (1937; 1957; 1967) that, in addition, are closer to Keynes' views about price flexibility and goods market clearing.[46]

APPENDIX

A rather interesting alternative interpretation may be given to possibility A2 (see p. 62).Starting from the observation that the first two steps of possibility A1 may be understood as reflecting the Walrasian price–into–quantity approach (resulting in $r = r(p)$), possibility A2 may be seen as reflecting the Marshallian quantity–into–price approach (resulting in $r = r(Y)$): start with an arbitrarily chosen level of output (real income) (Y_1); the supply *price* function (the inverse function of the aggregate supply function) tells us that firms will want to supply this level of output at supply price P_1^S; at what level of the rate of interest $\left(r_{IS_1}\right)$ will the Marshallian goods market equilibrium condition (demand price = supply price) be fulfilled? With Y_1 and P_1^S given, at what level of the rate of interest $\left(r_{LM_1}\right)$ will the real quantity of money $\left(M_0 / P_1^S\right)$ be willingly held? Table 4 shows the necessary modifications of Table 1 to capture the Marshallian quantity-into-price approach.

Furthermore, if $P^S Y$ is identified with the *aggregate* supply price, $P^D Y$ with the *aggregate* demand price (Keynes 1936, 24-25) and $P^D Y = P^S Y$ as the "point of effective demand" (Keynes 1936, 25, 27), then the IS curve emerges as the locus of alternative "points of effective demand" (on this see Barens (forthcoming)). Without intending to place too much emphasis on the distinction between the Walrasian and the Marshallian approach in the context of the present paper, nevertheless the question may be raised whether the use of (r, Y) space by IS–LM analysis – implying $r = r(Y)$ – might not be considered as evidence of Marshallian elements in Hicks' IS–LM model and/or of the Marshallian heritage of Keynesian macroeconomics.[47]

Finally, it may be pointed out that because the Marshallesque IS curve represents alternative Marshallian short-period equilibria on the goods market (demand price equal to supply price of output), the Marshallian AD (demand price) curve used by Buiter and Lorie (1977) and Dutt and Skott (1996) is not needed to determine the equilibrium price level and could not be derived from the Marshallesque IS and LM diagram.

Dutt (1997) argues that a Marshallian *interpretation* of the textbook AD curve, i.e. as showing the demand price for any given output level instead of the quantity of goods demanded at any given price level,[48] could mend the price level flexibility inconsistency discussed by Barro (1994) and thus save current textbooks from a recall action. But the *construction* of such a demand price curve implies solving the IS and LM equations not for alternatively given price levels, resulting in a single downward-sloping IS curve and a family of upward-sloping LM curves in (r, Y) space, but for alternatively given output levels, which leads to a *family* of IS *points* and family of *vertical* LM curves in (r, Y) space (see possibility B2 on p. 64). To the knowledge of the present author, no macroeconomic textbook makes use of such an IS-LM diagram. Therefore, if the Marshallian *interpretation* of the AD curve is based, as it indeed should be, on its *construction* along the Marshallian quantity-into-price approach, this would not save macroeconomic textbooks from a recall action—by contrast, it would be an extremely forceful argument that such a recall is needed.

BIBLIOGRAPHY

Barens, I. (1996). Zur Interpretation der IS-Kurve und der Aggregierten Nachfragekurve. *Wirtschaftswissenschaftliches Studium*, 25: 591-3.

Barens, I. (1997a). *Destruction by Simplification: IS-LM after 60 Years. Paper presented at the 1997 Annual Conference, Charleston, SC, June 27–June, 1997.* unpublished, June, Bergische Universität Wuppertal, Wuppertal.

Barens, I. (1997b). *The Use and Abuse of Aggregate Demand and Supply Functions: A Comment on Nevile/Rao.* unpublished, January, Bergische Universität Wuppertal, Wuppertal.

Barens, I. (1997c). What Went Wrong with IS-LM/AS-AD Analysis—and Why? *Eastern Economic Journal*, 23: 89-99.

Barens, I. (1998). *Makroekonomie--Lehrbücher im Elch--Test. Einige Anmerkungen zur jüngsten US--amerikanischen Debatte um die (In)Konsistenz von AS-AD—Modellen.* unpublished, February, Bergische Universität Wuppertal, Wuppertal.

Barens, I. (forthcoming). From Keynes to Hicks—An Aberration? IS-LM and the Analytical Nucleus of the *General Theory*. In Elisabetta di Antoni, Peter Howitt and Axel Leijonhufvud (eds), *Money, Markets and Method. Essays in Honor of Robert Clower*, Cheltenham, UK; Lyme, US: Edward Elgar.

Barens, I. and Caspari, V. (1997). *Commodity Market or Capital Market Equilibrium: What Does the IS Curve Represent? A Clarification.* unpublished, August, Bergische Universität Wuppertal; Technische Hochschule Darmstadt, Wuppertal; Darmstadt.

Barens, I. and Caspari, V. (1999). Old Views and New Perspectives: On Re-Reading Hicks' "Keynes and the Classics". *The European Journal of the History of Economic Thought*, 6.

Barro, R. J. (1984). *Macroeconomics*, 1st ed., New York: John Wiley & Sons.

Barro, R. J. (1994). The Aggregate-Demand/Aggregate-Supply Model. *Eastern Economic Journal*, 20: 1-6.

Barro, R. J. and Grilli, V. (1994). *European Macroeconomics*, 1st ed., London: Macmillan.

Barron, J. M., Loewenstein, M. A. and Lynch, G. J. (1989). *Macroeconomics.* Reading, MA: Addison-Wesley.

Benassy, J.-P. (1983). The three regimes of the IS-LM model: A non-Walrasian analysis. *European Economic Review* 23: 1-7.

Benassy, J.-P. (1986). *Macroeconomics. An Introduction to the Non- Walrasian Approach*, 1st ed., London: Academic Press.

Benassy, J.-P. (1993). Nonclearing Markets: Microeconomic Concepts and Macroeconomic Applications. *Journal of Economic Literature*, XXXI: 732- 61.

Benavie, A. (1972). Prices and Wages in the Complete Keynesian Model. *Southern Economic Journal*, XXXVIII: 468-77.

Brownlee, O. H. (1948). Money, Price Level, and Employment. In F. M. Boddy (ed.), *Applied Economic Analysis*. New York: Pitman Publishing Corp.

Brownlee, O. H. (1950). The Theory of Employment and Stabilization Policy. *Journal of Political Economy*, 412-24.

Buiter, W. H. (1979). *Temporary and Long-Run Equilibrium.* New York: Garland.

Buiter, W. H. and Lorie, H. (1977). Some unfamiliar properties of a familiar macroeconomic model. *Economic Journal*, 87: 743-54.

Burda, M. and Wyplosz, C. (1997). *Macroeconomics. A European Text*, 2nd ed., Oxford: Oxford University Press.

Clower, R. W. (1989). Keynes' *General Theory*: the Marshall connection. In Donald A. Walker (ed.), *Perspectives on the History of Economic Thought.* Aldershot, Hants: Edward Elgar.

Clower, R. W. (1990). Keynes's *General Theory*: A Contemporary Perspective. *Greek Economic Review*, 12: 73-84.

Clower, R. W. (1991). Ohlin and the *General Theory*. In Lars Jonung (ed.), *The Stockholm School Revisited.* Cambridge: Cambridge University Press.

Clower, R. W. (1994). The Effective Demand Fraud. *Eastern Economic Journal*, 20: 377-85.

Colander, D. (1986). *Macroeconomics. Theory and Policy*, 1st ed., Glenview, Ill.: Scott, Foresman.

Colander, D. (1994/1995). *Macroeconomics*, 2nd ed., Burr Ridge, IL: Richard D. Irwin.

Colander, D. (1995). The Stories We Tell: A Reconsideration of AS/AD Analysis. *Journal of Economic Perspectives*, 9: 169-88.

Crouch, R. L. (1972). *Macroeconomics.* New York: Harcourt Brace Jovanowich.

Darity, W., Jr. and Young, W. (1995). IS-LM: An Inquest. *History of Political Economy*, 27: 1-41.

Dornbusch, R. and Fischer, S. (1984). *Macroeconomics*, 3rd ed., New York: McGraw-Hill.

Dornbusch, R. and Fischer, S. (1994). *Macroeconomics*, 6th ed., New York: McGraw-Hill.

Dutt, A. K. (1997). *On an Alleged Inconsistency in Aggregate-Supply/Aggregate-Demand Analysis.* unpublished, March, University of Notre Dame, Notre Dame, IN.

Dutt, A. K. and Skott, P. (1996). Keynesian Theory and the Aggregate- Supply/Aggregate-Demand Framework: A Defense. *Eastern Economic Journal*, 22: 313-30.

Felderer, B. and Homburg, S. (1992). *Macroeconomics and New Macroeconomics*, 2nd ed., Berlin: Springer-Verlag.

Fields, T. W. and Hart, W. R. (1990). Some Pitfalls in the Conventional Treatment of Aggregate Demand. *Southern Economic Journal*, 676-85.

Fields, T. W. and Hart, W. R. (1996). The AD AS Model in Introductory Macroeconomics Texts: Theory Gone Awry. In Nahid Aslanbeigui and Michele I. Naples (eds), *Rethinking Economic Principles.* Burr Ridge, IL: Richard D. Irwin.

Froyen, R. T. (1993). *Macroeconomics. Theories and Policies*, 4th ed., New York: Macmillan.

Fuhrmann, W. (1991). *Makroekonomik. Zur Theorie interdependenter Markte*, 3rd ed., München; Wien: Oldenbourg.

Geithman, D. T. (1994). A Note on Teaching the Aggregate-Supply/Aggregate-Demand Model. *Eastern Economic Journal*, 20: 475-7.

Hellwig, M. F. (1993). *The Conceptual Structure of Macroeconomic Models: I. The Income Equation.* WWZ-Discussion Papers, Nr. 9308, Juli, Wirtschaftswissenschaftliches Zentrum der Universität Basel, Basel.

Henry, K. and Woodfield, A. (1985). Aggregate Demand Curves in Macroeconomic Theory: Some Curiously Antipodean Controversies. *New Zealand Economic Papers*, 19: 21-34.

Heubes, J. (1996). Zur Interpretation der IS-Kurve. *Wirtschaftswissenschaftliches Studium*, 25: 94-5.

Hicks, J. R. (1936). Mr. Keynes' Theory of Employment. *Economic Journal*, 46: 238-53.

Hicks, J. R. (1937). Mr. Keynes and the "Classics"; A Suggested Interpretation. *Econometrica*, 5: 147-59.

Hicks, J. R. (1939). *Value and Capital. An inquiry into some fundamental principles of economic theory*, 1st ed., Oxford: Clarendon Press.

Hicks, J. R. (1946). *Value and Capital. An inquiry into some fundamental principles of economic theory*, 2nd ed., Oxford: Clarendon Press.

Hicks, J. R. (1957). A Rehabilitation of "Classical" Economics? *Economic Journal*, 67: 278-89.

Hicks, J. (1967). The 'Classics' Again. In John R. Hicks (ed.), *Critical Essays in Monetary Theory*. Oxford: Clarendon Press.

Hicks, J. R. (1973). *Letter to J. M. Keynes, 9 April 1937.* In Donald Moggridge (ed.), *Collected Writings of John Maynard Keynes*, Vol. XIV. London: Macmillan.

Hicks, J. R. (1980-81). IS-LM: An Explanation. *Journal of Post Keynesian Economics*, 3: 139-54.

Issing, O. (1973). Marginalien zum LM-IS Konzept. *Jahrbücher für Nationalekonomie und Statistik*, 188: 349-62.

Johnson, H. G. (1972). *Macroeconomics and Monetary Theory.* London: Gray- Mills Publishing Ltd.

Keynes, J. M. (1936). *The General Theory of Employment, Interest, and Money.* London: Macmillan.

Keynes, J. M. (1973). *Letter to J. R. Hicks, 31 March 1937.* In Donald Moggridge (ed.), *Collected Writings of John Maynard Keynes*, Vol. XIV. London: Macmillan.

Klein, L. R. (1947). *The Keynesian Revolution*, 1st ed., New York: Macmillan.

Laidler, D. (1993). *The Demand for Money. Theories and Evidence*, 4th ed., New York: HarperCollins.

Leijonhufvud, A. (1974). Keynes' Employment Function. *History of Political Economy*, 6: 164-70.

Leijonhufvud, A. (1984). Hicks on Time and Money. In David A. Collard, N. H. Dimsdale, C. L. Gilbert, Dieter R. Helm, Maurice FG. Scott and Amartya K. Sen (eds), *Economic Theory and Hicksian Themes.* Oxford: Clarendon Press.

Leijonhufvud, A. (1994). Hicks, Keynes and Marshall. In Harald Hagemann and Omar F. Hamouda (eds), *The Legacy of Hicks. His contributions to economic analysis.* London; New York: Routledge.

Lipsey, R. G., Steiner, P. O. and Purvis, D. D. (1984). *Economics*, 7th ed., New York: Harper & Row.

Marschak, J. (1951). *Income, Employment, and the Price Level. Notes on Lectures Given at the University of Chicago, Autumn 1948 and 1949.* New York: Augustus M. Kelley.

McKenna, C. J. and Rees, R. (1992). *Economics. A Mathematical Introduction*, 1st ed., Oxford: Oxford University Press.

McKenna, J. P. (1955). *Aggregate Economic Analysis*, 1st ed., New York: Dryden Press.

Meade, J. (1937). A Simplified Model of Mr. Keynes' System. *Review of Economic Studies*, IV: 98-107.

Meyer, L. H. (1980). *Macroeconomics. A Model Building Approach.* Cincinnati: South-Western.

Modigliani, F. (1944). Liquidity Preference and the Theory of Interest and Money. *Econometrica*, 12: 45-88.

Modigliani, F. (1963). The Monetary Mechanism and Its Interaction with Real Phenomena. *Review of Economics and Statistics*, 45: 45-88.

Modigliani, F. (1968). Liquidity Preference. In David Lawrence Sills (ed.), *International Encyclopedia of the Social Sciences*. New York: Cromwell, Collier and MacMillan.

Monissen, H. G. (1972). Some Theoretical Issues in Keynesian Stabilization Policy. *Schweizerische Zeitschrift für Volkswirtschaftslehre und Statistik*, 108: 523-54.

Neumann, M. (1988). *Theoretische Volkswirtschaftslehre I. Makroekonomische Theorie: Beschiftigung, Inflation und Zahlungsbilanz*, 3rd ed., München: Vahlen.

Nevile, J. W. and Rao, B. B. (1996). The Use and Abuse of Aggregate Demand and Supply Functions. *Manchester School of Economic and Social Studies*, LXIV: 189-207.

Owen, P. D. (1987). Aggregate Demand Curves in General-Equilibrium Macroeconomic Models: Comparisons with Partial-Equilibrium Microeconomic Demand Curves. *New Zealand Economic Papers*, 21: 97-104.

Parkin, M. and Bade, R. (1988). *Modern Macroeconomics*, 2nd ed., Oxford: Philip Allan.

Patinkin, D. (1958). Liquidity Preference and Loanable Funds: Stock and Flow Analysis. *Economica*, 25: 300-18.

Patinkin, D. (1965). *Money, Interest and Prices. An Integration of Monetary and Value Theory*, 2nd ed., New York: Harper & Row.

Phelps, E. S. (1985). *Political Economy. An Introductory Text*, 1st ed., New York: W. W. Norton & Company.

Rabin, A. A. and Birch, D. (1982). A Clarification of the IS Curve and the Aggregate Demand Curve. *Journal of Macroeconomics*, 4: 233-8.

Rao, B. B. (ed.) (1998). *Aggregate Demand and Supply. A Critique of Orthodox Macroeconomic Modelling*. London: Macmillan.

Richter, R., Schlieper, U. and Friedmann, W. (1973). *Makroekonomik. Eine Einführung*, 1st ed., Berlin; Heidelberg; New York: Springer-Verlag.

Romer, D. (1996). *Advanced Macroeconomics*. New York: McGraw-Hill.

Samuelson, P. A. (1955). *Economics*, 3rd ed., New York: McGraw-Hill.

Samuelson, P. A. and Nordhaus, W. D. (1995). *Economics*, 1st ed., New York: McGraw-Hill.

Shapiro, E. (1978). *Macroeconomic Analysis*, 4th ed., New York: Harcourt Brace Janovich.

Shapiro, E. (1982). *Macroeconomic Analysis*, 5th ed., New York: Harcourt, Brace & World.

Smith, G. (1984). *Macroeconomics*. New York: W.H.Freeman & Company.

Young, W. (1987). *Interpreting Mr Keynes. The IS-LM Enigma*, 1st ed., Oxford: Polity Press/Basil Blackwell.

ENDNOTES

[1] Although the AD–AS framework apparently was introduced to augment IS–LM analysis in macroeconomic textbooks only at the end of the 1960s, the first textbook making use of it was McKenna (1955) building upon Brownlee (1948; 1950). Interestingly, this textbook was published the same year that IS–LM made its first appearance in the third edition of Samuelson's influential textbook; see Samuelson (1955). In lectures given at the University of Chicago in 1948 and 1949, Marschak used AD and AS curves; see Marschak (1951).

[2] See for example Barro (1984), Barro/Grilli (1994), Romer (1996) and Felderer/Homburg (1992). Felderer/Homburg instead interpret the IS curve as the equilibrium curve of the "capital market"; see Barens/Caspari (1997) for a critical discussion of this interpretation. For example, in Chapter 10 of Burda/Wyplosz (1997) three different notions of goods market equilibrium are used.

[3] For a discussion of additional inconsistencies of the textbook AS-AD model see Barens (1997b; 1998).

[4] For a most recent but unsuccessful attempt to clarify the relation between the IS curve and the AD curve see Heubes (1996), who inadvertedly reproduces exactly the dilemma raised by Rabin/Birch (1982) which he sets out to resolve (Barens 1996).

[5] See as well Fields/Hart (1990; 1996) and Rao (1998).

[6] A fourth variant, fixed price level and flexible money wage (see Benassy 1983; 1986; 1993), as well as the Liquidity Trap and the Investment Trap cases will be neglected in the present paper.

[7] See the latest edition of Samuelson's influential textbook (Samuelson/Nordhaus 1995) that no longer makes use of IS–LM analysis.

[8] Hicks (1937) originally called both curves the SI and LL curve respectively and only later adopted the now common lables. See Young (1987) for the origins of IS-LM and Darity/Young (1995) for its later development.

[9] See Barens (forthcoming) and Barens/Caspari (1999) for a discussion of Hicks' comparison of "classical" theory and Keynes' theory.

[10] "The expression `money market equilibrium' is something of a misnomer. There is no single market in which money ... is bought and sold. Money changes hands against all other goods in all other markets. The expression `money market equilibrium' which is too convenient a shorthand to do without, therefore simply means equality of demand for and supply of money" (Buiter 1979, 13n11).

[11] In addition, in 1937 Hicks, not being interested in the employment implications of Keynes's *General Theory*, did not discuss the labour market explicitly; on a problem regarding the applicability of Walras' Law that is raised by this procedure and Hicks' solution, see Hicks (1980-81) and, in addition Patinkin (1958).

[12] Hicks (1937) does not address this aspect of Hicksian IS–LM; but this argument was already put forth in Hicks' review of the *General Theory* (Hicks 1936, 246), elaborated in a letter to Keynes (Hicks 1973, 82) and finally in Hicks (1980-81, 143). In addition, Hicks (1980-81, 141-2) stresses that the 1937 IS–LM model was an application of his representation of three–way exchange on a two–dimensional diagram (see Hicks 1939; 1946, Chap. V)

[13] Dropping *any* of the three market equilibrium conditions (or curves) and still being able to show simultaneous equilibrium geometrically is only possible if the three market equilibrium curves are *distinct*; see (Patinkin 1958) and Buiter (1979, 51, 56). Some textbooks have a BB curve coinciding with the LM curve (see, for example, Felderer/Homburg (1992), Dornbusch/Fischer (1994) and Burda/Wyplosz (1997)). In this case, either the LM or BB curve, but not the IS curve may be dropped (Buiter 1979, 46). This is evidence that in these textbooks an equilibrium specification for the "money market" and the bond market different from the one used by Hicks is adopted; see as well Hicks (1980-81, 143).

[14] Ironically, Hicks and Keynes were talking at cross purposes (Hicks (1973), Keynes (1973)); on this see Barens (forthcoming) and Barens/Caspari (1999).

[15] See Hicks (1937); from the equilibrium rate of interest r^* and the investment function we know nominal investment demand $I_N^* = p_I^* I^*$, from this and the supply function of the investment goods sector we can derive (p_I^*, I^*); from equilibrium nominal income Y_N^* and I_N^* we know nominal consumption demand $C_N^* = Y_N^* - I_N^* = p_C^* C^*$, from this and the supply function of the consumption goods sector we can derive (p_C^*, C^*).

[16] Below it will be shown that the textbook aggregate demand curve not only is not needed but cannot be derived from the Hicksian IS and LM curves.

[17] In this simplified one–sector model, the IS curve is the equilibrium curve of "the" good market.

[18] Following Hicks, bond and labour markets are neglected in what follows.

[19] Eq. (3) may seem to imply that the consumption component of aggregate demand is assumed to depend on aggregate supply, instead of current real income Y as is the case in most macroeconomic textbooks (but not all, see, for example, Fuhrmann (1991) and Richter/Schlieper/Friedmann (1973)). Indeed, the assumptions (real wage equal to marginal productivity of labour or, equivalently, price of output equal to marginal costs of production) made by Hicks (1937), Modigliani (1944; 1963; 1968)

and Klein (1947) are equivalent to assuming that firms *always* are on the aggregate supply curve. In the context of the present paper this assumption is unnecessarily strong, because by constructing the IS curve as the goods market equilibrium curve, *only those* situations are considered that are characterised by firms finding themselves on the aggregate supply curve. But for situations of goods market equilibrium ($Y^S = Y = Y^D$), it makes no difference whether consumption demand is assumed to depend on Y or Y^S (see Hellwig 1993).

[20] See Benavie (1972, 469); surprisingly, Benavie does not mention Hicks (1937).

[21] See as well Patinkin (1965, 259); but as Patinkin (1965) does not discuss a flexprice–fixwage model, only his flexprice–flexwage model is presented in this manner (see below section IV).

[22] See the appendix for a Marshallian interpretation of this possibility.

[23] The validity of both curves is restricted to situations of excess supply of labour. For simplicity, throughout this essay all curves are assumed to be linear.

[24] This had been hinted at, somewhat cryptically, by Hicks (1957, xxx).

[25] This determination of P^* resolves the problem encountered by Henry/Woodfield (1985, 32) in their attempt to construct an alternative to the textbook AD curve. At the same time it becomes clear that, with P^* determined in this manner, their alternative AD curve, just as the conventional AD curve, is not really needed.

[26] There is an ambiguity in the textbook treatment of IS–LM/AD–AS models. In the fixprice–fixwage model the exogenously given price level can be considered to enter the "money market" equilibrium condition as a shift parameter. But in the flexprice–fixwage and flexprice–flexwage variants of IS–LM the price level is endogenous, so, strictly speaking, the price level can no longer be a shift parameter in the textbook LM function $M/P_o=L(Y,r)$. Nevertheless – because Y is considered to be independent of P – (endogenous) changes in P only effect real money supply but not real money demand (Froyen 1993, 207), so a given change in P will – at an unchanged Y – lead to a fall of r, a result that may be geometrically represented as a shift of the LM curve.

[27] See Meyer (1980, 126ff) and Patinkin (1965, 259). It should be noted that in Patinkin (1965) the goods market equilibrium curve is not horizontal because of wealth effects which are neglected here.

[28] This IS–LM diagram does not allow to show the determination of P^* even if combined with a (P, Y) diagram showing the vertical flexprice-flexwage AS curve. To see this, assume that the AS curve in Fig. 1b) is vertical; with Y^* determined in the IS–LM diagram, it is impossible to link equilibrium output to any specific price level.

[29] Modigliani (1944, 59) already had emphasized this "important property" of the IS curve. In his fig. 3, the IS curve becomes horizontal as soon as full employment is established and the money wage becoming upwardly flexible. Thus Modigliani in this respect anticipated the results of Hicks (1957;1967).

[30] The price level implied by equilibrium nominal income Y_N^* may be determined by combining, in (P, Y) space, the vertical aggregate supply curve above Y_F^S with a hyberbola defined by $P = Y_N^* / Y$; the point of intersection of both curves then determines the equilibrium price level P^* (see Johnson 1972, 9-10).

[31] "Here at last we have the rate of interest solely determined in real terms (by productivity and thrift); for the height of the horizontal line is solely dependent upon the real factors in the system; it cannot be affected by the position of the *LM* curve. All that the *LM* curve here determines is the level of money incomes. The famous 'dichotomy' between real and monetary economics has appeared." (Hicks 1967, 149; the label of the "money market" equilibrium curve has been changed from *LL* in the original).

[32] See, for example, Dornbusch/Fischer (1984, 123-4), Colander (1986, 100), Crouch (1972, 47), Shapiro (1982, 130, 244-5), Parkin/Bade (1988, 171), McKenna/Rees (1992, 276). Taken to its extreme, this assumption will lead to the conclusion that the aggregate demand function $Y^D = C(Y) + I(r)$ may be interpreted as the aggregate supply function; see Monissen (1972, 525).

[33] Possibility C1 is only listed for the sake of completeness and will be neglected in what follows, because every point except one on the resulting IS and LM curves would imply $r_{IS_i} \neq r_{LM_i}$, while the equilibrium point $r_{IS_i} = r_{LM_i}$ could not be determined geometrically.

[34] Eq. (6) is taken from Hellwig (1993).

[35] Comparison of eqs. (7) and (8) shows that in this view notional (planned) aggregate supply – a choice–theoretic notion – takes the place of the capacity constraint – a purely technical notion.

[36] For an ingenious way to integrate both views geometrically, see Neumann (1988, 79).

[37] At least insofar as the horizontal AS curve indeed can be considered to be a supply curve; see Clower (1990).
As pointed out in Barens (1996; 1997b) and Nevile/Rao (1996), every point on the textbook AD curve would be intersected by a horizontal AS curve if the price level is constant and endogenous.

[38] The only author to point this out – although only for the IS curve – has been Issing (1973).

[39] It would be tempting to label the original IS-LM model as presented in Hicks (1937)—but basically taken from Meade (1937) (see Young (1987)—as Meade-Hicks-IS-LM, the IS-LM model based on an endogenous but constant price level as Hansen-IS-LM and, finally, the IS-LM model based on an exogenously given price level as Patinkin-Barro-IS-LM.

[40] See, for example, Barro (1984), Barro/Grilli (1994), Felderer/Homburg (1992).and Romer (1996).

[41] This is frequently pointed out, see for example Barro (1994), Barro/Grilli (1994), Barron/Loewenstein/Lynch (1989), Colander (1986; 1994/95), Felderer/Homburg (1992), Laidler (1993), Lipsey/Steiner/Purvis (1984), Shapiro (1978), Smith (1984), Stobbe (1987) and especially Owen (1987).

[42] And equilibrium in the bond market, if the bond market equilibrium curve is constructed to coincide with the LM curve; see, for example, (Felderer/Homburg 1992, 90).

[43] This implies a somewhat weird assumption about the behaviour of money wages. They must be (i) sticky regarding the state of excess supply on the labour market but (ii) perfectly flexible regarding changes in the sticky price level. Without (ii), the real wage would diverge from its labour market clearing value and the vertical AS curve would not be operative.

[44] This problem is sometimes recognized, see Felderer/Homburg (1992, 103n25). The same arguments apply to the flexprice–fixwage model as well.

[45] In addition, it may be noted that, strictly speaking, the textbook IS and AD curves do not exist for price levels *below* the equilibrium price level.

[46] On this see Leijonhufhud (1974), Hellwig (1993) and Clower (1994).

[47] On the Marshallian roots of Keynesian macroeconomics, see Clower (1989; 1991; 1994) and Hellwig (1993); see Barens (forthcoming) and Leijonhufvud (1984; 1994) for Marshallian features in Hicks'IS-LM analysis.

[48] To the knowledge of the present author the only textbook that explicitly gives a Marshallian interpretation to the AD curve is Phelps (1985).

5

ON 'MONEY' IN ISLM AND AD/AS MODELS[1]

Colin Rogers and T.K. Rymes

5.1 INTRODUCTION

Hicks's ISLM model interpretation of Keynes's theory[2] is subject to much controversy.[3] In this paper, we focus upon the 'real balance' effect and its role in ISLM and AD/AS analyses.[4] We shall argue that ISLM and AD/AS require 'nominal anchors'. We live in a world where, increasingly, the 'money' in the ISLM and AD/AS model no longer exists (as Keynes imperfectly understood in his *Treatise on Money*). There are no longer any nominal anchors, rather they have been replaced by discretionary policy. As Professor Ferris nicely sums up our position, we argue that central banks are fundamentals.

5.2 A REVIEW

In any standard ISLM analysis, the IS schedule is

$$y = \phi(i, y, \overline{K} + \overline{M}/P) \qquad (1)$$

where y is output in 'real' terms or constant prices, i is (a complex of) the 'real' rate(s) of interest, $\overline{K}$ is the given 'real' stock of capital, $\overline{M}$ is a given nominal stock of money, such as circulating currency issued by the central bank and the nominal stock of (say, demand) deposits held by the nonbank public as liabilities of the banks. While the expected rate of change of prices is taken to be zero in our discussion, it can be easily adapted to expectations of inflation or deflation. One can rewrite (1.1) as

$$y = \phi(i, y, \overline{K} + \overline{H}/P) \tag{2}$$

where $\overline{H}$ is a given nominal stock of fiat, base or outside money made up of circulating currency and the nominal stock of reserves held by the banks, both liabilities of the central bank.[5]

It is assumed that $\phi_1 < 0, 0 < \phi_2 < 1$ and *crucially* $\phi_3 > 0$.

The LM schedule is
$$\frac{\overline{H}}{P} = \mu(i, y, \overline{K} + \overline{H}/P) \tag{3}$$

where $\mu_1 < 0, \mu_2 > 0, 1 > \mu_3 > 0$

The two schedules determine i and y for any given P. A lower P will be associated with a higher y and a higher/lower i (see appendix).[6] The negative relationship between P and y gives the AD curve, shown (in the appendix) convex in (P, y).

Figure 1.

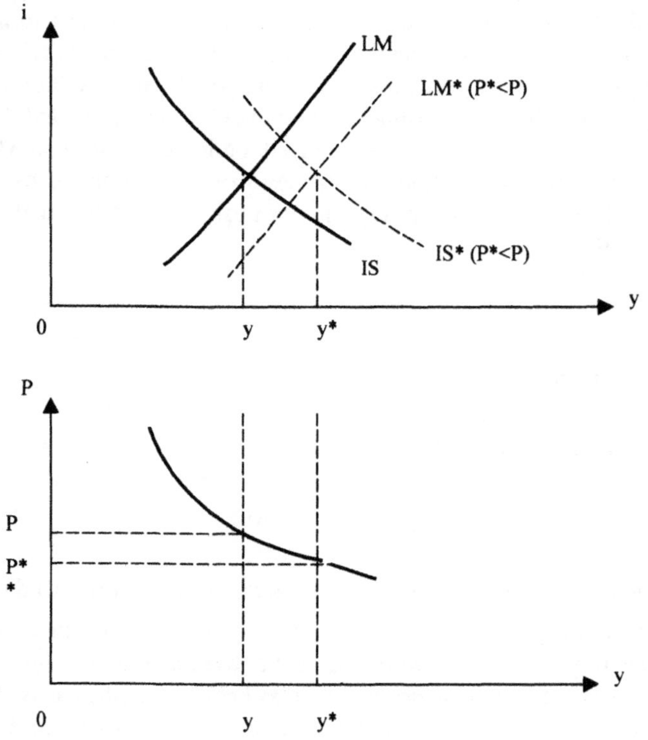

The relationship between ISLM and AD/AS, when the (money wage rate and) price level is lower at P* than at P, is illustrated in Figure 1.

It is well known that one is dealing with lower price levels *not* with falling price levels, the latter perhaps being associated with lower aggregate demand.[7]

Ignoring negative interest rates, the so-called Patinkin 'real balance' effect (and the so-called Keynes effect, which is really just part of the Patinkin effect) means there is necessarily a level of prices (and money wage rates) such that y is at full employment, contrary to Keynes's basic position that such a level may, not must, exist. One quotation is enough to represent a widely held view.

> "But in [t]his admirable attempt at formal theory, Keynes failed. His top-priority goal of articulating a model with an unemployment equilibrium ... foundered on the Pigou-Patinkin real balance effect" [8]

5.3 INITIAL CRITICISM

Keynes knew of the Pigou effect and dismissed it as empirically unimportant.[9] So do Friedman and McCallum.[10] Here is a curious argument. While it is stated that one would not rely upon 'real balance' effects in the real world, they nevertheless prove that Keynes's contention that there may exist a less than full employment equilibrium is without theoretical foundation. As Friedman (321) says,

> "The Pigovian and [Friedman's] the more far-reaching answer to Keynes's proposition have been extremely important on a theoretical level in assuring that there is *no basic flaw* in our theoretical analysis. But I hasten to add that in my opinion neither corresponds to effects that are empirically important in the kind of economic fluctuations that actual economies experience." (our italics)

One of our objectives in writing this paper is to eliminate the mental tensions such extraordinary statements must create.[11]

One can also say that, since H includes circulating currency, which modern central banks do not control but rather allow to expand or contract to meet changes in the nominal (and real) demand for circulating currency, the partial endogenization of money undercuts the empirical and *theoretical* rational for the role of 'real balances' in the IS-LM model and the implication that differences in the price level can have equilibrating properties in the AD/AS models. While it is undoubtedly true that no modern monetary authority operates on the stock of circulating central bank notes or fiat coin to control price levels, they still have, according to the traditional position, the stock of reserves in the form of deposits held by private banks with the central banks on which to operate. While it can be argued that private agents, in a world of lower price levels, will use their holdings of circulating currency to pay off overdrafts and loans so that deposits and currency, M, in the hands of the public and price levels P, will be positively correlated, there need exist no such positive correlation between reserves of banks with the central bank and price levels. That is, while it might be argued that $M = M(P)$ such that $M_P > O$ so that lower prices are associated with lower 'money' supplies, one cannot argue that H = H (P) and $H_P > O$ with similar conviction.[12]

5.4 MAJOR CRITICISM

The major point of this paper is that the stock of nominal fiat high powered money has vanished in modern monetary economies. There is no nominal anchor! There is no H which will be a co-determinant of P nor is there an H which will ensure, via the 'real balance' effect, a full employment price level. Keynes's conjecture that there may exist less than full employment monetary equilibria remains correct.

It is now increasingly established that central banks exercise control over nominal and real magnitudes, in regimes where banks desire to hold zero reserves, not by altering the stock of reserves nor by fixing interest rates but rather by operating upon the spreads or the relative price of banking services. Central banks always affect the price of banking services which are essentially the supply of liquid, and accessible-at-least-cost, intertemporal transactions services. Central banks are always operating upon this real relative price so that the set of all relative prices cannot be ascertained independently of the activity of the monetary authorities. Just as Keynes argued[13] we must now work with a monetary theory of value.

Modern central banks, such as the Bank of Canada and the Reserve Bank of Australia, have learned that by 'setting spreads', i.e., by charging higher than market interest rates on banks' negative settlement balances and paying lower than market rates on banks' positive settlement balances, they enforce banks to pursue overdraft and deposit policies such that the banks *expect* to be in zero settlement balances position in their clearings with the central Bank (hereafter just the Bank), unless the Bank is taking non-neutral action. Unless the Bank takes what we shall call enforcement actions, such as open market operations or repos or redeposit and drawdown of government deposits (or overdrafts) with the banks, the banking system, i.e., the set of all financial intermediaries offering transactions services, will always be in balance, in an overall *zero* settlement balance position with the Bank. Set aside circulating currency for a moment. In a world of paper transactions or increasingly electronic debits and credits, one individual's debit (an increase in her overdraft or decrease in her deposit) must be matched by another individual's credit (an increase in his deposit or decrease in his overdraft). If the individuals transact through different banks, her bank will be experiencing a negative settlement balance with the Bank while his bank will be recording an equivalent positive settlement balance. A market in settlement balances will exist, such that through their private clearing arrangements, a House, her bank will borrow his bank's positive clearing balance at a rate lower than the Bank would charge while his bank would loan its positive settlement balance at a rate higher than could be earned with the Bank. Hence, unless the Bank puts the banking system as a whole into non-zero settlement balance positions, the interbank market (or House) in settlement balances will clear at spreads or 'service prices' below those of the Bank.

Private non bank agents transact with banks and face interest rates on overdrafts which exceed rates paid by the banks on deposits, the spread said to be the 'price' of banking services. Of course, the 'spread' the banks charge their customers is greater than that charged by the banks' House and the 'spread' charged by the Bank.

From Baltensberger[14], the liquidity costs of a competitive bank are given as

$$L = iR + \int_{R}^{\infty} \rho(X - R)f(X)dX \tag{4}$$

where i is the opportunity cost of reserves, R is precautionary reserves, ρ is the penalty rate charged (say) by the Bank for being in reserve deficiency, X is the net loss experience, f(X) the density function of such withdrawals assumed normal so that E(X) = ö. The liquidity costs are minimized when

$$i - \rho \int_{R}^{\infty} (X)dX = 0 \tag{5}$$

so that if R is zero, $\rho = 2i$, or what emerges is the '2 for 1' rule at one time imposed by the Bank of Canada.[15] That is, in order for a bank to conduct its overdraft and deposit policies such that it expects to be in a zero settlement balance position in the clearings, the penalty rate must be twice the opportunity cost rate, for example, the rate banks could earn on demand overdrafts.

The structure of interest rates implied by the '2 for 1' rule is that the Bank would pay a zero rate on positive settlement balances, i_{cr} = o. This implies that the cost of holding a positive settlement balance with the Bank is $i - i_{cr} \equiv ä_{CB}$ and that the penalty rate, designated i_{dr} (=2i), implies that the cost of holding a negative settlement balances with the bank is $i_{dr} - i \equiv ä_{CB}$. The expression $ä_{CB}$ is the carrying cost, spread or service charge the Bank is levying for the provision of clearing and liquidity services.

When the Bank raises i_{dr} without altering i_{cr} it raises the charge it makes for the provision of services to the banks. The service charge is composed of two parts: the trivial debit and credit fees which 'price' the number of transactions; and the carrying cost, the 'price' for the provision of liquidity serves to them. Similarly, the House charges its members fees for its final clearing, as the banks swap settlement balances and for the monitoring costs involved in the provision of the liquidity services the House provides its member banks.

Individuals use the transactions services of banks since they (i) delegate the monitoring of persons to whom they would lend and from whom they would borrow to the banks because it is less costly for the banks, specializing in this activity, to do so; (ii) they use overdrafts and deposits for the execution of transactions (and may use private bank notes as well) because, unlike other financial intermediaries, banks promise to keep unchanged the nominal value of such overdrafts and deposits[16] and (iii) subject to known costs (the debit and credit fees and carrying costs) they debit and credit their deposits and overdrafts because of immediacy of access on the part of depositors and non-immediacy of call experienced by overdrafters.[17] Banks provide monitoring, a common service of financial intermediaries, but their assets and liabilities used in transactions are fixed in nominal terms with clear terms of accessibility and established interest rates, debit-credit fees and carrying costs.

A bank is able to offer immediacy of access to demand depositors and non-callability to overdrafters because it can tap the provisions of liquidity by the House. A bank will not necessarily demand payment of an overdue overdraft if it thinks the overdrafter's credit is good but is merely in an illiquid position if it can in turn borrow, at a cost in the House, in turn not subject to immediacy of call. Thus, the bank's overdrafters and depositors are using indirectly the immediacy of accessibility at-least-cost services supplied by the House. Ultimately, of course, the banks and their House fall back on the services of liquidity, provided at cost, by the Bank.

Banks, though increasingly less so, charge for their services through 'spreads'. A simple revenue statement for a bank, with respect to overdrafts and deposits would be

$$i_o O - i_D D;$$

for a House

$$i_B B - i_L L;$$

and for the Bank

$$i_{Dr} Dr - i_{cr} Cr$$

where O and D are the banks' overdrafts and deposits, with their rates, i_O and i_D; B and L are the borrowings from and lendings to the House by its members, with their rates i_B and i_L; and D_r and C_r are the negative and positive settlement balances of banks with the central Bank, not swapped in the House, with their respective rates i_{Dr} and i_{Cr}. We observe, in general, for demand overdrafts and deposits,

$$i_{Dr} > i_B > i_O > i_D > i_L > i_{Cr}$$

One argues that i_O - i_D is the service charge levied on overdrafters and depositors by banks,[18] i_B - i_L is that levied by Houses on their members while i_{Dr} - i_{Cr} is the service charge levied by Banks on banks unable to obtain accommodation through the House, that is, the price charged for the ultimate liquidity provided by them.

Suppose the 'spreads' are such that the House and banks are producing a volume of nominal overdrafts and deposits - that is, are producing a volume of services - with which the Bank is content. Suppose the banks begin an expansion of overdrafts and deposits with which the Bank is not in accord. The expansion in banking output is too great. Modern Banks raise their spreads, i.e. they raise i_{Dr} keeping (say) i_{Cr} unchanged. The Bank's spread is higher, and the House and clearing banks know the price of the liquidity services offered by the Bank is higher. To the House and clearing banks, the cost of straying from zero to negative settlement balances, compared with straying from zero to positive settlement balances, has risen.[19] Competitive banks (and their House) will therefore try to unbalance their portfolios away from overdrafts towards deposits which of course, they cannot do. Their spreads, their service charges, will rise. Non banks will find therefore intertemporal surplus compared with deficit positions less costly and planned investment will contract relative to savings.

The Bank has not reduced reserves (there are none to reduce) by neither open market operations nor drawdowns, nor has it raised interest rates per se. Rather it has raised its spread[20] and the House and its banks follow suit. The whole set of intertemporal transactions services banks provide has increased in relative price and the volume of bank output contracts.

Since banking output is used by firms and households as inputs into final demand components and as intermediate inputs in production the decline in banking output is associated with a contraction in final demand and the net output of the whole economic system.

The Bank attempts to thwart the expansion in banking, and aggregate output, not by contracting the growth of some particular definition of money or high-powered money nor by raising interest rates. Rather it does it by raising the price of liquidity - the charge for the service the Bank ultimately provides. Since the demand for liquidity provided by the banks, the House and the Bank is continually changing in a Keynesian world of uncertainty, the Bank must always be operating with the relative price of banking services and output. *Central Banks therefore have unrelenting real effects in the economy.* Earlier views which had Banks changing some costless stock of fiat money can easily be shown, with model-consistent expectations, to ensure that Banks have no 'real' effects. Such views are, however, no longer applicable. Similarly, those views which had central Banks setting interest rates and able somehow to affect not just nominal but real interest rates seem questionable. No doubt by encouraging banking expansions which could be associated with higher growth rates, Banks might raise real rates of return, given positive links between growth rates and real rates of return, but the relationship between central Banking, charges in banking output and real rates of growth requires more theoretical and empirical study.

Figure 2.

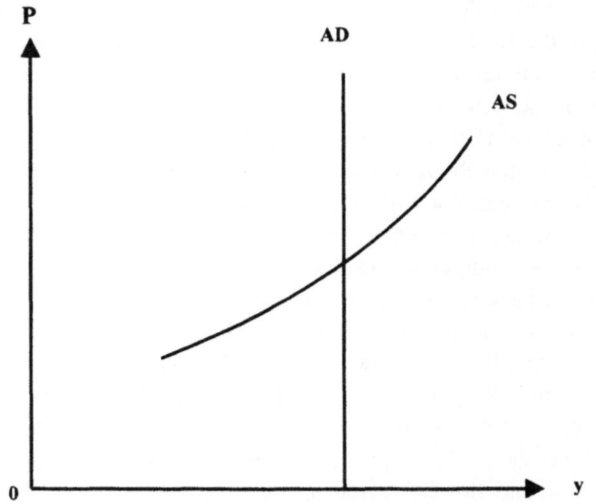

5.5. RECONSTRUCTION OF ISLM AND AD/AS ANALYSIS

Consider a simplified set of balance sheets in a banking equilibrium.

Assets	Liabilities
Government of Canada	
Deposits at Bank of Canada	Bonds held by Bank of Canada
Deposits at banks	Other bonds
Bank of Canada	
Bonds of the Government of Canada	Government of Canada deposits
Negative settlement balances	Positive settlement balances
Banks	
Positive settlement balances	Negative settlement balances
Government Bonds	Deposits (including Government of Canada)
Overdrafts	
$P_K K_B$ Bank capital	
Non-banks (households and firms)	
Deposits	Overdrafts
$P_K K$ (non bank capital)	Net worth

It is to be noted that no nominal anchor exists. In nominal terms all magnitudes could be raised or lowered without any 'real' effects. It is only the liquidity services of the Bank which pin down nominal (and real) magnitudes in the economy. There is no H doing this. This being the case, the level of money wage rates and prices are indeterminate without Bank activity. In terms of AD analysis, one starts with Figure 2.

The position of the AD curve is a function of real variables including the provision of liquidity services by the Bank. The lower its service charge the higher will be AD for any given level of prices. For a given level of money wages and Bank services charges we have a given AS curve. The gross output of the economic system is Q = Q (L, K, (O + D) where Q is gross output, L and K are non banking labour and capital and (O + D) is the output of the banking sector. However, banking output, (O + D) = $F(L_B, K_B, (D_r + C_r))$, is a function of labour and capital in banking and the services supplied by the Bank. Thus net output is Q = Q (L, K, (Dr + Cr). In a Keynesian short run, costs are WL + δ_{CB} (Dr + Cr) where δ_{CB} is the central Bank spread. For given W and δ_{CB}, the marginal cost or supply price of net output rises in the shortrun because of diminishing marginal products of labour and banking services as inputs. For a decrease in δ_{CB}, aggregate demand will increase and also the aggregate supply will shift to the right subject to dimin-

Figure 3.

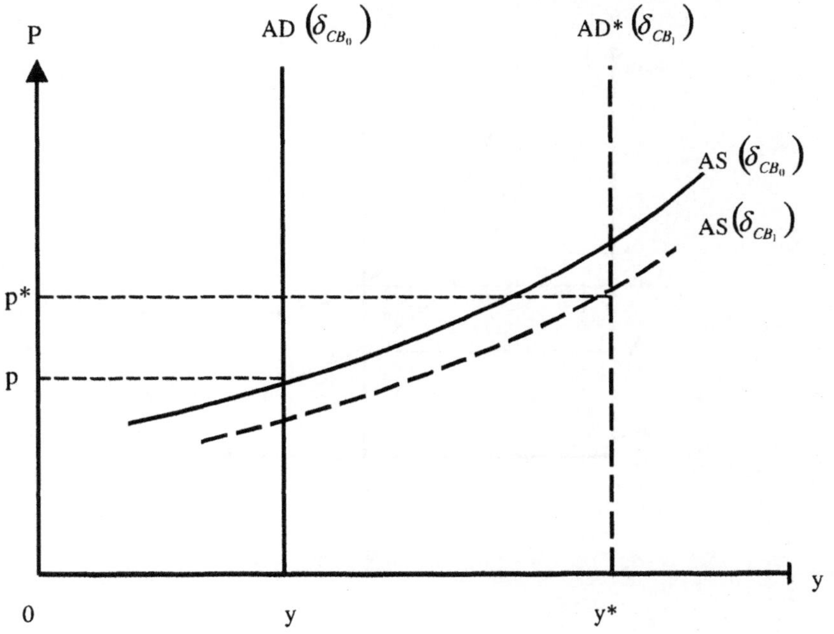

ishing returns to the provision of liquidity services. See Figure 3 for an illustration of this case.

Full employment levels of output, y_f, cannot be defined independently of the level of banking output. Since banking output cannot be defined independently of the flow of liquidity services from the Bank, no precise definition of full employment level of output is possible. There is thus no precise natural level of output because there is no natural level of outputs of banks, Houses and Banks.

We contrast our AD/AS analysis with those of new classical and new Keynesian economics in Figure 4.

In new classical economics, AS is given at the natural level of output, the AD is drawn to reflect the existence of 'real balance' effects. A reduction in AD by monetary contraction from AD_0 to AD_1 results only in lower prices with equilibrium at full employment assured by 'real' balance' effects. See top panel of Figure 4. In new Keynesian economics, with sticky money wages and prices, a reduction in AD by monetary contraction may result in some initial contraction in real output from y to y_x and a reduction in prices form P_o to P_x. 'Real balance' effects will overcome the 'rigidities', however, and the economy will recover to the full employment level of output and at price level P_o, replicating, *with sluggishness only*, the new classical case. See bottom panel of Figure 4.

The Keynesian case, for comparison purposes can be read from Figure 5.

The AD and AS curves, with increases in $ä_{CB}$, can be read as dealing with a monetary contraction. The level of output and price levels are lower the higher the service charges, spreads or carrying costs of the Bank. But given the AD function is perfectly vertical

Figure 4.

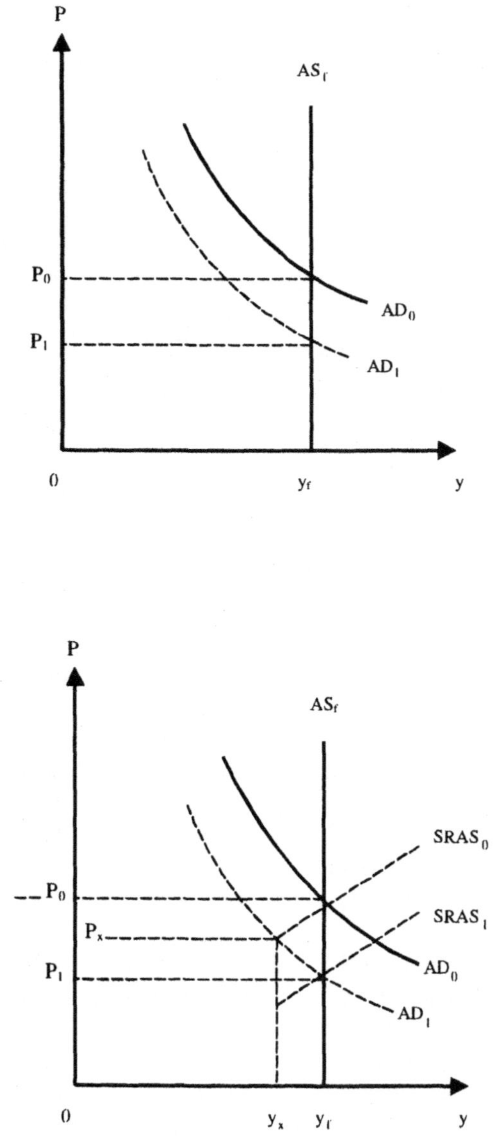

because there are, in an anchorless world, no 'real balance' effects, there are no price level forces re-equilibrating the economy.[21]

Since, in this simple model, one cannot determine the effects of changes of the level of banking output on the growth rate, no analysis connecting the level of output and the rate of interest is possible. If one argues that the spread is positively related to (say) the overnight rate, the cash rate or the Bank rate, then one could interpret ä$_{CB}$ in Figure 5 as

Figure 5.

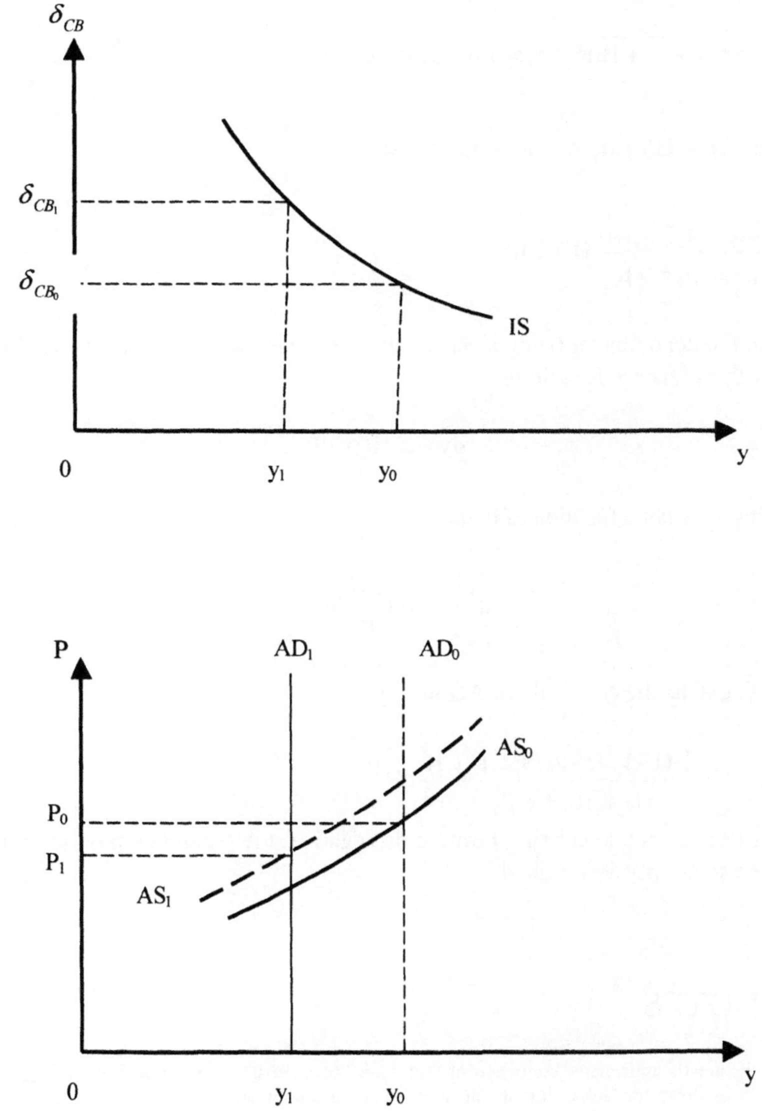

being equivalent to the overnight rate, where, in the IS diagram, δ_{CB}, the Bank's charge for the provision of liquidity services is replaced by the rate of interest.

One thing is clear. There is no LM function to contemplate because there is no nominal outside anchor. In Keynesian economics monetary policy is the anchor and is always real. It is in this sense that the LM portion of ISLM has vanished.

APPENDIX

From $y = \phi(i, y, \overline{K} + \overline{H}/P)$ $1\ \phi_1 > o, o < \phi_2 < 1, \phi_3 > o$

$$\frac{\overline{H}}{P} = \mu(i, y, \overline{K} + \overline{H}/P)\ \mu_1 < o, \mu_2 > o, o < \mu_3 < 1$$

$$dy = \frac{[-\phi_3\mu_1 - \phi_1(1-\mu_3)]}{(1-\phi_2)\mu_1 + \phi_1\mu_2} \overline{H}/P^2 dP$$

such that the denominator being negative and the numerator positive, a lower P is associated with a higher y. Rewriting as

$$dy = Z\overline{H}/P^2 dP$$

and taking Z as not a function of P, then

$$d^2 y = Z - [\frac{2\overline{H}}{P^3}](dP)^2$$

and z < O entails the convexity of AD in (P,y).

$$\text{Since } di = \frac{[-(1-\phi_2)(1-\mu_3) + \phi_3\mu_2]}{(1-\phi_2)\mu_1 + \phi_1\mu_2} \frac{\overline{H}}{P^2} dP$$

with the term in brackets being positive or negative, the relationship between i and P cannot be so simply ascertained.

ENDNOTES

[1] Despite the greatly appreciated comments of Professors Steve Ferris and Nicholas Rowe and general remarks by Professor Jack Galbraith, all error and confusion remain ours.

[2] Warren Young, *Interpreting Mr. Keynes: The IS-LM Enigma* (Cambridge: Polity Press, 1987).

[3] See, for instance, D. Patinkin, "In defense of IS-LM", *Banca Nazionale del Lavoro Quarterly Review*, 1990, CLXXII, 119-134; Robert G. King, "Will the new Keynesian macroeconomics resurrect the IS-LM model?" *Journal of Economic Perspectives*, VII, Winter 1993, 67-82, Paul Mizen and John R. Mesley, "A new perspective on the Keynesian revolution and IS-LM", University of Nottingham Discussion Paper #94, September 1994, and William Darity Jr. and Warren Young, "IS-LM: An inquest", *History of Political Economy*, XXVII, Spring 1995, 1-41.

[4] See David Colander, "The stories we tell: A reconsideration of AS/AD analysis", *Journal of Economic Perspectives*, IX, Summer 1995, 169-188.

[5] One does this by means of the standard well known formula, implying that H is considered as part of the wealth of the private sector. Though it is a liability of the government sector, it is assumed in standard analysis that changes in its real value do not affect the expenditure of the public sector. Our paper argues that this formula no longer has any content in modern monetary economies.

[6] By means of writing y as a function of L(and K) and the price level being equal to the money wage rate divided by the marginal physical product of labour, the whole analysis can be cast in terms of interest rates and levels of employment, with the levels of employment being inversely related to the level of money wage rates. Such a presentation indicates clearly how different such analyses are from that of Keynes.

[7] For different conclusions, see J. Tobin, "Price flexibility and output stability: an old Keynesian view", *Journal of Economic Perspectives*, VII, 1993, 45-65 and M. Friedman, *Price Theory* (1976), 319-321. Tobin argues that falling prices will create instability because of exacerbated Fisherian debt-deflation effects, excess demand for money because nominal interest rates cannot go negative and consequently even greater falls in prices, in short, price and output instability. Friedman distinguishes between output and real private income, out of which expenditure on output takes place. Private real income is output plus (minus) real capital gains (losses) from holding outside fiat money, with debt-delation effects offsettingly distributional. The faster prices fall the greater is real private income and the greater are expenditures on output. In the extreme case of no capital formation, real private income, by Friedman's dynamic version of the real balance effect, would be greater the greater the fall in prices and real consumption expenditure would approach the full employment level of output. At that point prices and money wages would stop falling and Tobin's spectre of instability set aside.

[8] B. McCallum, "The development of Keynesian macroeconomics", *American Economic Review*, May 1987, 125 quoted in Boris D. Pesek, *Microeconomics of Money and Banking and Other Essays* (Hemel Hampstead: Harvester-Wheatsheaf, 1988).

[9] Keynes thought the Pigou-Kalecki effect was "... too fantastic for words". See Robert Dimand, "Keynes, Kalecki, Ricardian equivalence, and the real balance effect", *Bulletin of Economic Research*, XLIII, July 1991, 289-292.

[10] Friedman, *op. cit.* and Bennett T. McCallum, *Monetary Economics: Theory and Policy* (1989). McCallum's views about the empirical unimportance of the real balance effect are drawn up in the context of evaluating the welfare costs of steady inflation. The basic conclusion in his summary analytical framework, which must follow from the assumed presence of nominal anchors and the belief that policy is concerned with the manipulation of such costless fiat creatures, is that most macroeconomists accept as a *theoretical principle* that deviations of output or employment "...cannot be affected permanently by monetary policy." (216).

[11] They are examples of what Coates calls scholasticism. See John Coates, *The Claims of Common Sense: Moore, Wittgenstein, Keynes and the social sciences* (Cambridge: Cambridge University Press, 1996).

[12] See Marc Lavoie, *Foundations of Post-Keynesian Economic Analysis* (Aldershot: Edward Elgar, 1992), See especially Chap 4 Credit and Money, Basil J. Moore, *Horizontalists and Verticalists: The macroeconomics of credit money* and Charles Goodhart, "Money supply control: Base or interest rates?", eds. K. Hoover and S. Sheffrin, *Monetarism and the Methodology of Economics* (Aldershot: Edward Elgar, 1995) reprinted in Goodhart, *The Central Bank and the Financial System* (Cambridge, MIT press, 1995).

[13] See J.M. Keynes, *The Collected Writings of John Maynard Keynes*, VI: The General Theory, xxii-xxiii. See also Thomas K. Rymes, *Keynes's Lectures, 1932-35: Notes of a Representative Student* (London and Ann Arbor: Macmillan for the Royal Economic Society and University of Michigan Press, 1989), 8.

[14] E. Baltensberger, Alternative approaches to the theory of the banking firm, *Journal of Monetary Economics*, VI, January 1980, 1-37.

[15] Bank of Canada, *The Implementation of Monetary Policy in a System with Zero Reserve Requirements*, Discussion Paper #3, revised September 1991. This '2 for 1' rule is now changed. See Bank of Canada, "A proposed framework for the implementation of monetary policy in the large value transfer system environment," Discussion Paper #2, 1 March 1996 and Kevin Clinton, "Implementation of monetary policy in a regime with zero reserve requirements", Bank of Canada Working Paper 97-8, April 1997.

[16] J. Chant, "The new theory of financial intermediation", eds. K. Dowd and M.K. Lewis, *Current Issues in Monetary and Financial Economics* (London: Macmillan, 1992).

[17] A demand deposit has immediacy of access, a time deposit has an option which inhibits immediacy of access (or makes it more costly), with a time overdraft a bank cannot call so the overdrafter is not subject to harassment while a demand overdraft is subject to call on demand.

[18] The UN (United Nations, *System of National Accounts 1993*) argues there exists a 'pure' rate i, such that i_o - i is the service charge paid by overdrafters and i - i_D is that service charge paid by depositors.

[19] In Canada, the Bank raises its borrowing and lending rates together, operating with 'bands'. The increases in its lending rate, the rate it charges for negative settlement balances, constrains banks to reduce their overdrafts. The increase in the borrowing rate, the rate the Bank pays on positive settlement balances, constrains banks to increase their deposits. Both represent an attempt by the banks to move towards positive settlement balances but, try as they may, unless the Bank accommodates, they cannot do so. Rates on overdrafts and deposits rise to the levels the Bank desires.

[20] If banks, the House and the central Bank reduced their spreads and substituted instead specific carrying costs (or service charges) on overdrafts and deposits on borrowing and lending and on negative and positive settlement balances, then it would be clear that the Bank exercises control by raising or lowering its spread and not raising or lowering an interest rate (such as Bank rate).

[21] Bank notes as theoretical anchors, though trivial empirically, are replaced by turning the note issue over to the private banks. If the Bank used its monopoly note issue as a device to enlist the public's support in the monitoring of private banks (e.g., the substitution to Bank notes from bank deposits), that can be replaced by the willingness of the Bank to accept deposits from any member of the public. The Bank would, of course, pay no interest on such deposits and they would therefore only be used by the public in the case of fear about the liquidity of the banking system as a whole. No nominal anchors are needed for the lender of last resort function by the Bank.

6

IS-LM AND LEIJONHUFVUD'S RE-APPRAISAL

Bruce Littleboy

6.1 INTRODUCTION

Many economists have reflected on the virtues and limitations of IS-LM. Axel Leijonhufvud has centered much of his work on the extent to which Keynes's insights can be, and have been, conveyed by mainstream economists and their textbooks. He has attributed much of the strength of the revival of some forms of classical economics to the innate susceptibility of neoclassical Keynesianism to attack. The weaknesses of US mainstream Keynesianism can be traced to the gradual drift away from emphasising the most importantly anti-classical features of Keynes's revolution, in particular, the multiplier and the malcoordination of saving and investment.

The IS-LM system has encouraged, or at least its use has resulted in, a theoretical and empirical focus on the elasticities of the curves.

Leijonhufvud maintains (1983, p. 65) that "IS-LM has served us ill in three long-lasting controversies": namely Keynes and the classics, loanable funds *versus* liquidity preference[1] and the empirical validity of monetarism. One could add that renewed interest in the business cycle has proceeded without IS-LM being integral. Dialogue with the Austrian school has not been fostered, but, at one level, real business cycle stories can be depicted.[2] But, despite its shortcomings, Leijonhufvud (1983, p. 64) accepts that "in the teaching of macroeconomics, a better mousetrap has yet to be invented".[3]

Leijonhufvud's first objection is the most well known: IS-LM came to view Keynes and the classicists as disagreeing primarily about the elasticities of the curves, and, in the long run, elasticities did not matter anyway because wage flexibility would ensure their intersection over full-capacity output. While Keynes devoted much of the *General Theory* to the determination of interest rates, textbooks ended up with the notion that, to Keynes, they did not matter. Whether elasticities were large or small was empirically testable. Formalism, the mode of analysis rejected by Keynes himself, became the academic and scientific style post-war. It resulted in a drift away from grasping the intuition, the essentialist overtones of which positivists distrust. The rise of the technocratic econometrician and the Walrasian theorist, with their quest for precision and rigour, facilitated the language, IS-LM, being appropriated by the users who had something else (better, in their minds) to say. Keynes's preoccupation with market speculation over interest rates in a deeply uncertain world was replaced by the banality of transactions costs as a means to flatten LM, for example. Pragmatism displaced insight.[4]

In his writings since his 1968 book Leijonhufvud has complained that IS-LM analysis has been used too mechanically insofar as the interdependencies and sympathetic shifts of the curves are typically suppressed. Increases in expenditure have clear and predictable financial implications of which wealth holders presumably could quickly become aware. Some post Keynesians, it may be said, use IS-LM to good effect; e.g. Davidson (1978) shows how Keynes's finance motive for holding money can be incorporated to show that shifts in IS caused by investor confidence leads to an immediate change in the demand for bridging funds. What perhaps doesn't make sense is the simultaneous belief by mainstream economists in IS-LM and in Walrasian notional demands. The question is whether spillovers and effective demands can be captured by IS-LM. One curve need not sit still while the other is manipulated. It becomes a question of learning and anticipation.

Leijonhufvud's point is that sometimes monetary disturbances have real consequences and sometimes real ones have monetary and financial consequences. One of the problems with IS-LM stories based on the standard, extreme assumptions about elasticities that are told by fiscalist Keynesians and monetarists is that their respective and rival consequences always are claimed to happen (1983, p. 75). For example, "monetarism" (flat IS, vertical LM) requires that IS shocks never change income. If the dynamics in reality instead depend on the state of knowledge and degree of learning (and no one would disagree with this), then the "same impulse need not produce the same response every time it is repeated" (1983, p. 76). Both IS and LM can shift depending on who knows what when.

But is any of this a valid criticism of IS-LM *per se*? All languages and doctrines are susceptible to capture and to evolutionary change. Was IS-LM peculiarly susceptible? One could even playfully suggest that Keynes's Chapter 12, which some regard as the axis around which the *General Theory* revolves, has been exaggerated and distorted, for example, by Shackle. Can a long-run[5] reversion to classical explanations of unemployment that centre on wage inflexibilities really be attributed to the use of IS-LM?

This paper argues that Leijonhufvud's critique of textbook Keynesianism is even more valid now than it was in 1968 when he wrote his book. Samuelson's spirited rejection of Leijonhufvud is explored briefly. Furthermore, Leijonhufvud's case can be extended: textbooks do a poor job of explaining classical economics both when IS-LM and the related AS and AD approaches are used. Too many recent controversies between Keynesians and classicists have little to do with empirical disagreements over elasticities. Leijonhufvud's more recent objections to IS-LM have received scant attention. Solow's reaction is examined, and some, though not all, of his counter-arguments appear sound. In careful hands, IS-LM still has some value as an instrument of analysis.

6.2 SAVING AND INVESTMENT: MISSING PRESUMED DEAD

Leijonhufvud complains that IS-LM fails to make coordination breakdowns central. Even the crude income-expenditure model did this job better than IS-LM. The multiplier and the paradox of thrift, both of which at least draw attention, albeit in an extreme way, to the role of saving and investment, have disappeared from high level discourse according to Leijonhufvud (1981, pp. 177-80). Debates with monetarists are on their terms and are not couched in terms of the "Hansenian verities" (1981, p. 177) stressing how interest rates fail to coordinate saving and investment. Wage flexibility and speed of learning have become central instead.

During the 1980s and 1990s textbooks have changed further. Standard models are presented, the equations are all there, the diagrams are drawn and students learn them by rote. But the intuition has gone. Many of the old verities have been editorially removed from modern textbooks. They are not refuted. They are simply never stated anymore. The paradox of thrift is disappearing. The speculative nature of the financial sector is taboo. These markets are efficient. Wage cuts do not reduce demand for goods; they increase the demand for labour. Leijonhufvud's criticisms may well be even more valid nowadays.

It is now routine for textbooks to introduce macroeconomics with a bland discussion of GDP. The circular flow of income concept is now used (misused) to establish national accounting identities. In earlier textbooks, the inequality of leakages and injections explained why the equilibrium flow could change. Circular-flow diagrams nowadays show household saving leakages that are now returned directly to businesses via financial markets. The *ex ante* (planned) equality is frequently conflated with the *ex post* (realized) identities. (Thankfully, at least the Latin has disappeared.) The notion that there can be problems with coordinating saving and investment flows is virtually invisible.

Policy debates about the conditions under which saving results in investment have died out. It is widely regarded as self-evident that higher national saving (public and private) results in higher national investment. Government deficits can always be beneficially cut, and if investment does not absorb the resources "released", the export and import replacing sectors will (the twin deficits hypothesis).

Mainstream Keynesians seem to stand mute in the face of assertions that high saving in free-market Asia has directly resulted in high investment. It is as though they don't believe in their own textbooks which contain models (nowadays only implicitly) severing the link between saving and investment, at least over the short to medium term. Either that or they are too embarrassed to transgress against what every "respectable" economist is saying. Would their students believe them if they ever did speak of saving leakages not offset by investment injections?

6.3 ON CLASSICAL ECONOMICS AND THE ECONOMICS OF THE CLASSICISTS

The grip of textbook simplifications has yet to weaken, and Keynes is not the only victim. Classical views of classicism are distorted too, if elasticities are posited as the line of demarcation between Keynes and the classicists. In the 1990s textbooks still talk about monetarism as involving a steep LM and flat IS while fiscalists hold the opposite. Of course, Friedman dismisses fiscalism not so much because of the elasticity of the IS curve but because the permanent income hypothesis knocks out the efficacy of the dynamic multiplier over the relevant policy period. Short-run MPCs are uselessly small. The IS curve is "too heavy" to move around easily. By contrast the LM curve is potentially "too light" or too hair-trigger. A change in the money supply tends to have powerful, but temporally unpredictable, effects on nominal income. The elasticities of the curves are almost irrelevant.

Neither does IS-LM portray classicism coherently. The IS curve is supposedly quite flat; if interest rates are high, output is low. But isn't textbook classicism based on Say's Law which states that the composition of output varies, not its total? If interest rates are high, investment is indeed lower, but according to classical loanable-funds theory, consumption rises to preserve full-employment levels of output, provided that inputs can be switched quickly to alternative uses. This would make IS *vertical* over Y* (full-employment output), wouldn't it? Perhaps the textbooks are referring to the rearguard classicists who accept that Say's Law is invalid in the short term and who prefer monetary policy to fiscal policy on empirical grounds. Maybe such pragmatic classicists, who accept that lags in structural adjustment do occur, are in mind. But there are New Keynesians who prefer monetary policy, so the focus on elasticities has ceased to be useful as a means of distinguishing Keynesians from classicists.

Similarly, regarding the vertical LM curve as capturing classicism has problems. The textbook vertical LM curve seems to be capable of being cut free, in the short run, from Y*. An expansion of money raises AD in a classical world. Here there is no problem incorporating money. Money is there to be spent. If prices lag, output surges as Hume pointed out. See Keynes (1936, p. 343n). But Keynes (1936, p. 209) was puzzled about how classical quantity theorists could believe, with logical consistency, that cutting the money supply through open market operations would cut output. For money to be sucked from the financial sector by bond sales, idle cash had to reside there, he reasoned, but classicists held that hoarding was a temporary aberration not a normal condition. Keynes (*CW*, vol. 29, p. 258) eventually concluded that a fixed amount of hoards could exist in the classical framework but that classicists tacitly assumed no interest elasticity of asset demand because they had no concept of speculative demands for cash and bonds. (Classical hoarding would be instinctive rather than motivated by making profits in the bond market.) He then generously attributed to them a belief in an implicit argument, the Keynes effect, that deflation would mean that the real money supply would grow in the long run to ensure, in near-Hicksian terms, that the LM curve, in the absence of the liquidity trap, would move and cut the IS curve directly over Y*. This became the standard textbook account. By textbook logic, the only reason why monetary policy would ever work is because wage-flexibility had not yet occurred. Keynes (1936, p. 267) dryly observed that by this reasoning union leaders had as much power over the real money supply as the central bank.

There is one case at least where Keynes did point to elasticities as partially relevant, but in a way quite different from the textbooks Leijonhufvud condemns. Keynes's argument was that the demand for money was not vertical. Textbooks still claim that Keynes's contribution was simply the liquidity trap, where the LM curve is flat. Keynes, however, invented liquidity preference theory to show why the demand for money was not vertical and why this mattered. The case of the "intermediate slope" is Keynes's, not the neoclassicists'. Textbooks sometimes give the impression that Keynes borrowed the standard neoclassical model and made an extreme and implausible assumption about the interest elasticity of the demand for money. By contrast, surely anything less than a vertical LM means that Keynes's more general theory is right. Keynes has somehow been marginalised to the point where he is claimed to uphold a special case without getting any credit for the very framework adopted by textbook. But it was Keynes who was responsible for raising the issue of the existence of a speculative demand for money.

The textbook emperor is still naked. What students are expected to learn by heart simply makes little sense. While elasticities can matter for policy purposes, they do not help clarify the underlying differences of vision, which separate Keynesians from classicists, about how well markets work.

6.4 SLIPPERY SLOPES

Textbooks have in no way improved since the 1960s when Leijonhufvud presented his critique of the Keynesian apparatus. Students are still exposed to accounts of Keynes and the Classics rendered in terms of possible extreme elasticities. Introductory textbooks rightly emphasise the need to distinguish between shifts of curves and movements along them. Frequently, however, textbooks are rather casual about how the basics are presented - at least from the point of view of people with a history-of-thought background.

The excessive weight given to elasticities in IS-LM carries over into AS-AD analysis with the same effect of facilitating the notion that wage and price flexibility are the central questions. In classicism the short-run aggregate supply curve presented in some textbooks is supposedly vertical over full capacity, but hasn't there been a confusion if the reason offered is that money wages and prices can free fall? It is more accurate to say that a positively sloped SAS shifts immediately resulting in a vertical locus. If the dynamics are benign - and textbooks don't talk about how wage-cuts reduce consumption spending any more - then movements along any SAS would never be observed if nominal wages were perfectly flexible.

Other problems go beyond pedagogical oversimplifications of this sort. In classicism, is the AD line in P-Y space better depicted as flat, or is it that a shift in some component of spending (e.g. investment) is offset by relative price changes (specifically, only interest rates adjust) to preserve its initial position? In the latter, slope is secondary. If the dynamics depend on whether further declines in P are expected, thereby shifting AD again, then here also slope is of secondary relevance.

Patinkin (1965, pp. 357-8) has wrestled with a related issue: does Say's Law mean that wage-price flexibility ensures the aggregate planned expenditure line never shifts from a position consistent with equilibrium at full employment or does it mean that the marginal propensity to spend is unity resulting in planned expenditure coinciding with the 45° line?

These are rather basic questions and standard accounts must be confusing to those students who are trying to understand what is going on. (Rote learners, by contrast, experience no difficulties and, in fairness, textbook writers may well simply be responding to a market demand by students for simple, neat classifications).

Perhaps textbooks can only change slowly. After all, it took 30 years for them to begin to replace "deflationary" gaps with "contractionary" or "recessionary" gaps. Deflation has not been seen since the Depression. Expecting less emphasis on elasticities asks for too much, if only because many instructors would stop choosing a book which deals with old debates differently from the way they themselves were taught. Besides, Keynes and Say are widely viewed by economists and by students as merely ancient history. The history of economic thought has little attraction for textbook writers when they are judged by their coverage of new developments. Indeed, Say's Law and its validity have become minor issues in many textbooks. Leijonhufvud has not succeeded in getting textbooks to improve. Elasticities can be measured. By contrast, coordination failures are more conceptual and difficult to explain to students.

6.5 SOLOW'S RESPONSE TO LEIJONHUFVUD

Solow (1984, p. 22) accepts that some of what Leijonhufvud says about the shortcomings of IS-LM is "quite wholesome", but the emphasis on information - about who knows what when - as a means to explain coordination failure is "seriously misleading" (p. 25). He argues that

> it would follow that macroeconomic policy could usefully be restricted to the production and dissemination of the missing information ... One could equally say that the second World War was an example of information failure: if Hitler had known what was going to happen, he would never have invaded Poland... (1984, p. 23)

The information issues surrounding a purely nominal disturbance, like an increase in the money supply, are simple enough to maintain plausibly that, if everyone understood what was happening, nominal prices would simply rise proportionally. But disturbances in the real sector involving a shift in the confidence of investors are not merely more complex to interpret:

> The opaqueness of economic events ... is an intrinsic characteristic of a decentralized market economy...
>
> No-one could *possibly* know what the new equilibrium would look like after the discovery of electricity (1984, pp. 23-24).

6.6 A RESPONSE TO SOLOW

Two issues need to be kept distinct: what Leijonhufvud says about the properties of the dynamics of conventional IS-LM stories and what he says about actual economies. Full-information models are a benchmark for comparison. They are not depictions of realizable states of the world. When Leijonhufvud criticises a model for making strict assumptions about information endowments he says nothing in particular about the role of information in reality.

It is questionable for Solow to attribute to Leijonhufvud the claim that macroeconomic policy in the real world could simply involve the dissemination of information. For a start, in Leijonhufvud's system this information would need to be provided before the multiplier came into operation. While conceptually possible, in practice it is implausible. Information about the existence of a problem emerges only after damage is becoming evident. Isolated agents react to actual problems rather than cooperate to solve them in advance of their impact. Insofar as savings buffers smooth consumption and forestall the multiplier, this only buys time for the correct information and decisions to emerge. When the multiplier is at work - and Leijonhufvud's view is that large enough disturbances take real-world economies out of the buffer zone, or corridor, around Y* - the prices and the actions required to restore full employment change. Knowledge of the "correct" vector become irrelevant once the multiplier-induced liquidity constraints prevent agents acting on it.[6] After you have missed the boat and are stranded on the jetty, information about the departure time is irrelevant. Even being told the ship's current location is of no use by itself. Intervention (a government speedboat) is required to restore the ability of the agent to board the ship. It is also strange for Solow to attribute to Leijonhufvud something resembling the new classical policy of simply supplying the private sector with information about the government's policy regime and the relevant statistics. Leijonhufvud is caustic about the failure of new classicism to take either current or intertemporal coordination failures and the resulting involuntary unemployment seriously. The lack of effective demand needs to be restored by demand stimulus and then true signals (information) about notional demands will begin to be generated.

It is important to note that many of the passages in "The Wicksell Connection" focusing on the importance of information relate to dynamics "within the corridor", i.e. multiplier-induced liquidity constraints preventing potential convergence to full employment have not been incorporated.[7] Presumably involuntary unemployment would complicate the story still further and add to the demands on judgement required for the judicious use of IS-LM, or any other model for that matter. It would then be less clear about whether improvements in information really would have the power to arrest the dynamics of routine applications of IS-LM. Conceivably the more powerful the multiplier, the more truly the routine use of IS-LM relates to reality. Any information lag would have a magnified effect. Whether the changes of information possessed by individual agents or groups (employers, employees) will change their behaviour and result in shifts of IS or LM curves not modelled in standard IS-LM, *ceteris paribus*, exercises depends crucially on the freedom of action of agents. The involuntarily unemployed have little such freedom.

One is left wondering though about how reasonable it is for Leijonhufvud in his writings in the 1980s to assume the multiplier away if the topic in question is the business cycle. How much of the cycle does Leijonhufvud regard as being "within the corridor"? If severe contractions, such as the Depression itself, show the catastrophic effects of disturbances too large for financial buffers to cope with, are more typical recessions characterised by a significant minority of agents being liquidity constrained but the majority acting on the information, right or wrong, they currently possess? Or are the dynamic multipliers normally observed mere artefacts, declines in consumption somehow really being "induced" voluntarily?

One must also have some misgivings about Leijonhufvud's views about the dynamics resulting from a shift in the MEC. He remarks (1981, p. 201) the notion of

> "Dark Forces of Time and Ignorance", as Keynes put it ... will make intertemporal economic activities the most difficult to coordinate.

Some (like Solow) would say that this considerably understates the problem. Success in business is arguably rather more haphazard. Animal spirits create enough investment and entrepreneurial flair (and advertising) create what are later regarded as the "right" products. A hardline fundamentalist, like Shackle, would say that systematic detailed coordination is impossible not merely difficult. The system does not solve given equations. Subsequent solutions endogenously create the equations later being apparently solved by markets whenever, or if ever, coherent outcomes emerge.

Leijonhufvud suggests that a downward shift in the MEC could plausibly in reality be offset by a decline in interest rates regarded as relevant, or normal, for the future. The LM curve could shift simultaneously and sympathetically with the IS curve if both the real and financial sectors interpreted events and circumstances in the same way (ie had the same "information" about the loss of investor confidence). Not all speculation is uninformed in this view.

Surely, however, in reality investors themselves do not know how valid is their loss of confidence or how long they will hold such views. The bears making portfolio decisions about their asset stocks have no great reason to give weight to the views of those expressing current flow-demands for finance, if experience shows there is considerable volatility of investor expectations. Electricity – Solow's example - is only introduced once, by the way. In some irrelevant and hypothetical world, if we did have this historically unique knowledge of the impact of electricity the dynamics would be different, wouldn't they? Leijonhufvud's point can be regarded as trivial rather than erroneous.

Leijonhufvud's views (1983, pp. 84-5) on information flows to and in the financial markets also deserve comment.

> With a bit more information ... agents would short-circuit the particular sequence assumed in the usual IS-LM exercise ...
>
> This price [interest rate] mechanism will work with well-informed speculators ... [i.e. those who realise that "permanent" lower profitability requires a lower interest rate]. The difference between the LP [liquidity preference] Keynesian and the loanable funds Keynesian [Leijonhufvud himself] is that between a system which cannot work properly [because interest rates *only* fall after Y falls] and one that can and presumably often does, work [if interest rates decline quickly enough to equate saving and investment flows at the initial income level], but cannot be counted on to do so without fail.

This is a rather sanguine view of the efficiency of financial markets in practice, but it is a question of what "presumably often" means. And financial markets only need to work well enough to keep the economy in the corridor around full employment where liquidity constraints are not a problem. Perfection is not required.

Leijonhufvud (1983, p. 87) concludes:

> So is the procedure of shifting LM, keeping IS constant - or vice versa - justified? The answer is sometimes; perhaps often; but not necessarily or always. And that very largely, is what is the matter with IS-LM.

Compare Solow's view that IS-LM is still "fit training for our intuitions" (1984, p. 15) and appropriate for application to many

> "routine macroeconomic events in an underemployed economy. It goes without saying that some questions force you well beyond the scope of the IS-LM apparatus right away."

But Leijonhufvud's misgivings about IS-LM are more pronounced:

> In the end, it is probably not a short-cut to understanding macroeconomics; for knowing when to use it and when not to rely on it seems to be more difficult than the subject matter itself. (1983, p. 65)

For Solow (1984, p. 14) by contrast:

> If I pick up the morning paper and read that the US Congress may soon pass a package of tax and expenditure measures intended to reduce the Federal deficit ..., my mind naturally draws IS and LM curves and shifts them.

Solow's example is, of course, "routine". Presumably he would accept that the line of demarcation about the appropriate domain of any model's applicability is always a "more difficult" higher-order judgement. For Solow, IS-LM is not obsolete. Leijonhufvud insinuates otherwise.

6.7 SAMUELSON VERSUS LEIJONHUFVUD

Harry Johnson (1970, p. 71) observed that

> both Milton Friedman...and Joan Robinson...can with a clear conscience commend Leijonhufvud's book to their students; Paul Samuelson...will find it embarrassing to do so.

Samuelson's (1983, p. 25) response is fairly abrupt:

> What James Meade, Roy Harrod, John Hicks, Brian Reddaway, A.P. Lerner, Oskar Lange, Paul Samuelson, A.C. Pigou, and Joan Robinson all agreed on as the analytical core of the General Theory, Mr Leijonhufvud decides is only a mathematical perversion of Keynes's thought. The real Keynes is rather to be found in the subtle nuances of Keynes's perceptions: the notions of "bearishness" and "liquidity"...
>
> Yes, Keynes was a genius. Yes, some of his ideas were inchoate and would not have lent themselves usefully to diagramming and symbolic manipulation...
> In science it is not the incoherent, inchoate and ineffable that has a cash value.
>
> What is remarkable is ... how strong was the latent demand in the 1970s for a work to debunk Keynesianism.

Samuelson has yet to respond to Leijonhufvud beyond this in any detailed way so far as I am aware.

In response to Samuelson, is an attack on Walras's Law really so "ineffable" or lacking in pragmatic "cash value"? If the intuition of an argument is important - and, with the partial release of the stranglehold of positivism, one can at last say this publicly - and if the textbooks stripped it away and left only the bare equations, then they have discarded something of value. Of course, it is not necessarily the use of mathematics that is to blame; it is the excessive focus by the technicians on elasticity coefficients, numbers that can be measured with the view to framing policy.

It is curious that Samuelson should strive to enlist Joan Robinson who used the term, "bastard Keynesian", to describe the sorts of works Leijonhufvud critiqued. Furthermore, Leijonhufvud hardly rejects the "analytical core" if it includes the set of ideas perceived by all of the authorities listed by Samuelson. Leijonhufvud simply complains that Lerner, Robinson and Harrod have been squeezed out by Pigou, Lange and Samuelson. When firing a rocket at the moon, a seemingly small navigational error at the outset becomes a large one much later in the journey. Samuelson's selection of the essentials brought considerable progress but only for a time. In 1968, Leijonhufvud announced that the Walrasian rocket was discernibly off-target.

While Leijonhufvud's work, by discrediting established Keynesian doctrine, could well have indirectly contributed to the respectability of monetarism, it is not clear that any of this was Leijonhufvud's intention. One could at least as reasonably argue that the success of monetarism stemmed from a lack of preparedness of mainstream economists. They had over-invested in a version of Keynesianism that was so narrowly based that it was liable to topple. Samuelson himself had been exposed to the power and excitement of reading the *General Theory*. Two generations later students were soulless number-crunchers. Technicians are seldom able to recognise and deal with implausible innovations when they hear them.

Samuelson's sensitivity is easy to understand and, at one level, is justifiable. Those criticised by Leijonhufvud are mostly winners of the Nobel Prize (Samuelson himself, Klein, Tobin, Solow, Modigliani). Furthermore, taking anything vaguely resembling a "liberal", leftist or interventionist position in the United States has always taken some courage and a thick skin. Indeed, when McCarthyism flared, Larry Klein understandably went to Oxford.[8] Emphasising market failures seems more muscular than emphasising information failures when it comes to tackling head-on the issue of whether market systems tend reliably to generate full employment. Information failures sound too close to the issues tressed by monetarists and new classicists.[9]

Leijonhufvud can be construed as accusing Samuelson and others as wimps when it was they that did the hard work in elevating and propagating at least some aspects of Keynes's theories. Samuelson's response is an entirely human one.

Some of Leijonhufvud's statements hit hard for all their elegance and diplomacy.

> It is clear, I think, that Keynesianism has had no Champion in the United States for quite some time. There have been no leading figures concerned to maintain a semblance of intellectual coherence in Keynesian macroeconomics. Nor has there been a Keynesian "research programme" for perhaps twenty years. The best people in the center have been neo-Walrasian all along...
>
> Well, no one was obliged to keep the Hansen school running. Nor could one argue that our intellectual resources would have been better allocated if, say, Paul Samuelson or Lawrence Klein had taken time out for the purpose. (1981, pp. 178-179)

Leijonhufvud makes two forthright criticisms of the neoclassical Keynesian Establishment. They inadequately represented Keynes to begin with and, besides, what have they done lately? No wonder Samuelson takes offence.

Samuelson (1985) recalls the times when the Keynesian revolution hit the US. He rejects the rarefied, intellectualised, rational reconstruction of Leijonhufvud in favour of recounting the confusion and frustration of the era and the pressing need for practical answers:

> All the more reason to have a Rip van Winkle like me tell a chronicler like Axel Leijonhufvud how it really was in history. (1985, p. 5)

However, it is simply hard to believe that, of all the explanations of mass unemployment circulating at the time, the most obvious one of all had eluded American economists. But Samuelson (1985, p. 6) states:

> Clearly I was ripe to accept...Keynes' proposal that money wage rates be accepted as if they were "sticky". This was not a perfect bicycle, but it was the best wheel in town.

This, of course, is what Leijonhufvud rightly views as a thoroughly classical statement: unemployment is caused by wages being too high. But that was the Keynesian revolution as Samuelson remembers it. There was no displacement of

Hansen's verities perpetrated during the 1950s if Samuelson's version of history approximates the facts.

Perhaps Hansen and Ackley were the outliers. Mainstream American thinking has always been sympathetic to the classical emphasis on wages. Patinkin did not subvert Keynesianism in America when he deflated Hick's attempt to show that Keynes said nothing new if a system could not settle into an unemployed state. Patinkin simply codified the instincts of the mainstream economist. It was natural that the *General Theory* was rapidly confined to a special case most relevant to the Depression.

6.8 IS-LM AND PRAGMATISM

Perhaps the primary appeal of Keynesian policies in the United States has always been pragmatic in nature. If, and while, the technocrats and econometricians can produce results, they will command respect. During this time, pragmatism and formalism can coexist. Perhaps many "Keynesians" have always been upholders of essentially classical conceptions. They simply had enough commonsense to realise that wages, prices and markets did not in reality have full flexibility. J. Ronnie Davis (1971) indicates that many ideas which became regarded as "Keynesian" were already being devised in the US (the multiplier, for instance) prior to the *General Theory*. He also notes how many classical economists urged Hoover to stimulate demand. Keynes's deeper critiques of capitalism never really caught on in the US. They were dismissed early on as florid, elitist, idiosyncratic exaggerations inessential to the revolution. See Schlesinger (1956) and Johnson and Johnson (1978).

Leijonhufvud describes the macroeconomic centre as viewing itself as "Keynesian" in some sense, especially so far as some cautious advocacy of short-term stabilisation is concerned.

> But...it is curiously difficult to say what the centrist position has become or what is "Keynesian" about it. The topnotch people in the center can only be described as "eclectic" in theory and "pragmatic" in policy. Those terms, however, are descriptive of judicious temperament rather than expressive of a shared and coherent system of beliefs. On occasion, Robert Solow or James Tobin will make it his business to explain where Joan Robinson or Milton Friedman go too far. But this is not enough - unless "anti-Monetarist" is to become the residual definition of "Keynesian". (1981, p. 178)

Leijonhufvud (1981, p. 179) also observes:

> Most astoundingly, Neoclassical Keynesianism has ended up in a position that has proven difficult to demarcate from Monetarism in any significant way. But, *how could that be*?

If many Keynesians were really pragmatic classicists to begin with - wages and prices are sticky in practice - then the debate is naturally over matters of speed of adjustment, of degree, questions of sizes of coefficients and, especially, elasticities.

But things have become more astounding since. Milton Friedman has increasingly become a respectable, if dated, figure of the centre. Rational expectations typically imply faster learning than Friedman feels can be inferred from the facts. The new classicists are the radicals now. The widening spectrum at the classical end has moved the stationary Friedman more to the pragmatic centre.

Many American New Keynesians embrace rational expectations preferring to do battle over wage and price flexibility, the old terrain. Some are prepared to favour rules over discretion. It is difficult to tell New Keynesians from New Classicists once you maintain that perceived wage-price inflexibilities are in fact outcomes of the free play of market forces. Barro (1984, p. 509) has observed that if free markets spontaneously create apparent impediments to price flexibility, there must be a good reason grounded in efficiency, so there really is no market failure to correct by demand stimulus. Agents have freely chosen price inflexibility and cyclical variations in employment. Even though manipulating demand would have real effects and GDP could be pumped up, there could be less social welfare as a result. It is hard to argue with this, if only because the reasoning is something of a closed loop. And IS-LM views all of this from a distance. It is not the language of the debate.

Pragmatism has its virtues. There is a distrust of grand theory and radical shifts in policy. Many economists simply did not believe that New Classicism could be right despite its orthodox formalism, but it became difficult in respectable circles to be sufficiently aggressive until the econometricians showed that even anticipated monetary policy in fact worked and had real effects.

But pragmatism has its faults - in economics and beyond. Pragmatism has resulted in a disregard of deep theory and its biggest fault, of course, is that in the long run it doesn't work. Eventually, it drifts too far from its inspirational source to continue drawing sustenance. The pragmatist roams and grazes. Pragmatism begins as an enthusiastic rejection of a failed dogma; here it has a dynamic energy. But, as the scientific "conversation" continues, new alliances of convenience emerge making it difficult to see what principles, if any, lie below the surface to separate the discussants. New entrants making bold "principled" claims - the policy ineffectiveness postulate, for example - rapidly seize market share. A beachhead is formed. When their principal arguments are countered and invalidated they move into an undefended terrain, real business cycle theory.

There are things worse than pragmatism, and IS-LM is illequipped to deal with them.

6.9 CONCLUSION

In matters of judgement the correct answer cannot be demonstrated and need not exist. Discussions about the validity of IS-LM merge quickly into ones concerning its legitimacy as a representation of Keynes.

There seems to be agreement that, in careful hands, IS-LM can be used safely. The language, however, cannot easily be separated from some message about the need for, and effectiveness of, counter-cyclical demand management.

Leijonhufvud is right insofar as mainstream textbooks still over-emphasise elasticities at the expense of examining why and whether the curves are likely in the circumstances to shift. The latter questions are by nature less empirical and more conceptual. After examining the views of Leijonhufvud, Samuelson and Solow, the impression emerges that progress in the debate is not being made. The issues get talked about, but it is not clear that even mutual understanding, let alone a consensus, is evolving.

This paper is imbued with a sense of vagueness and frustrating inconclusiveness. While this could in some part be the fault of the writer, the authorities in question seem objectively to disagree over mere matters of emphasis yet they clearly remain divided about something that is difficult to identify. They seem to agree that IS-LM has specific advantages and shortcomings, but they somehow remain in somewhat prickly disagreement. It seems that IS-LM has a symbolic value; to accept or to criticise it is apparently to have some implicit agenda.

Perhaps Leijonhufvud's real sin was to write such a well received PhD which was so dismissive of so much of what Samuelson and his allies stand for. Leijonhufvud searches for intuitive meaning and he wrote a history of economic thought intended for contemporary relevance. He transgressed the rules of the establishment: positivism, mathematics and empirics are the proper means to scientific advance, and studying earlier thinkers is just a way of taking a rest from serious research.

Possibly the early success of Leijonhufvud's book resulted from a bored dissatisfaction of segments of the academic establishment with mainstream "Keynesian" economics. If Leijonhufvud ever returns to popularity, it would be more likely to stem from a bored dissatisfaction with the content and style of mainstream economics as a whole.

BIBLIOGRAPHY

Robert Barro (1984). *Macroeconomics*, Wiley, New York, 2nd ed.

William Breit and Roger Spencer (eds) (1986). *Lives of the Laureates: Seven Nobel Economists*, MIT Press, Cambridge, Mass.

Robert W. Clower (1975). "Reflections on the Keynesian Perplex", *Zeitschrift für National_konomie*, vol. 35, pp. 1-24.

Paul Davidson (1978). *Money and the Real World*, Macmillan, London.

J. Ronnie Davis (1971). *The New Economics and the Old Economists*, Iowa University Press, Ames, Iowa.

Elizabeth S. Johnson and Harry G. Johnson (1978). *The Shadow of Keynes: Understanding Keynes, Cambridge and Keynesian Economics*, Basil Blackwell, Oxford.

Harry Johnson (1970). "Keynes and the Keynesians: Some intellectual legends", *Encounter*, vol. 34, Jan., pp. 70-2.

John Maynard Keynes (1936). *The General Theory of Employment, Interest and Money*, Macmillan, London.

Axel Leijonhufvud (1968). *On Keynesian Economics and the Economics of Keynes; a study in monetary theory*, Oxford University Press, New York.

Axel Leijonhufvud (1981) *Information and Coordination; essays in macroeconomic theory*, Oxford University Press, N.Y.

Axel Leijonhufvud (1983). "What was the matter with IS-LM?" in Jean-Paul Fitoussi (ed.) *Modern Macro-economic Theory*, Basil Blackwell, Oxford, pp. 64-90.

N. Gregory Mankiw (1992). *Macroeconomics*, Worth Publishers, New York.

Donald Moggridge (ed.) (1979). *The Collected Writings of John Maynard Keynes*, vol. 29, Macmillan, London.

Don Patinkin (1965). *Money, Interest and Prices*, Harper and Row, New York, 2nd ed.

Paul Samuelson (1983). *Economist*, vol. 287, no. 7295, June 25, pp. 21-5.

Paul Samuelson (1985). "Succumbing to Keynesianism", *Challenge*, vol. 27, no. 6, Jan.-Feb., pp. 4-11.

James R. Schlesinger (1956). "After Twenty Years: The General Theory", *Quarterly Journal of Economics*, vol. 70, no. 4, November, pp. 581-602.

Robert M. Solow (1984). "Mr Hicks and the Classics", *Oxford Economic Papers*, vol. 36 (n.s.), supp., Nov., pp. 13-25.

ENDNOTES

[1] For an attempt to disentangle this debate and to assess Leijonhufvud's specific objections to the details of the explanation of the dynamics in standard IS-LM stories, see Littleboy (1990, Ch. 5).

[2] See Mankiw (1992, ch. 14-2) for a rather strange attempt to dispense with the LM curve thereby not drawing attention to the very change in interest rates that account for the intertemporal substitution crucial to the explanation.

[3] Barro's (1984) textbook treats IS-LM, and Keynesianism, somewhat dismissively. Keynesianism occupies one chapter. More classically oriented textbooks have little trouble dispensing with IS-LM.

[4] One suspects that Leijonhufvud's close colleague, Robert Clower (1975, p. 10), would not regard the partnership of IS-LM and Walrasianism as a victory of pragmatism. Rather, the Walrasian system is a "fairy-tale" and "science fiction".

[5] By "long run" I mean a period of time sufficient for "sage flexibility" to ensure that mainstream economists are fully employed demonstrating how macroeconomics must return to its initial classical position.

[6] However, I am puzzled by Leijonhufvud's (1983, p. 67) remark:

> The temporal order of decisions is of analytical significance if, *and only if*, transactors have to act on incomplete information. (Emphasis is added.)
> If agents are trapped by liquidity-constraints, the sequencing of actions within the "transactions structure" (1968, p. 90)

presumably also matters. See the following footnote also.

[7] Leijonhufvud (1981, pp. 134 n. 4, 183 n. 87, 201). This point, however, is not clearly made in Leijonhufvud (1983).

[8] Breit and Spencer (1986, p. 28).

[9] And Leijonhufvud (1981, p. 199, n. 109) confesses, as if to provoke attack:

> The basic outlook that [I share] with Rational Expectations theory can be simply put: Unless there is an information failure inconsistent of some sort, economic activities will be properly coordinated. ...My emphasis on beliefs [cf. (1981, p. 140, n. 5] is foreign to...Lucas [where all agents]...must have the same beliefs. In contrast, Monetarist unemployment theory a`la Friedman is of "my" variety...[where] firms learn about the rising inflation before workers do.

7

IS-LM AND MACROECONOMETRIC MODELS

Bert G. Hickman

7.1 INTRODUCTION

After nearly sixty years, Hicks' (1937) mathematical formulation of the core of Keynes' *General Theory of Employment, Interest and Money* (1936) remains solidly lodged in macroeconomics textbooks as the basic theoretical paradigm for the simultaneous determination of national income and the rate of interest and for the analysis of the short-run impacts of monetary and fiscal policies. When the IS-LM model of aggregate demand is augmented with a model of aggregate supply, moreover, the combined AD-AS system also incorporates simultaneous price-level determination and the capability of analyzing the macro impacts of supply shocks.

The principal theme of this paper is that the IS-LM, AD-AS apparatus provides a fruitful approach to the analysis of the structures of mainstream macroeconometric models and their forecasting and simulation properties. The majority of contemporary macroeconometric models of developed economies are comprised of a (sometimes highly) disaggregated IS system of demand equations for final goods, a more or less disaggregated monetary (LM) bloc, and an aggregate supply (AS) structure usually based on a labor-market Phillips curve for wage determination, a labor demand function linking output and employment, and a markup hypothesis of price setting in imperfectly competitive markets. These often complex and sometimes huge models may conceptually be reduced to a central core with estimated implicit elasticities for the IS, LM, AD and AS locuses. The method lends itself to comparative studies of the properties of different macroeconometric models, but it is also a useful tool in the process of individual model verification which should be undertaken in any model-building or model-using project. It has the added advantage of showing that the large and complex system of equations typical of many operational macroeconometric models need not be regarded as a black box but can be understood as a disaggregated version of the simplified core.

7.2 A PROTOTYPE IS-LM MODEL

The fix-price IS-LM framework taken by itself determines the real interest rate (r) and real GDP (Y) levels consistent with simultaneous equilibrium in the markets for goods and money, for given monetary and fiscal policies and a given price level (P). Since P is fixed, the real interest rate is identical to the nominal rate.

In a simplified linear model, the quantity of aggregate demand (A) depends on exogenous government expenditure $\overline{G}$ and responds positively to real income and negatively to the interest rate:

$$A = \overline{G} + a(1-t)Y - br \; ; \; 0 < a < 1, b > 0, 0 < t < 1. \tag{1}$$

The response of consumer expenditures to real income depends on the tax rate, t, and the marginal propensity to consume, a. Investment responds negatively to the interest rate, but so also may consumer durables and state and local government spending.

Goods market equilibrium requires Y = A. Substituting Y for A in (1) and solving for r yields the IS curve (expenditure equals income, or investment equals saving):

$$r = \frac{\overline{G}}{b} - \frac{Y}{\overline{a}b} \tag{2}$$

where $\overline{a} = 1/(1 - a(1-t))$ is the Keynesian expenditure multiplier.

The IS curve is negatively sloped in r-Y space and is steeper, the smaller is the multiplier and the sensitivity of aggregate demand to the interest rate. An exogenous increase in government spending or a reduction in the tax rate will shift the IS curve rightward. Net exports are ignored for simplicity, but their inclusion in (1) would introduce export demand as a shift variable in (2) and also reduce the expenditure multiplier by an amount depending on the marginal propensity to import.

The LM curve is a similar locus of combinations of r and Y that equilibrate the supply and demand for real money balances. In linear form, the demand for real money balances L depends positively on real income through the transactions motive and negatively on the rate of interest, or the opportunity cost of holding money balances:

$$L = cY - dr \; ; \; c, d > 0. \tag{3}$$

Assuming a given nominal stock of money, $\overline{M}$, and a given price level $\overline{P}$, the real money supply is $\overline{M} / \overline{P}$. Equating real money balances and L and solving (3) for r yields the LM curve:

$$r = -\frac{(\overline{M}/\overline{P})}{d} + \frac{cY}{d}. \tag{4}$$

An increase in the nominal money stock will shift LM rightward. The LM curve is positively sloped and is steeper, the larger is the transactions demand and the smaller is the interest sensitivity of demand for real money balances.

The IS-LM construct is a useful paradigm for the analysis of the effects of fiscal and monetary policies under conditions of less than full employment and inflexible prices. Simultaneous equilibrium in the markets for goods and money occurs at the intersection of the IS and LM curves, as at point A in Figure 1. An increase in G or reduction in t shifts the IS curve rightward to a new equilibrium at B. The resulting increase in GDP will be larger, the flatter the LM curve and the steeper the IS curve. A model with these characteristics will respond strongly to fiscal policy and weakly to monetary policy. Monetary policy, in contrast, will be more powerful than fiscal policy in models with a flat IS curve and steep LM curve.

The rudimentary IS-LM model can provide useful guidance about key parameters affecting output responses to fiscal and monetary policies when output supply is highly elastic and the price level is therefore insensitive to demand shocks. Prices are flexible in the long-run if not in the short-term, however, and even short-term supply

Figure 1.

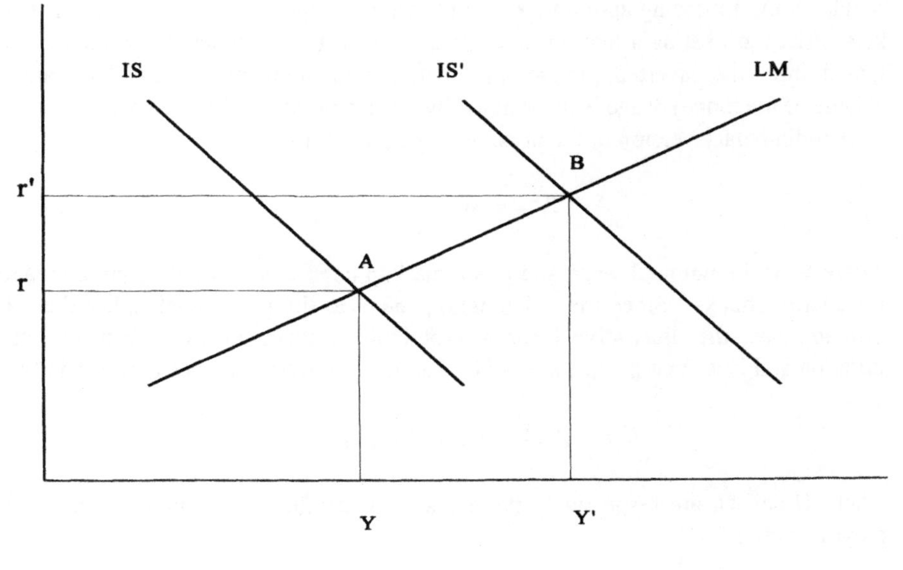

may be relatively elastic in some models. The core model must be broadened to include the interaction of AS and AD for simultaneous determination of P and Y and for the analysis of supply shocks.

7.3 A MODEL OF AGGREGATE DEMAND AND SUPPLY[1]

The AD function is easily derived from the IS-LM model. Solving the equations (2) and (4) simultaneously yields the reduced form equation for Y:

$$Y = \frac{\bar{a}\, d}{d + \bar{a}\, b\, c}\bar{G} + \frac{\bar{a}\, b}{d + \bar{a}\, b\, c}\frac{\bar{M}}{\bar{P}} \tag{5}$$

As long as G, M and P are exogenous, as in the IS-LM model, this is the appropriate reduced form to determine Y. When the system is broadened to include endogenous determination of P, however, (5) becomes an AD locus defining alternative pairs of P and Y consistent with equilibrium in the goods and money markets. A simple economic rational underlies the negative slope of AD. Given $\bar{M}$, a reduction in P increases the real money supply, reduces the interest rate, raises investment, and increases consumption through the multiplier process. This is the Keynes effect, operating through an automatic increase in real money balances when prices fall.[2] The AD curve will be flatter, the steeper underlying LM curve and the flatter the IS curve. An increase in $\bar{M}$ or $\bar{G}$ or a reduction in the tax rate t will shift the AD function rightward, and vice-versa.

The theoretical specification of the AS function is less settled in the literature.[3] A simple approach appropriate for the interpretation of a typical econometric model builds on the following assumptions. Firms are imperfect competitors in goods markets. Prices are set as a markup over unit labor cost. The demand for labor is obtained from the inverted production function with adjustment lags. The rate of change of the money wage is determined by a labor-market Phillips curve.

A rudimentary version of the price setting equation is:

$$P = e\, W \;; e > 0, \tag{6}$$

where W is the nominal wage and e is a markup coefficient including an allowance for energy shocks.[4] Since the AS function refers to the price level rather than the inflation rate, the illustrative labor market Phillips curve abstracts from expected inflation and is written in absolute rather than relative wage changes for simplicity:

$$W = -\, g\,(U - U_f) + W_{-1} \;; g > 0, \tag{7}$$

where U and U_f are respectively the actual and natural or full-employment unemployment rates.

The relation between output and labor input may be represented by an Okun's Law equation:

$$U - U_f = h\,(1 - Y/Y_p);\, h > 0, \tag{8}$$

where Y_p is the potential output corresponding to full employment of labor and the parameter h encapsulates several behavioral responses of unemployment to changes in output, including induced changes in labor supply (discouraged worker effect), labor productivity, and the average work week.

Substitution of (7) and (8) into (6) yields the short-run AS function:

$$P = -\ egh(1 - Y / Y_p) + e\,W_{-1}; \tag{9}$$

The AS function will be flatter, the smaller the reduction of unemployment for a given increase of Y ($\delta U/\delta Y = -\ h\ /\ Y_p$), the smaller the increase in the wage rate for a given unemployment reduction ($\delta W/\delta U = -\ g$), and the smaller the increase in P for a given increase in W ($\delta P/\delta W = e$). A flat AS curve will imply a small price and large output response to a shift in AD stemming from a monetary, fiscal, or other demand shock. The long-run supply curve is vertical at $Y = Y_p$, however, since that is the only output level at which P can remain constant over time. The short-run AS curve crosses LRAS at a price equal to P_{-1} ($= e\ W_{-1}$), and it will shift up or down if the lagged price term changes from one period to the next.

The long-run interaction of AS and AD is illustrated in Figure 2. The model is in long-run equilibrium at point A. A negative demand shock shifts AD downward and price and output fall to a new short-term equilibrium at B. This is an unstable point, however, because the shortfall of output from potential generates excess unemployment and a reduction in the wage and price levels from their preceding values. AS therefore shifts downward in the next period, reducing P but increasing Y. The process continues as long as $Y < Y_p$, driving P and Y back to long-run equilibrium at point C, where AD again equals AS at the potential output level, U again equals U_f, and P is again stable. Unfortunately, the precise timepath to long-run equilibrium cannot be analyzed rigorously in this framework, since it depends on unspecified adjustment lags in the various markets.

7.4 EMPIRICAL APPLICATIONS OF THE METHODOLOGY TO ECONOMETRIC MODELS

The insight that large mainstream models could be regarded as enhancements of an underlying IS-LM system originated with Michael McCarthy and was applied to the Wharton Model Mark III in Duggal, Klein and McCarthy (1975). The authors set forth a theoretical one-good prototype model to illustrate the concept. On the IS side, they assumed monopoly pricing by a single firm with a Cobb-Douglas technology,

Figure 2.

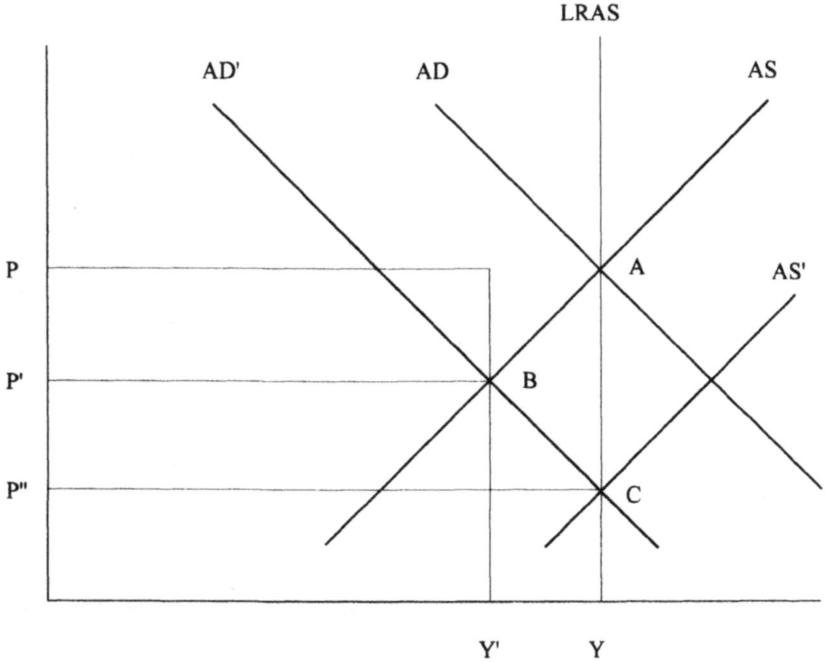

facing a market demand curve and maximizing profits in its choice of inputs, output and product price. The first order conditions led to four equations that represented (a) the demand functions for the good and the capital and labor inputs, and (b) a pricing equation in the form of a markup over unit labor cost. It was then pointed out that the large model was comprised of disaggregated sector equations corresponding to each of these prototypes. Similarly, the LM side of Mark III consisted of a disaggregated model of the demand and supply of money.

This pioneering application divided the Mark III model between the real and monetary sectors, with the entire real sector regarded as the IS construct. Hence, the equations linking inputs and outputs, the Phillips curve, and pricing decisions were all discussed as part of the IS bloc even though they are supply- side relations.

In a subsequent article entitled *Simplification of Large Scale Macroeconometric Models,* Klein, Doud and Sojo (1985) returned to the topic with a later (1983) version of the Wharton Quarterly Model, this time reducing the large system to IS and LM equations. They solved the liquidity preference equation for the values of Y consistent with alternative values of r to derive an empirical LM equation, and similarly solved the remaining 1166 equations in the model (the real sector) for an empirical IS equation. Both r and Y were denominated in nominal terms for the exercise. The resulting LM curve was quite flat, whereas the IS curve was relatively steep, and the authors noted that this is a stability condition according to Hicks (1950). They also directly estimated a simplified six-equation model, which yielded similarly sloped IS and LM locuses, providing further evidence of the validity of the approach to large-model reduction.

In conclusion, they observed that "Contrary to the expressed opinions of some economists, large scale macroeconometric models do have a simple interpretation in familiar terms, and simple systems for pedagogical use in a micro computer environment can readily be constructed."

The use of nominal values for the IS and LM curves reduces the total system to only two equations, but at the cost of violating the theoretical objections to money illusion. The authors opted for simplicity in this regard, since they were estimating the small model as well as reducing the large one: "The choice is either to build a more elaborate model that does a better job of avoiding several relationships with money illusion and also explaining the price level, or a simple model with money illusion." The choice is not without cost in other contexts, however, not only from the theoretical standpoint, but also because it does not readily lend itself to the isolation and analysis of shocks to aggregate supply or of the long-run adjustment to either supply or demand shocks. Both of these considerations were important in the next study to be considered.

7.5 A MODEL COMPARISON STUDY

The first use of the approach to compare the properties of a set of econometric models is documented in *Macroeconomic Impacts of Energy Shocks and Policy Responses: A Structural Comparison of Fourteen Models* (Hickman, 1987).[5] For the most part, the 14 models were large-scale, general purpose macroeconometric models, including all the well-known forecasting systems. The paper presented a comparative analysis of the macroeconomic impacts of an adverse oil shock, as estimated in coordinated simulation studies of the various models, organized under the auspices of the Energy Modeling Forum (EMF) at Stanford University. The mitigating effects of monetary and fiscal policies to accommodate the energy shock were also analyzed, along with other energy shock and policy simulations not studied in the Hickman paper. The simulations covered a four-year span.

The principal contributions of the paper were the development of practicable methods for estimating the local slopes or elasticities of the *implicit* IS, LM, AS, and AD curves in the various models from the outcomes of the oil shock and policy scenarios, and the use of these estimated parameters to analyze the similarities and differences in the simulation results. It was obviously impractical to aggregate directly the individual structural equations of the models or to examine their individual parameters in depth, except possibly in the LM sector, but even then, some of the monetary sectors were highly disaggregated. Moreover, the comparative analysis was undertaken after the simulations were finished, and it was not possible to undertake partial simulations of the various sectors of the models. Instead, it was necessary to work with the data from the complete-model simulations.

The method is illustrated in Figure 3 for the case of a fiscal shock which disturbs the initial equilibrium at point A in the IS-LM and AD-AS panels. The shock shifts the IS and AD curves to the right, inducing an increase in Y, r and P. The rise in P induces a decline in real money balances and shifts the LM schedule upward, augmenting the increase in r and reducing that in Y. The new equilibrium is at point B in both diagrams. If instead of being positively sloped, the AS curve had been perfectly elastic, no induced increase would have occurred in P, the LM curve would not have shifted, and the new equilibrium would have been at point C.

What may be said about the slopes (or elasticities, if we assume that the scales are logarithmic) of the implicit IS, LM, AD and AS curves of a given econometric model from this simulation experiment? First, since the points A and B lie on an unshifted AS curve, an unbiased measure of the supply elasticity may be obtained from the observed values of P and Y in the baseline and shock scenarios. Second, an estimate of the elasticity of the LM schedule can be obtained from the corresponding changes in r and Y between points A and B of the IS-LM diagram, but it will be a biased measure, since point B lies on a shifted LM schedule. The measure of the LM elasticity would be unbiased only if the AS curve were perfectly elastic, in which case the new equilibrium would be at point C with an unchanged price level and hence an unshifted LM curve. Third, nothing can be learned about the slopes of the IS and AD curves from a fiscal shock simulation, since they are necessarily shifted by the research design.

The estimated elasticities of the short-run AS and LM curves for the various models were tabulated and compared in the paper, with the short-run defined as a two year interval. There was a considerable range in both the LM and AS elasticities across the models. Some of the short-run LM elasticities were biased, of course, but in many of the models the observed changes in P were negligible or small, indicating rather elastic short-run AS schedules, and hence rather small biases in the estimated

Figure 3.

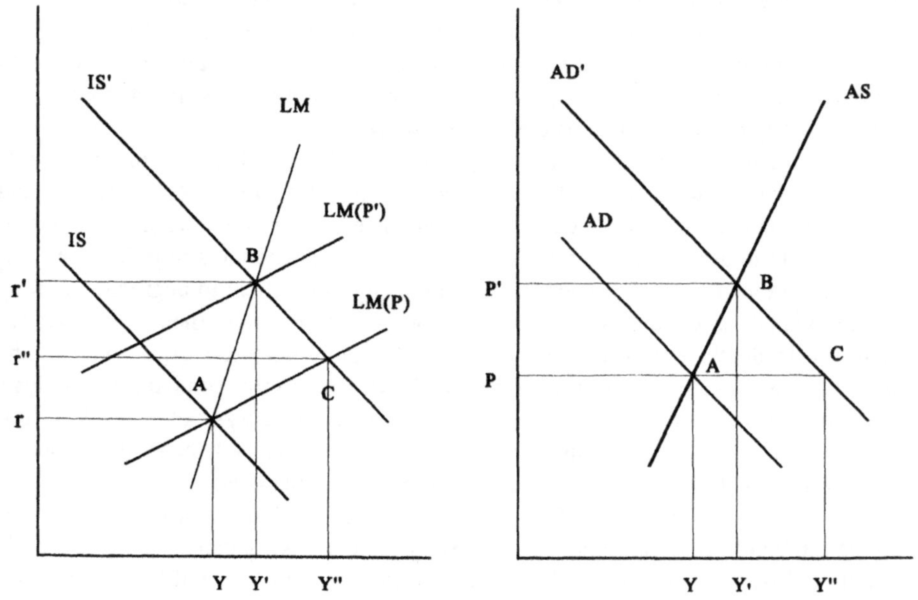

LM elasticities. The LM elasticities were all positive as expected, but the AS schedules were negatively sloped in two of the models.

In similar fashion, the results from the scenario for an accommodating monetary policy, defined as a once-for-all increase of $\overline{M}$ during the first two years of the simulation horizon, were used to provide estimates of the slopes of the IS and AS curves. For most of the models, unbiased estimates were obtained for the IS elasticities, but four of the models included real wealth terms in the consumption equations, together with positively sloped AS curves, so that the induced increases in P from monetary expansion shifted their IS curves leftward, thereby augmenting the decline in r, mitigating the expansion of Y, and biasing the estimated IS elasticities downward. The IS elasticities were all negative as expected, but the AS schedules were negatively sloped in four models.

The negative slopes of AS found in a few models in the demand shock scenarios were subjected to further analysis. A numerical decomposition of the response of price to output under a demand shock was based on the following equation, using dot notation to symbolize percentage changes in the variables:

$$\dot{P} / \dot{Y} = \dot{W} / \dot{Y} \text{ x } U\dot{L}C / \dot{W} \text{ x } \dot{P} / U\dot{L}C, \tag{10}$$

where ULC is unit labor cost. Normally, all three right-hand components are positive, yielding a positive elasticity of AS. Cyclical productivity gains may offset wage increases early in an expansion, however, and in some models are sufficiently large to cause an actual decline in unit labor cost, giving a negative sign on the second term of (10) and a negative slope to AS. In two of the models, the sign of the first term was negative under an expansionary monetary shock, owing to the inclusion of interest rates as direct arguments in the pricing equations and to a positive feedback between price and wage changes. Anomalous results such as these can alert model builders and users to possible specification biases.

The oil shock scenario was also analyzed in the EMF study. The basic theoretical analysis using the AD-AS paradigm is illustrated in Figure 4. The initial equilibrium at point A is disturbed by the exogenous increase in energy costs, shifting the short-run AS curve upward. If AD were unaffected by the oil shock, a new temporary equilibrium would be established at B, with the price level increasing in the face of falling output - the hallmark of a (positive) supply shock.

The AD curve is likely to be adversely affected by a so-called supply shock, however, especially in the case of an international oil shock. Such a shock will shift the terms of trade against net oil importers, including the U.S., redistributing income abroad and depressing domestic demand. An OPEC shock will also depress economic activity abroad, reducing the demand in non-OPEC countries for U.S. exports.[6] In Figure 4, it has been assumed that the AD shifts downward in response to the oil shock, so that the new short-term equilibrium is at point C instead of B, mitigating the rise in P and amplifying the fall in GDP.

Figure 4.

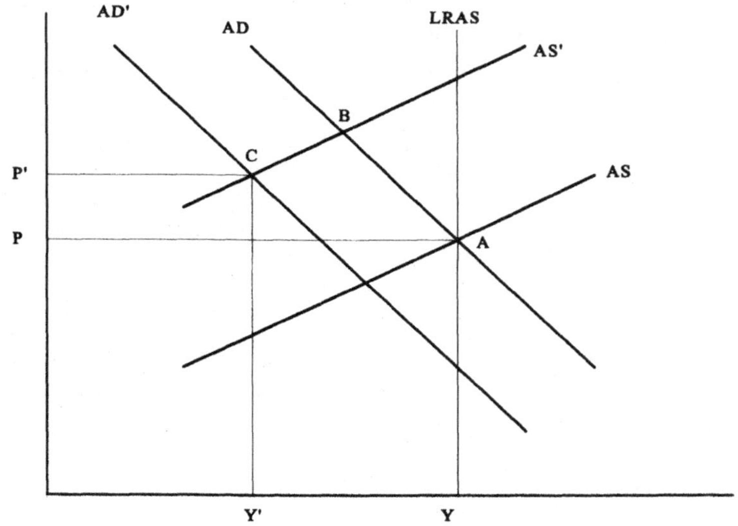

The economy is out of long-run equilibrium at C, however, with excess unemployment putting downward pressure on wages and prices, shifting AS downward as the economy equilibrates from the shock. The AD curve will tend to return to its original position as well, as OPEC income gains and the recovery of incomes in other countries augments U.S. export demand. Thus the price and output levels would tend to revert to their preshock levels at point A through automatic adjustment processes, provided that potential output were unaffected by the energy shock.[7]

The empirical results of the simulated oil shock were compared using the foregoing model as a theoretical guide. First, the elasticities of the implicit AD locuses were estimated from the changes in P and Y induced by the common oil shocks. These direct estimates were then compared for each model with the estimates of the IS and LM elasticities previously garnered from the fiscal and monetary scenarios, since a model with an inelastic LM and elastic IS curve will tend to have a rather flat AD locus, indicating a strong Keynes effect from a price change. The comparisons indicated that in the majority of the models the Keynes effect operates as predicted, and that the independently estimated IS and LM elasticities for these models were consistent with their relative AD elasticities as inferred from the supply shock scenario.[8]

Second, the model responses to the assumed oil price shock were decomposed into three elements corresponding to (1) the size of the upshift of AS under the energy shock, (2) the elasticity of the AS curve, with a more elastic supply aggravating the price increase and output decrease, and (3), the elasticity of the AD schedule, which governs the division between price and output responses for a given upshift and elasticity of AS. It was found that these elements differed across the models and that the relative size of the multiplier effects of the oil price shocks in the various models could be understood in terms of the magnitudes of the three components of the response. Despite the observed differences, there was a considerable consensus among the models about the direction and magnitude of the short-run changes in real incomes and prices in response to an oil shock without active policy intervention. There was also agreement among most models about the qualitative responses to stimulative monetary and fiscal policies, although the quantitative estimates ranged more widely than for the oil shock.

7.6 LATER STUDIES

The EMF study was conducted with stand-alone national models which ignored interactions with other economies. In a later conference organized by the Brookings Institution (Bryant, et.al., 1988), common monetary and fiscal simulations were undertaken on 12 multinational models to study the international transmission of economic fluctuations. The conference included a contribution by Hickman (1988) using an open-economy model of aggregate demand and supply for a comparative analysis of the short-run impacts of unilateral shocks in the U.S. on aggregate activity at home and abroad.[9] As before, the methodology provided a fruitful approach to explaining the similarities and differences in the multiplier results for the various models.

The last paper to be cited is *The IS-LM Cores of Three Econometric Models* (Green, Hickman, Howrey, Hymans, and Donihue, 1991), in which the methodology is extended in several directions. In the first section, the present author compares the estimation of the implicit short-run IS, LM, and AS locuses of an econometric model by partial simulation techniques and full-model-comparative static experiments and illustrates the methodology using the Hickman-Coen Annual Growth Model of the U.S. Economy. Next, Green estimates the IS and LM curves of the Indiana University Econometric Model of the United States (EMUS) in both the short-run (same quarter) and the long-run (3 or 4 quarters of sustained shocks), using partial simulation techniques. Similarly, he directly estimates both the short- and long-term (up to 35 quarters) AD and AS locuses of the EMUS model, and shows that the AD elasticities increase and the AS elasticities decrease over the long-run. Finally, Howrey, Hymans and Donihue derive the IS and LM curves for the Michigan Quarterly Econometric Model of the U.S. Economy (MQEM), again by the appropriate partial simulations of the relevant blocs of the model and for various adjustment periods of up to 40 quarters. They do not estimate AD or AS locuses for the MQEM model, but instead analyze the role of price change in the complete-model response over 40 quarters to a sustained fiscal shock by isolating the additional shifts in the derived long-term IS and LM locuses resulting from endogenous wage and price feedbacks.

7.7 CONCLUDING REMARKS

Among other attributes, the credibility of a macroeconometric model is dependent on consistency of its basic properties with macro theory. Most structural econometric models are disaggregated IS-LM systems on the demand side and assume imperfect labor and product markets and sticky wages and prices on the supply side, so that it is natural to interpret their properties in terms of the IS-LM, AD-AS model.

Estimation of the elasticities of the IS and LM curves provides a useful diagnostic tool for characterizing the predicted responses to fiscal and monetary policies in a given model, and it may direct attention to specific equations or parameters in either sector in need of further testing.

Most macroeconometric models involve sticky wage and price adjustments to shocks. They equilibrate largely through induced changes in the price level - the Keynes and Pigou effects - rather than by a neoclassical process of real wage adjustment, and hence their response patterns depend heavily on the elasticity of the AS curve in the short- and long-runs. These implicit elasticities may be determined by the various methods discussed in the references.

The simple IS-LM model dichotomizes completely between the monetary and real sectors, and when solved as an AD model, is also independent of the AS sector. This is not necessarily true of macroeconometric models, however, which differ in the degree of decomposability between the IS and LM and the AD and AS blocs. The results contained in the literature, however, indicate that the interdependencies are sufficiently weak so that the IS-LM and AD-AS decomposition is an informative methodology for diagnosing individual models and for standardized model-comparison exercises.

The method can accommodate a wide range of model specifications in aspects such as degree of disaggregation, lag distributions, modeling of expectations, functional forms, and methods of parameter estimation.[10] It can be applied even to avowedly nonstructural VAR models which incorporate prices and interest rates along with real variables, on the hypothesis that they are directly-estimated reduced forms of an underlying structural model of the IS-LM type.

BIBLIOGRAPY

Bryant, Ralph C., Dale W. Henderson, Gerald Holtham, Peter Hooper, and Steven A. Symansky, eds. (1988), *Empirical Macroeconomics for Interdependent Economies*, Washington, D.C.: The Brookings Institution.

Dornbusch, Rudiger and Stanley Fischer (1987), *Macroeconomics*, 4ed., McGraw-Hill, Chapter 13.

Duggal, Vijaya G., Lawrence R. Klein, and Michael D. McCarthy (1975), "The Wharton Model Mark III: A Modern IS-LM Construct" in Lawrence R. Klein and Edwin Burmeister (eds.), *Econometric Model Performance*, University of Pennsylvania Press, 188-210.

Green, R Jeffery, Bert G. Hickman, E. Philip Howrey, Saul H. Hymans, and Michael R. Donahue (1991), "The IS-LM Cores of Three Econometric Models," in Lawrence R. Klein (ed.), *Comparative Performance of U.S. Econometric Models*, New York: Oxford University Press, 89-124.

Hickman, Bert G. (1983), *EMF 7 Model Comparisons: Key Relationships and Parameters*, EMF 7.3, Energy Modeling Forum, Stanford University, Stanford, California, December.

Hickman, Bert G. (1987), "Macroeconomic Impacts of Energy Shocks and Policy Responses: A Structural Comparison of Fourteen Models," in B.G. Hickman, H.G. Huntington, and J.L. Sweeny (eds.), *Macroeconomic Impacts of Energy Shocks*, Amsterdam: North-Holland, 125-198.

Hickman, Bert G. (1988), "The U.S. Economy and the International Transmission Mechanism," in Bryant et. al., eds., 1988, 92-130.

Hicks, J.R. (1937), "Mr Keynes and the 'Classics': A Suggested Interpretation," *Econometrica*, 5: 147-159

Hicks, J.R. (1950), *A Contribution to the Theory of the Trade Cycle*, London: Oxford University Press.

Keynes, John Maynard (1936), *The General Theory of Employment Interest and Money*, New York: Howard Brace and Co.

Klein, L.R., A. Doud, and E. Sojo (1985), "Simplification of Large Scale Macroeconomic Models," *Eastern Economic Journal,* xi, 28-40.

Mankiw, N. Gregory (1994), *Macroeconomics*. 2ed., New York: Worth Publishers, Chapter 11.

ENDNOTES

[1] This section and the one following are adapted from Hickman (1987), sections 2 and 3.

[2] If real money balances were included as an argument in the expenditure functions, the Pigou or real balance effect would also stimulate aggregate demand.

[3] See Mankiw (1994) for a description of four theories of aggregate supply with output adjustment based on a discrepancy between the actual and expected price levels. The formulation in the present text follows Dornbusch and Fisher (1987) with minor modifications.

[4] The normal productivity level, which is assumed constant for simplicity and eliminated from explicit calculation of unit labor cost, may be thought of as absorbed in e.

[5] This paper was condensed from Hickman (1983).

[6] Discretionary changes in fiscal or monetary policy may also be adopted in response to the shock, but these can go either way depending on the objectives of policy makers, and are ignored here for convenience.

[7] A permanent oil shock will in fact tend to depress the level of potential output by increasing the real price of energy. Six of the models in the EMF study included endogenous equations for potential output and estimated potential declines by the fourth year ranging between 0.5 and 2.8 percent (Hickman, 1987, Appendix 2-D). With potential output reduced, long-run equilibrium would be attained at a point to the left and higher than A in Figure 4.

[8] This correspondence holds despite the fact that the estimates of the AD elasticity from the oil shock scenario are biased to the extent that the AD curve is itself shifted by the oil shock. The bias was judged to be small enough to neglect, however, insofar as the comparisons among models was concerned.

[9] For this purpose the theoretical IS structure was augmented to include endogenous export and import terms, with exports depending on income abroad and the real exchange rate, and imports depending on domestic income and the real exchange rate. An equation was also added determining the exchange rate from the interest parity condition. The IS and AD curves now include the foreign price and income levels and the exchange rate as shift variables. The LM curve is unchanged. The AS schedule now incorporates the foreign price level and the exchange rate as shift variables, together with the lagged domestic price level to represent the wage-price dynamics as before. The theoretical graphical analysis includes the IS-LM and AD-AS curves for both the domestic and the (aggregated) foreign economies, allowing for the study of both the foreign and domestic adjustments to a shock, including mutual feedbacks.

[10] For example, of the 12 multicountry models included in the Brookings conference, 11 were disaggregated IS-LM constructs and one was a VAR. All but one of the structural models shared a disequilibrium approach to labor and product markets similar to that underlying the concept of a short-term AS function. Four models featured rational expectations in financial markets, but only one of the four also imposed instantaneous market clearing. One of the four was a general equilibrium model with calibrated parameters.

8

MACROECONOMICS WITHOUT IS-LM: A COUNTERFACTUAL

Robert W. Dimand

8.1 BACKGROUND

The teaching of intermediate macroeconomics, and until fairly recently of graduate macroeconomics, has been dominated by the IS-LM representation of the determination of aggregate demand by equilibrium conditions for the goods market and the money market. Robert Solow agreed with James Tobin that this framework in "the trained intuition of many of us" (Young 1987, 1). Its influence was so pervasive that even Milton Friedman used the IS-LM framework when he wished to explain to the economics profession at large the essence of the revived quantity theory of money and its differences from Keynesian economics (Gordon 1974). Robert Barro's intermediate macroeconomics textbook (Barro 1993), which relegates IS-LM to the twentieth and final chapter on the Keynesian theory of fluctuations, remains an outlier even among textbooks with a strong New Classical flavour, as the habit of thinking in an IS-LM framework has become ingrained in successive generations of economists, even when they transform the model by assuming full employment. The IS-LM apparatus provides a convenient way of organizing analysis of income and interest determination, at the cost of diverting attention from formation of expectations of an uncertain future (stressed by Keynes 1937) to determination of current income given expectations. Macroeconomic argument was not always conducted in that framework, however, and IS-LM is absent from Keynes's *General Theory* and from Hicks's *Economic Journal* review (1936) of the *General Theory*. One can imagine macroeconomics advancing from the *General Theory* and from pre-Keynesian monetary and business cycle theory had Hicks never "done a Marshall" with his graph.

Several attempts at simplified representation of the *General Theory* produced systems of simultaneous equations either equivalent to or leading close to the familiar Hicks diagram. Articles in June 1936 by David Champernowne (1936) and W. Brian Reddaway (1936) were followed by three papers presented to an Econometric Society session at New College, Oxford on 26 September 1936 by Roy F. Harrod (1937), James E. Meade (1937), and J. R. Hicks (1937). Meade (1936) provided a verbal counterpart in a textbook exposition without writing out the system of equations. While all five articles reduced the aggregate demand analysis of the *General Theory* to small systems of simultaneous equations (see Young 1987), economics teaching was shaped by the diagram that Hicks labelled SI-LL (suggesting perhaps that he did not take it quite seriously), and that Alvin Hansen (1949, 1953) relabelled as showing IS and LM curves. As with the multiplier or the accelerator, more than one economist contributed to the development, and Young (1987) shows how Hicks (1937) may be indebted to Harrod's paper for the system of equations and to Meade's paper for notation, while the famous diagram is Hicks's own (Hicks had seen the Harrod and Meade papers for the session before writing his own). The multiplicity of closely-related formalizations of the *General Theory* published or presented within a year of the book's publication gave the impression that such formalization was an inevitable or natural reading of Keynes. This impression was strengthened by the personal links with Keynes of the earliest IS-LM theorists (other than Hicks), although Keynes himself was absent from the Oxford session giving a lecture to the Political Economy Club in Stockholm about liquidity preference and then going on with his wife to visit her family in Russia.

Meade had been a member of the "Cambridge Circus" in 1930-31 before returning to Oxford, while Harrod had studied with Keynes for a year in the early 1920s and commented on successive drafts of the *General Theory*. Champernowne and Reddaway were recent Cambridge graduates who had attended Keynes's lectures (see Rymes 1987 for Champernowne's notes of Keynes's 1934 lectures) and his Political Economy Club, Keynes had been their supervisor, and Champernowne was a Cambridge Apostle (Lekachman 1964, vii-viii, Straight 1983, 67, 92). They might be presumed to know Keynes's thought, since from his return to Cambridge in 1919 Keynes's annual course of eight lectures was about his own research, in effect a condensed annual draft of whatever book he was writing at the time. That was why the twenty-three-year-old Reddaway, returning to Australia in March 1936 as a research fellow at the University of Melbourne, was asked to review the *General Theory* for the *Economic Record* (Reddaway, interview quoted in Young 1987, 75).

Champernowne's and Reddaway's 1936 articles would have been deeply affected by their experience as students of Keynes in Cambridge while he writing the *General Theory*. Keynes presented a summary of his theory as a system of four simultaneous equations in his 1933 and 1934 Michaelmas term lectures (Rymes 1987, 1989) and in a 1934 draft (Keynes 1973, XIII, 439-42), but abandoned this approach in the final version of his book. Champernowne and Reddaway heard Keynes expound this approach in lecture (although Champernowne's notes survive only from the 1934 lectures, he also attended the 1933 lectures). On 4 December 1933, in the concluding lecture of that year's series, Keynes defined W as "state of news" and offered a four equation system, equating the quantity of money M to a function of W and the interest rate, consumption C to a function of W and income Y, and investment I to a function of W and the interest rate, with $Y = C + I$ for closure. Reading and reviewing the *General Theory* in the light of their notes and recollections of Keynes's lectures and supervisions, they built upon the simultaneous-equations approach that Keynes had discarded, but without his repeated explicit inclusion of the state of the news (expectations) as an argument in the liquidity preference, consumption and investment functions. Champernowne recalled that his paper was submitted for publication "some time before the publication of the *General Theory*" and "was based on Keynes' lectures and supervisions" (Young 1987, 82-83). Had Champernowne and Reddaway built instead upon the distinction between a cooperative economy and an entrepreneur economy that Keynes essayed in a 1933 draft but then abandoned, they would have focussed attention instead on the coordination problem.

Champernowne (1936, 155), by writing about "Failure to notice immediately the fact that the real wage rate has fallen" and "The habit of thinking in terms of the price level of some earlier date", also contributed to the myth that the effect of aggregate demand on employment in the *General Theory* was due to money illusion, for all of Keynes's emphatic denial in Chapter 2. This provoked Joan Robinson (1937a, 2n) to remark that "Mr. Champernowne adheres, on the whole, to the Pigovian school, but much of his argument is vitiated by a failure to distinguish between real wage rates and real earnings."

Such an influence of Keynes's lectures on the first two articles leading to IS-LM would not be the only instance of Keynes's brilliant exposition influencing developments distinct or uncongenial to his message to the economics profession. R. S. Sayers (1972, 595-96) has traced seeds of the "Treasury view" of the 1920s to Keynes's Treasury memoranda during the First World War (Keynes 1971, XVI), in which Keynes argued forcefully that exchange depreciation and demand stimulus could not increase real output *in a fully-employed wartime economy*. Later Treasury officials neglected the context and qualification.

Let us assume that the four-equation system in Keynes's 1934 draft remained as devoid of contemporary influence as the discussion of cooperative and entrepreneur economies in his 1933 draft, and also assume away the papers presented one Saturday morning in Oxford. What else might have become, or remained, the trained intuition of macroeconomists, in the absence of IS-LM?

8.2 OTHER PATHS FROM KEYNES

The tractable, teachable IS-LM diagram and, for introductory courses, the even simpler single-equation 45-degree "Keynesian"-cross proved so convenient that economists neglected to develop Keynes's own presentation in Chapter 3 of *The General Theory* of an aggregate demand function D and aggregate supply function Z, each a function of employment N. D(N) is the aggregate proceeds expected by entrepreneurs to result from a given level of employment, while Z(N) is the aggregate proceeds the expectation of which would be just sufficient to induce entrepreneurs to offer an amount N of employment (taking money wage rates as given). Keynes referred to the intersection of these two functions determining the level of employment and output, but did not illustrate this by a diagram. Keynes devoted Chapter 20 to the employment function, identified as the inverse function of the aggregate supply function, with the algebra of Chapter 2 reflecting his acceptance (in Chapter 2) of the "first classical postulate" that the real wage equals the marginal product of labour (that is, the economy is on the labour demand curve determined by the profit-maximizing decisions of competitive firms).

Eventually, IS-LM became joined in teaching with a different aggregate supply and demand diagram (AS-AD), with real output (Y) and the price level (P) on the two axes, rather than aggregate proceeds (PY) and employment (N) as in Keynes's Chapter 3. With an aggregate production function linking Y and N, each point on Keynes's aggregate demand function D(N) corresponds to a point of intersection of the IS and LM curves at a particular value of P, with a comparable correspondence between Keynes's aggregate supply function Z(N) and the later, standard AS curve (drawn upward-sloping for a given money wage), as shown diagrammatically by Lorie Tarshis (1984). Keynes's Z-D formulation focussed attention more directly on expectations than the AS-AD version does, but analytically a Z-D diagram need not be in any way inconsistent with a set of IS-LM/AS-AD diagrams.

Don Patinkin (1982, 156-57) noted that, although Dennis Robertson discussed the aggregate supply function in his review article on the *General Theory*, it passed unmentioned in Hicks (1937), in Robinson (1937b) and in review articles by Champernowne, Hawtrey, Leontief, Lerner, Pigou, Reddaway, Taussig, and Viner, and in Keynes's surviving correspondence with these reviewers (again excepting Robertson).

There is one piece of evidence of an Z-D diagram being used shortly after the publication of the *General Theory*. The diagram appears on a page of notes that Daniel Fusfeld took in Arthur E. Burns's course at George Washington University in June 1941 (Fusfeld 1985, Darity and Young 1995, 4). That single sheet, folded into Fusfeld's copy of the *General Theory*, remains after the loss of the rest of Fusfeld's notes from that course with his other personal papers in fire in the Economics Building of the University of Michigan on Christmas Eve 1981. An exchange between Fusfeld, Don Patinkin, and Paul Davidson in *History of Political Economy* (Fall 1989, 537-53) raised questions about whether Burns correctly represented the curvature of the D aggregate demand function and whether Burns obtained Keynes's approval of the diagram after a lecture Keynes gave at the Federal Reserve. Neither of these issues is relevant to the point that it could occur to an early reader of the *General Theory* to draw a Z-D diagram and base a macroeconomics course on it, nor are whatever minor slips Keynes made in his own exposition. The influence and importance of the IS-LM analysis does not depend of whether, in reading Keynes's 31 March 1937 letter to Hicks, the reader concentrates on the remark that Keynes found Hicks (1937) "very interesting and really have next to nothing to say by way of criticism" (Keynes 1973, XIV, 79) or on Keynes's "objection ... that is over-emphasises current income. In the case of the inducement to invest, expected income for the period of investment is the relevant variable" (1973, XIV, 80-81). What matters here is that reader of Keynes's Chapter 3 could very naturally think of drawing Z and D curves to illustrate the argument, not whether, as Patinkin (1989, 541) suggested, Keynes gave Burns "an answer to which he did not give much thought." The Z-D diagram (with D drawn concave to the horizontal axis, unlike Burns's diagram) was revived by Sidney Weintraub (1957, 1958), used in a textbook by Paul Davidson and Eugene Smolensky (1962), and expounded by Paul Wells (1977) and Lorie Tarshis (1979, 1984). Wells (1977) distinguished an expected proceeds function D* from the aggregate demand or expenditure function D, with D* and D coinciding only in an equilibrium in which short-period expectations are realized. Douglas Vickers (1985) is a rare example of a later textbook version of Z-D. The Z-D diagram has found a home in the *Journal of Post Keynesian Economics*, founded by Weintraub and Davidson. It was absent from Joan Robinson's *Introduction to the Theory of Employment* (1937b), a simplified exposition of the *General Theory* emphasizing verbal exposition of liquidity preference and the multiplier process. Even Lorie Tarshis, later a careful expositor of Keynes's aggregate supply and aggregate demand functions and of their microeconomic foundations (Tarshis 1979, 1984), used a 45-degree Keynesian cross diagram in a textbook (Tarshis 1967, 372-73) and a verbal discussion consistent with the 45-degree diagram in his first textbook (1947, 360-65, cf. Darity and Young 1995, 5n).

Had Hicks not drawn his SI-LL diagram, Burns would almost certainly not have been the only economist to be moved by reading about the intersection of the Z and D functions in Chapter 3 of the *General Theory* to draw the diagram showing that intersection. The obliteration by the IS-LM analysis (and 45-degree cross diagram) of Keynes's own notation and his aggregate supply and demand functions was a remarkable phenomenon. In the absence of the handy IS-LM diagram for goods and money market equilibrium, the vast controversial literature about Keynes's *General Theory* would very likely have used Keynes's own Z and D notation, and drawn the diagram implied by his remark about the intersection of the function. This would have had two advantages for Keynesian macroeconomics. Placing expected proceeds on one axis would have been a constant reminder of the crucial role of expectations. Consideration of the proper curvature for the Z aggregate supply function would have directed attention to the importance of Keynes's analysis of the supply side and labor market (emphasized in Dimand 1988), whereas the IS-LM diagram shows only the determination of aggregate demand. The Z-D diagram would not, however, have been nearly as convenient as IS-LM for considering the relative effectiveness of monetary and fiscal policy, or for extending the analysis to an open economy (as in the IS-LM-BP framework).

The 45-degree cross diagram (a translation from changes to levels of the simple multiplier process relating changes in equilibrium income to changes in autonomous spending) holds too many variables constant to have been a viable rival to the Z-D diagram above the introductory level, in the assumed absence of IS-LM. Joan Robinson's essay "Diagrammatic Illustrations" (1937a, 119-33) tentatively offered a representation of the General Theory of Employment in terms of short-period and long-period labor supply and demand curves, with real wages and employment on the (unlabelled) axes, but this essay had little influence, nor would it have been likely to have much even in the absence of IS-LM. Another short essay, on "Indeterminacy" (Robinson 1937a, 171-74), more persuasively criticized approaches like IS-LM for unjustified insistence on a determinate, unique equilibrium, a view in keeping with the emphasis on fundamental uncertainty in Keynes (1937). Such a criticism, however telling, does not provide an alternative. Her *Introduction to the Theory of Em-*

ployment (1937b) eschewed diagrams and equations, and, though an able and lively exposition, had no device to "do a Marshall" and capture the intuition of the economics profession. The only readily apparent Keynesian alternative to IS-LM was the Z-D framework.

8.3 CYCLES AND THE QUANTITY THEORY

The model of the trade cycle as due to the interaction of the multiplier and accelerator, given a lag between income and consumption, was developed in the late 1930s by Harrod, Tinbergen and Samuelson without drawing on the IS-LM framework. Without the pervasiveness of the IS-LM analysis in intermediate and higher macroeconomics courses, economists would likely have continued to a much greater extent to think in terms of models of cycles, instead of turning so strongly to static models of short-period equilibrium. Without the Harrod, Hicks and Meade versions of IS-LM presented at the September 1936 Econometric Society session in Oxford, macroeconomic argument might have been more deeply influenced by trends epitomized by another Econometric Society session, that in Leiden in October 1933 at which Ragnar Frisch, Michal Kalecki and Jan Tinbergen presented papers on mathematical models of business cycles, all published in *Econometrica* in 1935. The older approach to economic fluctuations as cycles of fixed periodicity associated with Juglar, Jevons, Beveridge and Kondratieff was fading in influence, due to the increasing number of superimposed periodicities needed to explain the data and to Slutsky's demonstration that apparent cycles could be due to summation of random shocks (see Dimand 1995b). The models of endogenous oscillations in economic activity developed by Frisch, Kalecki and Tinbergen could have had a much greater influence on macroeconomic teaching and thought had the IS-LM framework for analyzing short-period equilibrium not become so widespread (and also if the Second World War had not disrupted Continental European business cycle research).

Along with emphasis on the dynamics of business cycles rather than the comparative statics of short period equilibrium, greater attention to Kalecki's work would have contributed a greater Marxian flavor to Western European macroeconomics. Together with Frisch's and Tinbergen's econometric approach to business cycles, this would have led to more pronounced differences between postwar macroeconomics in Western Europe and in North America than actually occurred.

Another approach to economics, influential before Keynes and returning to influence later, might have had a much more direct role in shaping postwar macroeconomics had it not been for the IS-LM framework: the monetary economics exemplified by Irving Fisher, including his monetary theory of fluctuations during transition periods as well as his use of the equation of exchange (MV + M'V' = PT) as a framework for examining the long-run effect of the money supply on the price level. Irving Fisher was the most cited macroeconomist in the 1920s, but he lost his audience with the spread of the IS-LM representation of Keynes, vanishing entirely from citation counts in the 1940s (Deutscher 1990, 188-94, cf. Dimand 1995a). The eventual revival of the quantity theory of money in the form of monetarism was in large part a return to Fisher's concerns. Fisher was cited more often in *Milton Friedman's Monetary Framework: A Debate with his Critics* (Gordon 1974) than any other economist other than Keynes or Friedman (if self-citations by contributors are excluded).

Fisher's importance as an available alternative source of a macroeconomic framework is shown in Champernowne's essay, "Expectations and the Links Between the Economic Future and the Present" (Lekachman 1964, 174-202), written in 1963 as a reconsideration of his 1936 article. Champernowne stressed the resemblance, recognized by Keynes, between Keynes's marginal efficiency of capital and Fisher's rate of return over cost (Lekachman 1964, 182-85, Fisher 1930, 159, Keynes 1936, 140). Comparing Fisher (1930, 216) and Keynes (1936, 167), Champernowne observed that "At first sight it might seem that in his treatment of liquidity preference, Keynes was again following Professor Irving Fisher" who had written about the liquidity of cash balances, the ability to dispose of money without prior preparation, as compensating for foregone interest, except that Fisher denied any lasting effect of the quantity of money on the interest rate (Lekachman 1964, 185-86).

Referring to Keynes's Chapter 19 argument that money wage flexibility, even if possible, could not be relied upon to restore full employment, Champernowne held that "It was indeed natural that Keynes should anticipate some such criticism, since Professor Irving Fisher had clearly stated six years before in his *Theory of Interest* the view that it was through price and money wage flexibility that the rate of interest was influenced towards that level which allowed the rate of investment to settle at figure which was consistent with full employment and the savings forthcoming from incomes at their full employment level" (Lekachman 1964, 189). Fisher's debt-deflation theory of depressions sharply altered his view of whether increased nominal flexibility would be stabilizing (Fisher 1933, Dimand 1994). Champernowne stressed in his conclusion that while "Economists such as Professor Irving Fisher had written as though each individual's decision to save now carried with it the decision when instead to spend the money on consumption goods", Keynes, crucially, rejected that view (Lekachman 1964, 201).

In Champernowne's mind, Fisher's work was a benchmark, offering both parallels and alternatives to the *General Theory*. Curiously, some of the impetus for Fisher to write *The Theory of Interest* came from a source close to Keynes: "I was encouraged to write this new exposition of the theory of interest by various economists and leading business men and especially by Mr. Oswald T. Falk, one of the representatives of Great Britain at the Versailles Peace Conference, who was kind enough to say that he had gained more insight into economic theory from *The Rate of Interest* [Fisher 1907] than from any other book." Falk, Keynes's colleague in "A" Division (external finance) of the wartime Treasury and then at Versailles, served with Keynes on the board of the National Mutual Life Assurance Society, and was his close friend and partner in several speculative ventures until they quarreled in 1930 over the losses of their Independent Investment Trust (M. Keynes 1975, 153, 224, 226-27, Lekachman 1964, 46).

Irving Fisher, far more than A. C. Pigou or Friedrich Hayek, provided an available non-Keynesian source for macroeconomics in a counterfactual world lacking the IS-LM representation of Keynes (see Dimand 1995b for a survey of possible non-Keynesian bases for the development of modern macroeconomics). What Fisher had to offer to catch the trained intuition of economists was the equation of exchange (which Fisher 1911 had extended to include bank deposits M' as well as currency M, with differing velocities of circulation), expected inflation as the difference between real and nominal interest rates, and the two-period diagram for consumption and saving decisions. The first two lead to later monetarism, the third to postwar permanent income and life-cycle theories of consumption and saving. Fisher also had (like Hawtrey) a monetary theory of economic fluctuations during transition periods, implemented empirically by correlating indices of output and employment with distributed lags of price level changes, in a series of papers including a 1926 article reprinted in 1973 as "I Discovered the Phillips Curve" (see Dimand 1993). Fisher (1930) used a distributed lag of past price changes to estimate expected inflation, as was later the case with the adaptive expectations hypothesis. What he lacked was a theory of the level of real output and of employment, and a simple graphical representation pulling his contributions together in a way that would be as intuitively appealing as Marshall's scissors of supply and demand or Hicks's IS-LM diagram.

The things that Fisher had to offer to appeal to the intuition of the economics profession were the equation of exchange, the real and nominal interest distinction, the two-period consumption diagram, adaptive expectations, long-run neutrality of money with short-run non-neutrality due to misperceptions and mistaken expectations, and the debt-deflation theory of depressions. Apart from the debt-deflation theory, these were building blocks for the monetarist revival of the late 1960s and the monetary misperceptions version of New Classical macroeconomics in the 1970s. Without the dominance of macroeconomic teaching above the introductory level by the IS-LM framework, economists might have built upon these aspects of Fisher's monetary economics at an earlier date than they actually did. Even though other aspects of Fisher's economics, such as his enthusiasm for applying mathematics to economics, did not appeal to the economists of the interwar and early postwar eras, and his losses in the stock market crash hurt a reputation already weakened by crusades for Prohibition and dietary reform, Fisher would have been much more likely to continue to hold a professional audience for his monetary economics had IS-LM not transformed the notation and graphical framework in which economists thought about such topics.

8.4 CONCLUSION

Counterfactual enterprises are necessarily highly speculative. I have identified three strands of macroeconomics that I believe would have been considerably more prominent in the postwar era had the conveniently teachable IS-LM framework not swept the discipline: a Z-D aggregate supply and demand analysis building on Chapter 3 of the *General Theory* and more focussed on expectations in its presentation than IS-LM was, business cycle theory extending the work of Frisch, Kalecki and Tinbergen, and a revival of the quantity theory of money and monetary theory of fluctuations, drawing on Fisher's foundations. Elsewhere (Dimand 1996), I have argued that several approaches, such as the writings of Pigou and Beveridge on unemployment, would have remained dead-ends even if Keynes's *General Theory* had never been published. If that argument is sound, it would hold *a fortiori* assuming away IS-LM but not the *General Theory*. What I do not see as likely to have emerged from the available macroeconomic literature of the time and shaped the trained intuition of the economics profession is an analytical apparatus viewing the essence of the *General Theory* as a coordination problem in which failure of markets to clear with full utilization of resources is not simply the result of arbitrarily assuming unexplained nominal rigidities or irrational money illusion. Such an apparatus would take seriously our limited and uncertain knowledge of the future and Keynes's insight that a decision to save does not signal a decision to spend on particular commodities at a definite date. Keynes's distinction between a cooperative economy and an entrepreneur economy, essayed in a 1933 draft but then dropped (Keynes 1979, XXIX, 76-102), points in that direction, as did his 1937 article stressing volatile long-period expectations subject to fundamental uncertainty as central to his theory. I do not think, however, that this line of theorizing would have developed much further in the absence of IS-LM than it did in the presence of IS-LM. Regardless of the importance of its insights, I do not see this approach leading to the sort of tractable, teachable apparatus that could become the trained intuition of economists.

BIBLIOGRAPHY

Barro, Robert J. (1993) *Macroeconomics*, 4th ed. New York: John Wiley & Sons.

Champernowne, David G. (1936) "Unemployment, Basic and Monetary: the Classical Analysis and the Keynesian," *Review of Economic Studies* 3, as reprinted in Lekachman (1964), 153-74.

Darity, William A., Jr., and Warren Young (1995) "IS-LM: An Inquest," *History of Political Economy* 27, 1-42.

Davidson, Paul, and Eugene Smolensky (1962) *Aggregate Supply and Demand Analysis*. New York: Harper and Row.

Deutscher, Patrick (1990) *R. G. Hawtrey and the Development of Macroeconomics*. Ann Arbor: University of Michigan Press.

Dimand, Robert W. (1988) *The Origins of the Keynesian Revolution*. Aldershot, UK: Edward Elgar, and Stanford, CA: Stanford University Press.

---- (1993). "The Dance of the Dollar: Irving Fisher's Monetary Theory of Economic Fluctuations," *History of Economics Review* 20, 161-72.

---- (1994) "Irving Fisher's Debt-Deflation Theory of Great Depressions," *Review of Social Economy* 52, 92-107.

---- (1995a) "Irving Fisher, J. M. Keynes, and the Transition to Modern Macroeconomics," in A. Cottrell and M. S. Lawlor, eds., *New Perspectives on Keynes*, annual supplement to *History of Political Economy* 27, 247-66.

---- (1995b) "Macroeconomics With and Without Keynes," *History of Economics Review*, 24, 23-42.

Fisher, Irving (1907) *The Rate of Interest*. New York: Macmillan. Reprinted, with introduction by Donald Dewey, New York and London: Garland, 1982, and in Fisher (1997), Vol. 3.

---- (1911) *The Purchasing Power of Money*, with H. G. Brown. New York: Macmillan. Reprinted Fairfield, NJ: A. M. Kelley, 1985, and in Fisher (1997), Vol. 4.

---- (1926) "A Statistical Relation between Unemployment and Price Changes," *International Labour Review* 13, 785-92. Reprinted as "I Discovered the Phillips Curve," *Journal of Political Economy* 81 (1973), 496-502, and in Fisher (1997), Vol. 8.

---- (1930) *The Theory of Interest*. New York: Macmillan. Reprinted Philadelphia: Porcupine Press, 1977, and in Fisher (1997), Vol. 9.

---- (1933) "The Debt-Deflation Theory of Great Depressions," *Econometrica* 1, 337-57, and in Fisher (1997), Vol. 10.

---- (1997). *The Works of Irving Fisher*, 14 vols., ed. William J. Barber assisted by Robert W. Dimand and Kevin Foster, consulting ed. James Tobin. London: Pickering & Chatto.

Fusfeld, Daniel R. (1985) "Keynes and the Keynesian Cross: A Note,"*History of Political Economy* 17, 385-89.

Gordon, Robert J., ed. (1974) *Milton Friedman's Monetary Framework: A Debate with his Critics*. Chicago: University of Chicago Press.

Harrod, Roy F. (1937) "Mr. Keynes and Traditional Theory," *Econometrica* 5, as reprinted in Lekachman (1964), 124-39.

Hicks, J. R. (1936) Review of Keynes (1936). *Economic Journal* 46.

---- (1937) "Mr. Keynes and the Classics: A Suggested Interpretation," *Econometrica* 5, 147-59.

Keynes, J. M. (1936) *The General Theory of Employment, Interest and Money*. London: Macmillan. Reprinted as Keynes (1971), VII.

---- (1937) "The General Theory of Employment," *Quarterly Journal of Economics* 51, 209-23, as reprinted in Keynes (1973), XIV, 109-23.

---- (1971-89) *Collected Writings*, ed. D. E. Moggridge and E. A. G. Robinson. 30 vols. London: Macmillan, and New York: Cambridge University Press, for the Royal Economic Society.

Keynes, Milo, ed. (1975) *Essays on John Maynard Keynes*. Cambridge, UK: Cambridge University Press.

Lekachman, Robert (1964) *Keynes' General Theory: Reports of Three Decades*. New York: St. Martin's Press.

Meade, James E. (1936) *Economic Analysis and Policy*. Oxford: Oxford University Press.

---- (1937) "A Simplified Model of Mr. Keynes' System," *Review of Economic Studies* 4, as reprinted in Seymour E. Harris, ed., *The New Economics*, New York: Knopf, 1947.

Patinkin, Don (1982) *Anticipations of the General Theory? And Other Essays on Keynes*. Chicago: University of Chicago Press.

---- (1989) "Keynes and the Keynesian Cross: A Further Note," *History of Political Economy* 21, 537-44, with reply by Daniel R. Fusfeld, 545-47.

Reddaway, W. Brian (1936) "The General Theory of Employment, Interest and Money," *Economic Record* 12, as reprinted in Lekachman (1964), 99-108.

Robinson, Joan (1937a) *Essays in the Theory of Employment*. London: Macmillan.

---- (1937b) *Introduction to the Theory of Employment*. London: Macmillan.

Rymes, T. K. (1987) *Keynes's Lectures, 1932-35: Notes of Students*. Ottawa: Department of Economics, Carleton University.

---- (1989) *Keynes's Lectures, 1932-35: Notes of a Representative Student*. London and Basingstoke: Macmillan, and Ann Arbor: University of Michigan Press.

Sayers, R. S. (1972) "The Young Keynes," *Economic Journal* 82.

Straight, Michael (1983) *After Long Silence*. New York and London: W. W. Norton.

Tarshis, Lorie (1947). *The Elements of Economics*. Cambridge, MA: Riverside Press.

---- (1967). *Modern Economics*. Boston: Houghton Mifflin.

---- (1979) "The Aggregate Supply Function in Keynes's General Theory," in Michael J. Boskin, ed., *Economics and Human Welfare: Essays in Honor of Tibor Scitovsky*. New York: Academic Press, 361-92.

---- (1984) "Appendix: An Outline of the Theory of Aggregate Output and the Price Level", in L. Tarshis, *World Economy in Crisis: Unemployment, Inflation and International Debt*. Ottawa: Canadian Institute for Economic Policy, 151-68.

Vickers, Douglas (1985) "A Model of the Macroeconomy," Chapter 19 of D. Vickers, *Money, Banking, and the Macroeconomy*, Englewood Cliffs, NJ: Prentice-Hall, 437- 67.

Weintraub, Sidney (1957) "The Microfoundations of Aggregate Demand and Supply," *Economic Journal* 67, 455-70; revised in Weintraub (1958).

---- (1958). *An Approach to the Theory of Income Distribution*. Philadelphia: Chilton.

Wells, Paul (1977) "Keynes' Disequilibrium Theory of Employment," in Sidney Weintraub, ed., *Modern Economic Thought*, Philadelphia: University of Pennsylvania Press, 93-101.

Young, Warren (1987) *Interpreting Mr Keynes: The IS-LM Enigma*. Cambridge, UK: Polity Press, and Boulder, CO: Westview Press.

9

WHAT KEYNES WOULD HAVE THOUGHT OF THE DEVELOPMENT OF ISLM

J.W. Nevile*

9.1 INTRODUCTION

ISLM was originally devised as a way of interpreting the core of the theory in Keynes' *General Theory of Employment, Interest and Money* and showing the differences between that theory and the theories of those that Keynes, in an admitted solecism, called classical economists (GT, p.3).[1] The ISLM model was so successful that for a generation of economists, and many generations of undergraduates, it became "Keynesian" economics as far as the conventional wisdom was concerned. However, some of Keynes' closest followers repudiated ISLM analysis; Joan Robinson going so far as to call it bastard Keynesianism (1976, p.128). Hicks himself, in later life, thought that, as an explanation of what Keynes was saying, ISLM

> "succeeded perhaps only too well. For it is no more than a part of what Keynes was saying, or implying, that can be represented in that manner, and it was easy to take it as the whole". (1982, p.100).

Thus, it is of considerable interest to speculate on what Keynes would have thought about the way ISLM became identified as "Keynesian" economics for most of the economics profession. We know, of course, what his first reaction to ISLM was in 1937. But Keynes' heart attack later in 1937, the demands of the war, planning for post war reconstruction and his untimely death in 1946, together ensured that Keynes did not have the length of time to reflect on the matter that is necessary for a mature judgement. Moreover, the way ISLM has developed and has been used over the last 50 years has gone far beyond the spirit of Hicks' original article. While Keynes may not have gone as far as some of his disciples in rejecting ISLM in the way it was used in the 1950s and 1960s, even then its use showed ways of thought contrary to some fundamental aspects of the *General Theory*. Be that as it may, the way ISLM has been used in the last decade or so would have been rejected outright by Keynes as completely against the central message of the *General Theory*.

In the previous paragraph mention was made of speculating on what Keynes would have thought about the development of ISLM. While any discussion of Keynes' views on methods of economic analysis developed decades after his death must entail some element of speculation, there is enough in the *General Theory* and subsequent writings by Keynes for speculation to be based on sound judgement. We can say with some confidence, which, if any, of the comment, made in his famous letter to Hicks, Keynes would have modified and which he would have emphasised if the letter had been rewritten decades later. We can also be confident about at least some of the things Keynes would have said about the development of ISLM and the way it has been used in recent times.

Before we do this it is helpful to remind ourselves (or even to learn for the first time) what Keynes was saying in the *General Theory*. It is over 30 years since Harry Johnson described the *General Theory* as a classic—a book "that everyone has heard of and no one has read" (1961, p.1). Moreover, just because ISLM became so widely accepted as the essence of "Keynesian" economics, for many economists understanding ISLM became a natural substitute for reading the *General Theory*. While this may not result in too much violence to Keynes' liquidity preference theory of interest, it certainly results in a significant misunderstanding of Keynes' way of doing economics and the nature of his theory of employment and output. Therefore these two things will be briefly set out in the next section.

9.2 KEYNES' THEORY OF EMPLOYMENT AND OUTPUT

Keynes claimed to have achieved in the *General Theory* his aim of showing "what determines the volume of employment at any time" (GT, p.313). Thus, even what he was trying to achieve was very different from the goal of most economic theorising today, including ISLM analysis. The major body of economic theory today, as taught in universities or as written in scholarly journals, is concerned with the determination of variables in equilibrium. Usually employment theory is about what factors influence the level of employment in equilibrium, and not about what determined its actual value in some actual month (or year). In Joan Robinson's terminology (1962, 23-29) most modern economic analysis is equilibrium analysis whereas the analysis in the *General Theory* is historical analysis. Equilibrium analysis can not tell us what the value of any particular variable will be at any particular point in time. It tells us what the values of several variables must be if the economy, or perhaps some part of it, is to be in equilibrium. Strictly speaking there is no causation. A number of variables are determined simultaneously. It is not valid to say *a* causes *b*, all we can say is that, if it has such and such a value, then, given the values of *d*, *e* and *f*, *b* must have such and such a value if equilibrium is to be achieved.

On the other hand historical analysis does have causal chains; it makes sense to say a causes *b*, whether or not the economy, or the part being analysed, is in equilibrium. Keynes spelled out causal relationships—some very simple to make basic points and some much more complex. The simplest and most basic is perhaps "the propensity to consume and the rate of new investment determine between them the volume of employment" (GT, p.30), but this is just one example among many.

Keynes then was not primarily concerned to lay down a set of conditions that must hold in equilibrium, but to show "what determined the volume of employment at any time". But of course, in doing this, he was very concerned to show that the existing theory of employment was fatally flawed. He was concerned to show that an equilibrium is possible in which there is involuntary unemployment, i.e., that there can, and may well be times in the real world in which employment is in equilibrium at a level at which the real wage is not equal to marginal utility of employment (GT, p.21).

Keynes assumed a given state of technique and resources (including the stock of capital). In other words his analysis was short period analysis in the Marshallian sense.[2] At different stages in the *General Theory,* Keynes also assumed a number of other key variables were constant, but often this was for convenience rather than an essential aspect of his analysis. In showing what determines employment Keynes starts with a very simple case and then relaxes various simplifying assumptions to arrive at his final theory (or model as we would say today).

The most important of these simplifying assumptions made initially for expository reasons is the assumption of constant money wages. Since there has been so much confusion about this assumption and so much discussion about the extent to which it is necessary for Keynes' conclusions to follow, it is worth a short digression to spell out what Keynes did say.

Keynes thought the assumption of rigid money wages realistic in a variety of circumstances (GT, p.14), but in Chapter 19 of the *General Theory* he discussed the effects of relaxing this assumption. Keynes acknowledged that a reduction in money wages with the nominal money supply unchanged can have the same effect on the real quantity of money and hence the rate of interest as an increase in the nominal supply of money with the wage rate unchanged (GT, p.266). He did qualify this by saying that it was at least so in theory, but equally important in his mind were the limitations of either a sole reliance on monetary policy or a sole reliance on wage cuts, to restore full employment.

> "Just as a moderate increase in the quantity of money may exert an inadequate influence over the long-term rate of interest whilst an immoderate increase may offset its other advantages by its disturbing effect on confidence; so a moderate reduction in money-wages may prove inadequate, whilst an immoderate reduction might shatter confidence even if it were practicable" (GT, pp.266-267).

Moreover, while a flexible wage policy and a flexible monetary policy might be the same thing analytically, in practice they are very different: the flexible wage policy being much more difficult to implement (GT, p.207). In the real world, far from rigidity of money wages being the cause of equilibrium with involuntary unemployment, Keynes found that flexible nominal wages were deleterious, possibly even reducing output and certainly causing "great instability in prices" (GT, p.269). Keynes concluded that "the money-wage level as a whole should be maintained as stable as possible, at least in the short period" (GT, p.270).

Keynes' simplest model[3] was one in which the rate of interest is exogenous (to put it succinctly in modern terms).

> "Our independent variables are in the first instance, the propensity to consume, the schedule of the marginal efficiency of capital and the rate of interest, though as we have already seen, these are capable of further analysis" (GT, 245).

With the rate of interest and the marginal efficiency of capital schedule determined, planned investment is also determined. Equilibrium occurs when there is no unintended investment or disinvestment in inventories. Keynes thought that unintended investment, or disinvestment in inventories would normally be a very temporary phenomenon (GT, pp.124-5) and often defined his period as long enough for actual investment to be equal to planned investment. This simple model of Keynes sounds very like the 45 degree diagram, and, Keynes' the axes suitably labelled, the 45 degree model can be a genuine representation of Keynes' simple model[4] rather than the special variant of ISLM which occurs when the rate of interest is exogenous and the quantity of money endogenous rather than vice versa.

The assumption of an endogenous money supply implied in this simple first model of Keynes is often more realistic in the modern world than the opposite assumption, of an endogenous interest rate and an exogenous money supply, that is widely made in modern textbooks. Whenever a small country fixes its exchange rate by tying its currency to that of a large economy, the interest rate in the small country will be determined exogenously by the interest rate in the large country. More generally whenever a country targets its exchange rate, the rate of interest will have to be used as an instrument and the money supply will become largely endogenous.

This is not the only situation in which, in effect, the rate of interest if exogenous. This also occurs when the famous, or infamous, low level liquidity trap is operating, i.e., when the rate of interest has fallen so far "that almost everyone prefers cash to holding a debt which yields so low a rate of interest" (GT, p.207) and there is no speculative motive to hold bonds since it is widely believed that the interest rate can hardly fall any further. Keynes himself thought that, even in his era of low interest rates, the low level liquidity trap rarely, if ever, came into play. The use of the rate of interest as the instrument of government policy, for exchange rate or other reasons, is the more likely reason for an exogenous interest rate. Be that as it may, it is clear that Keynes' simple model can be more than an expository device. It can be a useful model for analysing real world problems in common situations in the modern world.

However, Keynes did not dwell on this simple model. It was adopted only in the first instance. As the title of his book implies the main model in the *General Theory* is one in which the rate of interest is endogenous, determined by liquidity preference and the money supply. In this model the independent variables are

> "(l) The three fundamental psychological factors, namely, the psychological propensity to consume, the psychological attitude to liquidity and the psycho-

> logical expectation of future yield from capital-assets; (2) the wage-unit as determined by the bargains reached between employers and employed; and (3) the quantity of money as determined by the action of the central bank" (GT, pp.246-247).

This model seems, at first glance, very like ISLM. The same variables are endogenous and the same or similar exogenous variables are important. However, as we shall see there is a subtle difference. ISLM is an equilibrium analysis in which everything is determined simultaneously. Keynes' theorising highlights the fact that production takes place over time and that fixed investment and production decisions made at the beginning of the period cannot be changed until the beginning of the next period. There can be unintended inventory investment and disinvestment, though, as already pointed out Keynes usually thought of the period as long enough for inventory investment to be at the level planned at the beginning of the period. As far as the short period is concerned (fixed) investment is predetermined and is not affected by what happens during the period. This could be because firms cannot change expenditure on fixed investment quickly; but more likely it is because in Keynes' mind the marginal efficiency of capital was constant in the short run and finance was arranged, through borrowing, at the beginning of each period at the rate of interest prevailing at that time (i.e., the rate determined by conditions in the previous period and ruling at the end of that period). Keynes did not think in terms of simultaneous determination of the dependent variables. For him it was a process and the process was as follows (GT, pp.248-9). Start with an assumed marginal efficiency of capital schedule and a predetermined rate of interest. These determine investment and, given investment, consumption is also determined, through the multiplier, determining aggregate demand. This, in conjunction with aggregate supply, determines employment, output, price and income for the period. If there is unintended inventory investment this leads to downward revision of expectations and a lower income in the next period (and vice versa for unintended inventory disinvestment). However, Keynes usually thought of the period as long enough for desired investment, and consumption, to be equal to actual investment and consumption. Once income is determined, given the stock of money and the liquidity preference function this will determine the rate of interest. If this is the same as the rate of interest at the end of the previous period the economy is in equilibrium. If the rate of interest is higher than this, in the next period investment and income will be lower leading to a fall in the interest rate and vice versa when the rate of interest is lower at the end of the period than at the beginning. There could be oscillations, but the system quickly converges to the equilibrium position in which the rate of interest, investment and income are constant from one period to the next.[5]

Keynes did not argue that the volume of employment was necessarily stable. On the contrary he stressed the volatility of the exogenous variables that determined the level of employment

> "there is not one of ... [these] factors which is not liable to change without much warning, and sometimes substantially" (GT, p.249).

In particular, Keynes thought that the marginal efficiency of capital could change dramatically, causing changes throughout the economy. Much of Chapter 22 of the *General Theory* is about the consequences of this. However, Keynes was concerned to demonstrate that a stable continuing position with substantial unemployment is possible. Above all Keynes considered that he had shown that the level of employment was determined by effective demand, not by equating the marginal disutility of labour with the real wage and that there was no tendency for the economy to move towards full employment:

> "the volume of employment is given by the point of intersection between the aggregate demand function and the aggregate supply function ... the point ... called *the effective demand* ... this is the substance of the *General Theory* of Employment" (GT, p.25, emphasis in the original).

9.3 KEYNES' REACTION TO ISLM IN 1936 AND 1937

In the light of the previous section it is not difficult to understand why Keynes gave cautious approval to Hicks' original paper with the words

> "I found it very interesting and really have next to nothing to say by way of criticism" (1973b, p.79).

To Keynes, Hicks' apparatus must have seemed to possess the supreme virtue of showing output and hence employment to be determined by effective demand. Although the graphical presentation makes clear that Hicks is presenting a system of simultaneous equations and not analyzing a process, the consequences of this are not emphasized. Keynes one real criticism of Hicks in his letter[6] is when Hicks is carried away by the simultaneous equation nature of his model and, prompted by "mathematical elegance", considers including current income as a determinant of the marginal efficiency of capital (1982, p.111). In the event this feature did not survive the transition of ISLM into the textbooks, but the importance of effective demand did, at least until the 1980s.

At the same conference at which Hick's 1937 paper was delivered, Harrod also gave a paper on Keynes and the classical economists. Keynes was very much more enthusiastic about Harrod's paper describing it as "instructive and illuminating" (1973b, p.84) and "extraordinarily good" (1973b, p.85). The mathematical equations in Harrod's interpretation of the *General Theory* are precisely those which underlie the IS and LM curves. Why then was Keynes so much more enthusiastic about Harrod's paper than about that of Hicks? If we can answer this question it may give us insights into what Keynes would have thought of how ISLM developed in the years after his death.

Hicks put forward three equations as the essence of the *General Theory* (1937, p.153). However, since investment and savings are identically equal he uses the same symbol for both. It is easier to follow what he is doing if we give each its own symbol and add the equation savings equals investment. If this is done, and modern notation is used, Hicks' equations are:

$$I = f_1(i)$$
$$S = f_2(Y)$$
$$M = f_3(i, Y)$$
$$I = S$$

The first is that investment is a function of the rate of interest, the second is the consumption function and the third is the liquidity preference function.

Harrod's model also had three equations and used the same symbol for savings and investment (1937, pp.76-78). Again in modern notation his equations are:

$$i = f_a(I)$$
$$Y = f_b(I, i)$$ but with the statement that Keynes usually simplified this to $Y = f_c(I)$
$$i = f_d(M, Y)$$
$$S = I$$

Harrod uses the same symbol for the rate of interest and the marginal productivity (or efficiency) of capital "since both the traditional theory and Mr Keynes hold that investment is undertaken up to the point at which the marginal productivity of capital is equal to the rate of interest" (1937, p.76). Thus, his first equation, that the marginal productivity of capital depends on the level of investment, is Hicks' first equation transposed. Similarly, (given S = I) his second equation in its simple form and his third equation can be obtained by transposing Hicks' second and third equations respectively. Thus, Keynes' much greater enthusiasm for Harrod's paper must be in the way the equations are presented and/or the discussion of them.

There are a number of notable differences in this respect. First, Hicks' exposition of ISLM reads like the exposition of a small Walrasian general equilibrium model. It was certainly taken that way by the economics profession and Hicks himself stated later that "the idea of the IS-LM diagram came to me as a result of the work I had been doing on three-way exchange, conceived in a Walrasian manner" (1982, p.32). Harrod, on the other hand, made very clear that he regarded Keynes' theory as a particular equilibrium model, a "short-cut" method that kept changes in a number of things out of consideration, at last temporarily, through the ceteris paribus assumption (1937, p.75).

Secondly, the presentation of Harrod's first equation as one for the marginal productivity (or efficiency) of capital led naturally to the point that for Keynes this was a psychological not a physical variable. Harrod noted (in two separate places) Keynes' emphasis that the value of the marginal productivity of capital depended on expectations. He commended this saying that it "constitutes a great improvement in the definition of marginal productivity" (1937, p.77). While expectations of future returns can underlie Hicks' IS curve, this is not explicit and in fact Hicks had no discussion of any difference between Keynes' theory of investment and that of the classics.

Thirdly, Hicks focused attention on liquidity preference as the important difference between Keynes and the classics and stated that the equation embodying the consumption function and the multiplier "is a mere simplification and ultimately insignificant" (1937, p.152). Harrod, on the other hand states that

> "the most important single point in Mr Keynes' analysis is that it is illegitimate to assume that the level of income in the community is independent of the amount of investment decided upon" (1937, p.76).

A fourth difference lay in the treatment of the determination of prices. Hicks explicitly assumed a constant nominal wage rate and implicitly assumed that prices were determined by a mark-up on wages so that there was also a constant price level (1982, p.323). Harrod had a long discussion of the matter, but concluded that (in Keynes' theory) nominal wages and the level of activity determined the money cost of production and that this in turn determined prices through marginal cost pricing "with suitable modifications for imperfect competition" (1937, p.82).

This difference in the way prices are determined means that aggregate supply had a role to play in Harrod's model, whereas it is virtually absent in Hicks' model. If, for ease of exposition, we clothe Harrod's ideas in modern concept and terminology, we can say that since Harrod assumed a quantity of money fixed in nominal terms, the higher the price level associated with any given level of real output, the higher the rate of interest. Harrod assumed that because of declining productivity and an increasing proportion of wages paid at overtime rates the general price level rose as the level of real output increased. In other words the aggregate supply schedule showed the price level rising as real output rose. Hence a higher level of output was associated with a higher interest rate, not only because of the shape of the liquidity preference function, but also because the quantity of money declined in real terms as output rose.

Given the marginal efficiency of capital schedule and the marginal propensity to consume, aggregate demand was given by the rate of interest. Equilibrium was reached when output is such that both the output and the resulting price level are consistent with the rate of interest which makes aggregate demand equal to that level of output. In Harrod's own words "the mutual interdependence of the whole system remains" (1937, p.83). In short, in Harrod the aggregate supply schedule played a significant role, whereas in Hicks it has all but disappeared since in Hicks' model the aggregate supply curve is horizontal (in price output space) at the exogenously determined price level.

While Keynes may not have consciously thought through the matter, each of these four differences probably partly explains the difference in his response to Harrod's paper as opposed to that of Hicks. Thus, a comparison of the papers of Hicks and Harrod has suggested four points to look for in considering what Keynes would have though of the development of ISLM. These are the use of general equilibrium analysis, the relative neglect of expectations, the importance of liquidity preference as opposed to the multiplier and the role played by aggregate supply. The marked difference in the degree of Keynes' enthusiasm for the two papers suggests that at least some of these four points must have been important to Keynes. In fact passages can be found in the *General Theory* that suggest Keynes, on reflection, would not be comfortable with any of these four aspects of Hicks' exposition. As we shall see in the next section the development of ISLM in the 1950s and 1960s emphasized three of the four points, but did not place the importance on liquidity preference, compared to the multiplier. that Hicks had done in 1937.

Before leaving Keynes' reaction to Harrod's paper one further point should be made. In his letter to Harrod, in commenting on things Harrod had left out, but which he himself would like to include, Keynes said

> "You don't mention *effective demand* or, more precisely, the demand schedule for output as a whole, except in so far as it is implicit in the multiplier. To me, the most extraordinary thing, regarded historically, is the complete disappearance of the theory of demand and supply for output as a whole" (1973b, emphasis in the original p.85).

That Keynes thought aggregate demand important is now a platitude. This quotation suggests that he also thought aggregate supply was far too important to be neglected.

9.4 KEYNES AND THE DEVELOPMENT OF ISLM IN THE 1950S AND 1960S

In the 1950s and 1960s ISLM was triumphant, both as an interpretation of what Keynes was saying in the *General Theory* and as the essential core of macroeconomics. It was correctly described, both in articles in professional journals and in textbooks, as a system of simultaneous equations whose solution gave the conditions necessary for an equilibrium situation. Those who actually read the *General Theory* recognised that Keynes had not presented a simultaneous equation system, but were more inclined to blame Keynes for not understanding the implications of what he was saying, than to acknowledge that, whatever the merits of ISLM, it was not an accurate representation of Keynes' theory. For example, in a paper published in the *American Economic Review* to mark the 25th anniversary of the *General Theory,* Harry Johnson complained about

> "Keynes's clumsy and misleading way of presenting what is essentially a general equilibrium model as a system of unidirectional causation. I refer to the order of analysis of the *General Theory,* in which income is defined as the sum of consumption and investment; consumption is determined by investment through the multiplier; investment is determined by the marginal efficiency of capital and the rate of interest; and the rate of interest is determined by liquidity preference and the quantity of money; but at the very last stage of the argument the level of income re-enters as a determinant of liquidity preference, so that the apparently simple line of causation from the demand for and supply of money to the interest rate to investment to consumption to income vanishes completely" (1961, p.4).

Johnson was so imbued with the general equilibrium approach to economics that he did not realize that Keynes had a system of uni-directional causation in substance, as well as in the way it was presented, and that this can be suitably represented by a recursive system, as was done earlier in this paper. This despite the fact that Wold (1954) had shown some years before that recursive systems can produce equilibrium situations just as much as simultaneous equation systems do.

However, the point here is not which is the best way to represent Keynes' theory, but that in the 1950s and 1960s a simultaneous general equilibrium system was taken to represent Keynes' theory of employment and output. It is useful to reinforce that point by quoting from a typical textbook since well regarded textbooks can be taken as presenting the conventional wisdom more surely than an original article, no matter how eminent the author. Ackley's *Macroeconomic Theory* has been selected as probably the most successful macro text book of the 1960s. In his presentation of ISLM Ackley makes it clear that it is a system of simultaneous equations that gives the conditions necessary for equilibrium. He states

> "Clearly at $r_0 y_0$ [the point of intersection of the IS and LM curves] both equilibrium conditions are satisfied: that saving equal investment and that the supply equal the demand for money. Any point on the line IS satisfies the first of these; any point on the line LM, the second; but only their intersection satisfied both conditions" (1961, p.370).

From the point of view of the economics of the *General Theory*, general equilibrium models have two problems. One is that they set out conditions necessary for equilibrium and hence say nothing about causation, about where the economy will be in the real world or what will be the likely effects of a specific change in policy at some actual point in time. Secondly the treatment of exogenous variables in general equilibrium analysis is completely incompatible with Keynes' approach.

We have already alluded to the first problem in our discussion of Keynes' theory of employment and output, but some elaboration is necessary. The emphasis in the use of the term equilibrium is different in general equilibrium theory to that in the *General Theory*. General equilibrium theorists tend to regard equilibrium as a situation in which all the actors plans are consistent so that no one's expectations are incorrect. Keynes thought short period expectations were usually largely correct, at least as far as output and employment were concerned. He spoke of unintended inventory investment or disinvestment as only momentary (1973b, pp.7 1-72). He thought that long period expectations were volatile. Hence, by the time that one knew whether or not they had proved to be correct it was probably irrelevant as they had changed in any case. He was just not interested in equilibrium as consistency of plans and fullfilment of expectations. For him the essence of an equilibrium situation was that it persisted and, in particular, of course, he was concerned about the persistence of unemployment.

This difference between Keynes and general equilibrium theory is not just a philosophical point, it is a very practical one. ISLM analysis can inform policy makers about the characteristics of a desired equilibrium situation, but there is nothing in it to tell them how to get there if the economy is not at that equilibrium situation. There was not in the 1950s and 1960s even much discussion of whether the equilibrium was stable, that is whether, if the economy reached it by chance or design, it was likely to stay there. In fact at the end of this era, Chang and Smyth (1972) show that the intersection of the IS and LM curves may not be a stable equilibrium position even with the plausible assumptions that "income changes at a rate proportional to excess demand in the goods market and ... the rate of interest changes at a rate proportional to excess demand in the money market" (p.372).

The basic problem is that general equilibrium models impart no information about an economy which is not in equilibrium. Of course, textbooks told "stories" about what happened when an exogenous variable changed throwing the economy out of equilibrium. However, the better ones were uneasy about this realizing that such "stories" are not, strictly speaking, supported by the theory that they have just expounded. For example, after tracing through the effects of a rise in the propensity to consume Ackley cautions

> "we tread perilously close to misleading statements in the foregoing, as well as being forced to bring dynamic considerations into what is supposed to be static analysis" (1961, p.372).

Keynes would have summarily rejected this kind of analysis. For him the whole point of theory was as a guide to policy, and especially in this case, policy with respect to employment. While he wanted to show that the economy did not automatically tend to full employment so that policy was necessary, he also wanted to show what policy actions were desirable, what was likely to move the economy from a situation with substantial unemployment to one of full employment. His theory did not aim to elucidate the conditions necessary for equilibrium but what determined the level of unemployment at any point in time. Hence, he would have been very critical of a theory that emphasized the conditions necessary for equilibrium.

Moreover, Keynes would have argued that the sort of presentation in Ackley (and virtually all the other textbooks of the time) was not just perilously close to being misleading, but was downright dangerous as being likely to lead to incorrect policy advice. This relates to the other problem of general equilibrium analysis, the treatment of exogenous variables, and can be neatly illustrated by contrasting Ackley's conclusions about the effects of an increase in the quantity of money with those of Keynes. Ackley sets out the standard analysis in which an increase in the quantity of money shifts the LM curve to the right. The new point of intersection with an unchanged IS curve is at a lower rate of interest and higher level of output. A summary of Keynes analysis of the effects of an increase in the quantity of money is contained in our earlier quotation about the effects of a reduction in money wage rates. To repeat, Keynes thought that

> "a moderate increase in the quantity of money may exert an inadequate influence over the long-term rate of interest, whilst an immoderate increase may offset its other advantages by its disturbing effect on confidence" (GT, pp.266-7).

In other words Keynes thought that an increase in the quantity of money could easily have no effect on output because it could, in ISLM terms, shift the IS curve as well as the LM curve. This reflects the difference between an exogenous variable and one that for the time being is included in the ceteris parabus assumption. The very name exogenous implies that such variables are outside the system and, their values can be changed at will in hypothetical cases to give useful insights into an actual economy. Variables under the ceteris parabus assumption are assumed constant for the purpose in hand. It is not assumed that their values can be changed at will. In discussing the demand curve for an individual commodity, say soap, it is often assumed that money income and the prices of all other commodities are held constant. This does not mean that it is useful to consider the effects of a large increase in money income on the demand for soap while keeping the assumption that the prices of all other commodities remain constant.

This difference between his way of thinking and the general equilibrium approach of ISLM was particularly important to Keynes, because he considered that there was one set of variables, assumed constant under the ceteris parabus assumption, whose values were likely to change if there were changes in the values of other variables assumed to be constant. This set was of course long period expectations. Keynes' discussion of the effects of a change in the quantity of money is an excellent example of the point. Keynes' emphasis on the key role of long period expectations was not part of his formal model but was a large part of the discussion in the *General Theory*. His emphasis is reflected in the complaint of some of his followers, most notably Joan Robinson, that ISLM neglects time. In a formal sense time has a large role in ISLM. The past is important as the determinant of the capital stock the state of technology and other factors. The future is important since expectations determine both the marginal efficiency of capital and liquidity preference. However, in ISLM both the past and expectations about the future are outside the model and can not be changed. For the past this is entirely appropriate, but at least in Keynes' view it is not appropriate for long period expectations. His stress on considering the way things may affect long period expectations would have made him critical of the way ISLM was used in the 1950s and 1960s.

Hicks' view that liquidity preference was more important than the multiplier as a distinguishing mark of Keynesian economics is not reflected in the way ISLM was used in the 1950s and 1960s, but his emphasis on aggregate demand rather than aggregate supply is. Indeed the assumption of a constant wage rate and mark up pricing, together with the implicit assumption of no rationing, make it impossible for aggregate supply to play a role in ISLM since the aggregate supply curve, drawn in price and outlet space, is horizontal at the exogenous price level. Keynes, in his letter to Harrod already quoted and elsewhere, maintained that he thought aggregate supply was important. Despite this there is little discussion of it in the *General Theory*. This may be because Keynes thought his aggregate; demand function was a new concept which needed a great deal of discussion whereas his aggregate supply function was "only a reconcoction of our friend the supply function" (1973a, p.513). It may also be that Keynes thought that the interesting things affecting aggregate supply were the state of technology and the capital stock which were already determined, could not be changed in the short period, and certainly should not be changed by policy in a way that would reduce unemployment in the short period. In any case it is likely he would have been disappointed that the use of ISLM in the 1950s and 1960s ignored the supply side completely, especially since in that period supply side issues were becoming increasing important compared to those on the demand side.

After a relatively lengthy discussion of the aspects of ISLM, as used in the 1950s and 1960s, which Keynes would have criticized, it is necessary to point out that, nevertheless, there were two features that Keynes would have found appealing. The first we have already alluded to, it is the clear-cut position that it is effective demand that determines the level of employment, not the balancing, at the margin, of the utility of wages against the disutility of work. Since we have already emphasized the importance Keynes gave to effective demand no more need be said on this point.

The second is that ISLM was used in the 1950s and 1960s in a way that stressed the effects of changes in the quantity of money on the real economy. As Keynes pointed out, in the letter to Hicks already quoted, a strict classical economist would not admit that a change in the quantity of money could have any effect on the level of employment or any other real variable. Keynes was keen to stress that it could. He stressed that the rate of interest was a monetary phenomenon (GT. Chap. 13. 1973b, p.80) and was proud to have reunited monetary theory with the rest of economic theory. He would surely have welcomed support for this in ISLM.

9.5 KEYNES AND THE DEVELOPMENT OF ISLM IN THE 1980S AND 1990S

Both these virtues that Keynes would have found in the way ISLM was used in the 1950s and 1960s largely disappeared in the way it was used in the 1980s and 1990s. Modem macroeconomics re-emphasized aggregate supply as well as aggregate demand, though it was a very different aggregate supply and demand analysis to that of Keynes. However, the majority of macroeconomists, both "neo-classical" and "neo-Keynesian" use ISLM as the basis of constructing an aggregate demand curve. The aggregate supply and aggregate demand curves are drawn on a graph with real output on the x axis and the general price level on the y axis. A fixed nominal supply of money is used so that for each price level there is a different real stock of money and a different LM curve. The aggregate demand curve plots the resulting equilibrium level of real output and income corresponding to each price level and its related LM curve. In the words of the very careful definition in one textbook, the aggregate demand curve

> "shows all the possible crossing points of a single IS commodity market equilibrium curve with all the various LM money market equilibrium curves drawn for each possible price level. Everywhere along the curve *both* the commodity and money markets are in equilibrium". (Gordon (1990, p. 159). Emphasis in the original).

We have already argued in the previous section that Keynes would have been critical of any analysis that assumes one can vary the value of one exogenous variable without considering the possible effects on other variables assumed to be held constant. Although the general price level is an endogenous variable in modern aggregate demand and supply analysis a similar argument applies. Whether the general price level is high or low may affect the values of variables assumed to be exogenous in the

ISLM analysis underlying the aggregate demand function. This is particularly likely in the case of the marginal efficiency of capital. Since last period's price is predetermined, each different price level represents a different rate of inflation. Keynes would have been very critical of a theory which maintained that the marginal efficiency of capital schedule does not change as the rate of inflation changes.

Secondly, Keynes would probably have stuck by his view that the concept of the general price level was too imprecise a measure to be of use in economic analysis. In the *General Theory* he commented that

> "to say that net output today is greater, but the price level is lower, than ten years ago or one year ago, is a proposition of a similar character to the statement that Queen Victoria was a better queen but not a happier woman than Queen Elizabeth—a proposition not without meaning and not without interest, but unsuitable as material for the differential calculus. Our precision will be mock precision if we try to use such partly vague and non-quantitative concepts as the basis of a quantitative analysis" (GT, p.40).

However, both these and the problems noted in the previous section that Keynes would have had with ISLM, pale into insignificance compared to the fact that in modern aggregate demand and supply analysis, ISLM is part of a theory which produces conclusions diametrically opposed to those of the *General Theory*. Not surprisingly this is most stark in the neo-classical version.

Again it is helpful to use a well regarded textbook to demonstrate the model in which ISLM is used. Parkin and Bade (1988) combine an aggregate demand curve based on ISLM, as described above, with a very classical (or neoclassical in modern terms) supply curve. In much of the analysis of the book the supply curve is drawn as vertical at the level of income corresponding to full employment output. Parkin and Bade think that this is the correct shape, both in the long run when, by definition, price expectations are correct, and also when any changes in prices are fully anticipated so that price expectations are correct in the short run. It is assumed that both the product market and the labor market are markets with flexible prices and that nominal wages will adjust to any price level so that the demand and supply of labor are equal. "If the price level doubled then the money wage would also have to double to preserve labor market equilibrium" (p.309). Output is determined solely by aggregate supply, as it is always at the level that obtains when there is equilibrium in the labor market, defined as occurring when the real wage rate is equal to the marginal disutility of work. Aggregate demand does not influence output (except possibly in the short run due to mistaken expectations) but is left to determine the price level and hence nominal wages.

Keynes would have completely rejected this as akin to the mistaken theories he was combating in the *General Theory*, only even less defensible. Not only does demand have no effect on the level of output, but the quantity of money also has little effect on the real economy.[7] The supply of money does affect aggregate demand and hence the price level. Not only would Keynes have rejected this outright, but he surely would have lambasted a theory in which the aggregate demand curve, based on ISLM, assumes a fixed nominal wage rate, but is combined with an aggregate supply curve which assumes that the nominal wage rate is perfectly flexible.

Parkin and Bade do allow for a case in which, due to mistaken price expectations on the part of employees the aggregate supply curve is not vertical. Hence aggregate demand can have some influence on the level of output, though the resulting equilibrium is temporary and can only last one period since by the end of the period the actual price level is known and the mistake realized.

This case is based on the assumption that, in any firm, employers have a good knowledge of their costs and the price of the firm's output, but employees often do not have a good knowledge of the price of wage goods in general. Hence, employees must make decisions on the basis of an expected real wage. It is assumed that both employers and employees know the money wage, so for employees the expected real wage is this money wage deflated by the expected price level. If employees expect a lower level of prices than actually occurs they will work for a lower actual real wage and employment and output will be higher than in the case when their expectations are correct. This last part follows because employers know both the money wage, their costs and the price of their product so that "the aggregate demand for labor depends on the *actual* economy-average real wage" (Parkin and Bade, 1984, p.327, Emphasis in the original). The result is an upward sloping supply curve with output increasing as prices increase, as long as prices expected by employees are held constant which can only be the case for one period at a time.

Keynes would have rejected this just as vehemently as he would the case of the vertical aggregate supply curve. Output is still determined by the level at which the marginal disutility of work is equal to the expected real wage. The aggregate demand curve is still based on ISLM which assumes that the nominal wage rate, the price level and hence the real wage rate are exogenous whereas the aggregate supply curve is based on a labor market with perfectly flexible wage rates. The glaring logical inconsistency still remains.

Although the neo-Keynesian aggregate supply curve is closer to the economics of the *General Theory*, Keynes would also have rejected the way it is combined with the same aggregate demand curve, based on ISLM, to determine output and the general price level. The very successful textbook by Dornbusch and Fischer (1987) will be used to provide an example of neo-Keynesian aggregate demand and supply analysis. Dornbusch and Fischer use the Phillips curve as the basis for the aggregate supply curve. They transform it from a relationship between employment and wage rates to one between output and prices by the use of a production function and the assumption of mark-up pricing. The resulting function, which is still about changes in output and prices, is then changed to a supply curve by transferring last periods' price to the right hand side of the equation where it joins last periods' output as a predetermined variable (1987, pp.477-480). In this model, in short period equilibrium real output and the general price level are determined jointly by aggregate demand and supply, but given the assumptions made about the quantity of money there is a strong tendency for real output to move to the full employment level which is defined as occurring when the rate of unemployment is consistent with a non-accelerating inflation rate.[8]

Keynes would have been critical of the way ISLM is used in the aggregate demand curve for the same reasons as he would have been in the neo-classical case. There is no difference between the neo-Keynesians and the neo-classical economists in their use of ISLM. Moreover, Keynes would have been dismayed that an analysis called Keynesian argued that the economy automatically returned to full employment.

9.6 CONCLUDING REMARKS

This paper has suggested a number of reasons why Keynes would have been critical of the way ISLM developed in the half century after his death. Three stand out as the most significant. The first is the use of ISLM in an analysis which argues that there is a strong tendency for an economy to return to full employment, especially since this type of analysis became dominant in the 1980s, the decade in which mass unemployment became a problem in most OECD countries.

The second is the neglect of aggregate supply in ISLM which led to its neglect in "Keynesian" economics generally in the 1950s and 1960s. Given the relative lack of discussion of aggregate supply in the *General Theory* this neglect is understandable. Keynes thought that he had little that was novel to say about aggregate supply, but he insisted that consideration of aggregate supply was important. If he had lived and kept at least some focus on aggregate supply in the 1950s and 1960s the discrediting of "Keynesian" economics, following stagflation in the 1970s, might not have occurred.

The third very significant difference between Keynes' approach and that of ISLM is the way time enters (or does not enter) into ISLM analysis and includes both the representation of Keynes' sequential analysis as a simultaneous equation system, and the neglect, in practice at least, of long period expectations. Keynes' formal model was not fully dynamic, but it did go further than comparative statics and lead easily into discussion of dynamic problems. Keynes though these important. The *General Theory*, he said, "has evolved into what is primarily a study of the forces which determine changes in the scale of output and employment as a whole" (GT, p.vii) and he commented favourably on the hints about a future dynamic theory at the end of Harrod's *Econometrica* paper (1973b, p.84).

Underlying this is the pervasive difference between Keynes' particular equilibrium, recursive method and the general equilibrium method of ISLM. Although he rejected the Cambridge School's use of Say's law and the quantity theory of money, Keynes' way of doing economics was fundamentally Marshallian. ISLM is not. Like most modern economic theory it is fundamentally Walrasian. As Friedman said of modern economic theory "We curtsy to Marshall, but we walk with Walras" (1953, p.89). But, as Friedman also pointed out, Keynes (himself as opposed to Keynesians) is an exception to this description (1953, p.92).

BIBLIOGRAPHY

Ashley, G. (1981), *Macroeconomic Theory*, New York, Macmillan.

Addison, J.T. and Burton, J. (1982), "Keynes's Analysis of Wages and Unemployment Revisited", *The Manchester School*, Vol. 50, No. 1, pp.1-23.

Chang, W. and Smyth, D. (1972), "Stability and Instability of IS-LM Equilibrium", *Oxford Economic Papers*, Vol. 24, No. 3, pp.372-84.

Dombusch, R. and Fischer, S. (1987), *Macroeconomics*, New York, McGraw-Hill.

Friedman, M. (1953), *Essays in Positive Economics*, University of Chicago Press.

Gordon, R.J. (1990), *Macroeconomics*, Boston, Little, Brown and Co.

Harrod, R.F. (1937), "Mr Keynes and Traditional Theory", *Econometrica*, Vol. 5, No.1 , pp.74-86.

Hicks, J.R. (1937), "Mr Keynes and the 'Classics': A Suggested Interpretation", *Econometrica*, Vol. 5. No. 2, pp.146-59.

Hicks, J. (1982), *Money, Interest and Wages, Collected Essays on Economic Theory*, Oxford, Basil Blackwell.

Johnson, H.G. (1961), "The General Theory after Twenty-Five Years", *American Economic Review*, Vol. 51, No. 2, pp.1-178.

Keynes, J.M. (1936), *The General Theory of Employment, Interest and Money*, London, Macmillan.

Keynes, J.M. (1973a), *The Collected Writings of John Maynard Keynes*, Vol. XIII, London, Macmillan.

Keynes, J.M. (1973b), *The Collected Writing of John Maynard Keynes*, Vol. XIV, London, Macmillan.

Nevile, J.W. and Rao, B.B. (forthcoming), "The Use and Abuse of Aggregate Demand and Supply Functions", *The Manchester School*.

Parkin, M. and Bade, R. (1988), *Modern Macroeconomics*, Oxford, Philip Allan.

Robinson, J. (1962), *Essays in the Theory of Economic Growth*, London, Macmillan.

Robinson, J. (1975), "What Has Become of the Keynesian Revolution" in Milo Keynes (ed), *Essays on John Maynard Keynes*, Cambridge University Press.

Wold, H. (1954), "Causality and Econometrics", *Econometrica*, Vol. 22, No. 2, pp. 162-97.

ENDNOTES

[*] The author would like to thank Peter Kriesler and John Lodewijks for commenting on a draft. The usual caveat applies.

[1] Page references preceded by GT are to any Macmillan edition of the *General Theory*.

[2] In his chapter "Notes on the Trade Cycle" this short period assumption was necessarily relaxed, as it was in discussion at other points in the *General Theory*. But the "Notes" and discussion remained just that and did not set out a formal model.

[3] For a summary of this discussion see Addison and Barton (1982).

[4] This is the case if output is measured on the *x* axis and expected deflated proceeds on the *y* axis.

[5] Particularly since Keynes thought that the rate of interest at the end of a period was unlikely to be so different from that holding at the beginning that a large change in investment occurred in the following period (GT, p.250).

[6] To be more exact, it was his one real criticism of Hicks' exposition of Keynes' theory. Keynes also criticises Hicks' version of classical economics as not being true to the genuine classical theory, but only to a slovenly modern version.

[7] It can affect the composition of output through its influence on the nominal interest rate.

[8] This is a very brief summary which does less than justice to Dornbusch and Fischer. For a detailed discussion see Nevile and Rao (forthcoming).

10

THE IS-LM MODEL: ITS ROLE IN MACROECONOMICS

L.R. Klein

10.1 INTRODUCTION

At the time of publication of J.M. *Keynes' General Theory of Employment, Interest, and Money* (New York or London, Harcourt Brace or Macmillan, 1936) the idea of mathematical modeling, especially in macroeconomics, was confined to a small group of mathematically-inclined economists, some of whom had just founded the Econometric Society. Ragnar Frisch, Michal Kalecki and a few others did for macroeconomics what Leon Walras and Vilfredo Pareto did for microeconomics; they formulated systems of equal numbers of equations and (endogenous) variables that would be able to determine the latter as solutions to simultaneous equations. They were seeking explanations of the business cycle during times of economic turmoil (stock exchange crashes and deep, prolonged depression).

Keynes dealt with the same problems, but paid less attention to cyclical dynamics and more to the depression. His analysis was brilliant but well understood mainly by economists in his narrow circle. A clear understanding of the Keynesian theory and message was provided through the medium of compact mathematical models that were capable of being solved for major macroeconomic magnitudes.

Among these mathematical renditions, including that of Kalecki, who independently anticipated Keynes' contribution, there were two outstanding contributions, one by Oskar Lange and the other by J.R. Hicks.[1]

These were both excellent presentations that clarified Keynesian ideas of the *General Theory*, but Hicks' paper produced the IS-LM diagram as a solution to a pair of equations in a pair of variables that served as a paradigm for the macro model that explained the determination of effective demand, in the aggregate. It was a beautiful virtuoso performance that stands on its simplicity, but a simplicity that escaped less nimble minds

$$\text{IS:} \quad I(r,Y) = S(r,Y) \quad r = \text{interest rate} \tag{1}$$

$$\text{LM:} \quad M = L(r,Y) \quad Y = \text{income aggregate} \tag{2}$$

Equation (1) is the equilibration between investment and savings (the *demand* for fixed capital and the *supply* of funds for financing the expansion of fixed capital, namely investment). Equation (2) is the equilibration of the demand for money balances and the (exogenous) supply of money balances by the monetary authorities.

The IS-LM diagram is the pair of *implicit* relations between r and Y, given by (1) and (2). If investment depends inversely on r, while savings depends positively, and if both investment and savings depend positively on Y with the savings slope in excess of the investment slope, then we shall find that the implicit relationship between r and Y defined by (1) should be negatively sloped. This accounts for the inverse relation between r and Y implied by (1). If money demand in (2) depends inversely on r and positively on Y, with M exogenously given, the implicit relation between r and Y from (2) will be positively sloped.

One curve slopes negatively in the r, Y plane, while the other slopes positively; this explains the fact that the curves normally are drawn so that they intersect in the positive quadrant, and the excess of the savings slope, w.r.t. Y, over the investment slope makes for stable equilibrium in the neighborhood of the point of intersection.

The positioning of the two curves depends on monetary and fiscal policy; that is another of the beautiful properties of this representation of the Keynesian system. The position of the LM curves in (2) depends directly on the (exogenous) money supply, set by the monetary authorities. This indicates the stance of monetary policy. In the investment-savings equalization in (1), we can split the investment magnitude into two additive parts, one being the endogenous response to r and Y, the other being the exogenous fixing of public expenditures on goods and services. This latter part of investment is set by fiscal policies of the treasury or budgetary authorities. A second dimension of fiscal policy is the tax-transfer system which can affect the separate slopes and positions of the two functions in (1) that imply the IS relationship.

We therefore find in the ISLM diagram the three pillars of the Keynesian system.

1. the propensity of save (or consume) in S(r,Y)
2. the marginal efficiency of capital in I(r,Y)
3. the liquidity preference relation in L(r,Y).

We also see, in two dimensions, their theoretical intersection in determining r and Y, as well as a means for policy evaluation.

But the ISLM approach has its problems, a deficiency. It makes sense in nominal terms, i.e. current priced investment, savings, and income. Also the interest rate is the nominal rate if the whole analysis is in nominal terms. This is all right for the problems of the 1930s, when these matters were being introduced. Large scale price changes were not the issue—not in fact and not for the situation of emergence from the recession. That is, however, a short run point of view. Once the economy entered a recovery phase in full swing, there were significant inflationary pressures within no more than 2 or 3 years. The recovery that did finally come was associated with World War II, an event that quite naturally carried many inflationary pressures in the process of restoring full employment. Even without all the trappings of a wartime mobilization economy, peacetime recovery would eventually have brought about some price rises.

Suppose that we take another route and think of the ISLM equations as a *real* system, stated without money illusion in terms of real investment, real savings, real income, real interest rate, and real money balances. In that case, the system would have to be stated as

(1')	IS:	$I(r - \Delta lnp, Y/p)$	=	$S(r - \Delta lnp, Y/p)$
(2')	LM:	M/p	=	$L(r - \Delta lnp, Y/p)$
		Δlnp	=	inflation rate
		$r - \Delta lnp$	=	real interest rate
		Y/p	=	real income
		M/p	=	real money balances

The problem is that we have 3 unknown (endogenous) variables, r, p, and Y but only two equations. In this case, if p is fixed and given, we have a system for determinate analysis, but this is not very satisfactory.

One approach for dealing with this problem is to add a pair of equations for real aggregate demand (AD) and real aggregate supply (AS), each depending on p, the general price level. In a separate diagram, the equating of AS and AD, each depending on p, provides a solution for p. This value is then supplied for the real ISLM diagram to determine real income and real interest rate, given real balances (M/p). The elegant simplicity of Hicks' original presentation is lost, and there is a problem in justifying

Aggregate demand = AD(p)

Aggregate supply = AS(p)

That is to say, one would be very hard put to derive these two functions explicitly from microeconomic principles and straightforward aggregation. Nevertheless, this is a popular pedagogical rendition.[2]

There is another way of dealing explicitly with the price-level problem, as it needs to be treated in connection with an ISLM analysis. My preferred route would be via the introduction of a wage-determination equation, known as the Phillips Curve, but present in economy wide econometric models since the latter part of the 1940s, and in theoretical analysis of Keynesian economics even earlier. This is not, however, an approach that lends itself to the great simplicity of Hicks' exposition.

If we enhance the ISLM model with equations for output, factor requirements, wage determination, and labor supply we can develop a theoretically based model that avoids the empirical short cuts of aggregate demand and aggregate supply, but we lose the graphical simplicity of ISLM analysis. We would need, schematically, such equations as production function: $Y/p = f(K,L)$ (3)

mark-up price formation: $p = g(rK/(Y/p), wL/(Y/p))$ (4)

wage equation: $\Delta \ln w = h((LF-L)/LF, \Delta \ln p)$ (5)

labor force: $LF = F(w/p)$ (6)

definition of capital: $\Delta K = I(r - \Delta \ln p, Y/p)$ (7)

K = fixed capital stock

L = employment

LF = labor force

w = wage rate

These five equations plus the two ISLM equations constitute a complete system to determine seven endogenous variables (r,Y,p, K, L, w, LF). The system represents a closed economy, and to make it open, with respect to the rest of the world, export and import equations would have to be introduced. That could be done in a variety of ways. The point of the extension, however, is to show how the demand-oriented ISLM model is related to the supply side of the economy, in which production and market determination of price level and wage level are included. Real variables and price ratios are introduced except in (5), where the relationship between w and p may not be proportional. Equation (5) is a dynamic bargaining or adjustment equation which need not be homogenous. This is the sense in which the Phillips Curve enables us to determine the price level.

Of course, the seven equations, although too complicated to be shown directly in two dimensions is enormously oversimplified. It is merely a stylized system. In actuality the model is large and complicated, consisting of hundreds or thousands of equations if it is to provide a suitable approximation to reality. That is what macroeconometrics is all about. Economists like simple bivariate relationships for pedagogical purposes, and simple models are very good in this respect, but they are not suited for the econometric application. All is not lost. however, for the beauty and simplicity of the ISLM exposition. It is possible, in many cases, to find the ISLM core of a large scale econometric model.[3]

In 1983, the Wharton Quarterly Model of the USA consisted of 1,167 equations, in 3 major parts.

1. A money demand equation relating nominal GNP and the nominal treasury bill rate to money balances—in this instance M_1 (exogenous). In this equation, there were also other variables such as real output growth, domestic asset stocks, and other interest rates.

2. A set of equations that related other interest rates to the treasury bill rate. These equations generated a spectrum of interest rates, much as a pure term structure (yield curve) does.

3. A remaining set of interdependent equations to determine real quantities and associated prices throughout the entire economy.

If the system were fully decomposable into one equation of the form

$$M_l = L(r, Y)$$

the procedure for constructing a plot of the underlying ISLM diagram would be straightforward, but since there are other variables in the liquidity preference equation (1), we must proceed approximately and iteratively to construct the ISLM diagram. As a first step, we fix values for real output change and domestic asset holding. We choose most recently observed values for these variables, just prior to the period for which the ISLM diagram is being constructed.

To establish the LM curve, we plot values of GNP_t for a sequence of assumed values for r_t . The values for the other interest rates that are needed in order to position this curve are easily obtained from their relationships to r_t . By choosing an entire sequence of values for r_t , given M_{lt}, we can calculate the corresponding values for GNP_t . We connect the sequence of points (r_t , GNP_t) in order to show the curve—in shape and in position.

The remaining equations in (3) can be solved for GNP_t , given r_t, . This is done for several values of r_t and a curve connects the solution, points (r_t , GNP_t,). This is the IS curve. The two plotted curves intersect near the observed values of (r_{83}, GNP_{83}). The solution will be associated with some new values for real output growth and domestic asset holdings. These new values, determined at the tentative intersection point can be used to re-set the LM curve and find a new solution. This step can be iterated to see if a closer and closer approximation to (r_{83}, GNP_{83}) can be found. This would be an improvement in the realism of the ISLM diagram for 1983, but is of second-order significance in a practical sense.

The realistic ISLM Core of the large scale equation system (1, 167 equations) is shown in Figure1.

This shows that a simple, meaningful interpretation of a large-scale system exists, in the form of an ISLM model and the two curves are related to one another in a stable dynamic relationship, according to Hicks' criteria; the absolute value of the LM slope is smaller than that of the IS slope.[4]

Another empirical approach to ISLM analysis can be constructed directly, from estimation of the relevant equations in a small system of four equations, based on nominal values alone. This has the advantage of compactness and simplicity but will track realistic values of the relevant variables over time less accurately than the large system of hundreds or thousands of equations.

The sample database for the direct estimation of the model is by annual observations, USA, 1960-86. The estimated equations are:

Figure 1. ISLM Curves, Wharton Quarterly Model 1983.

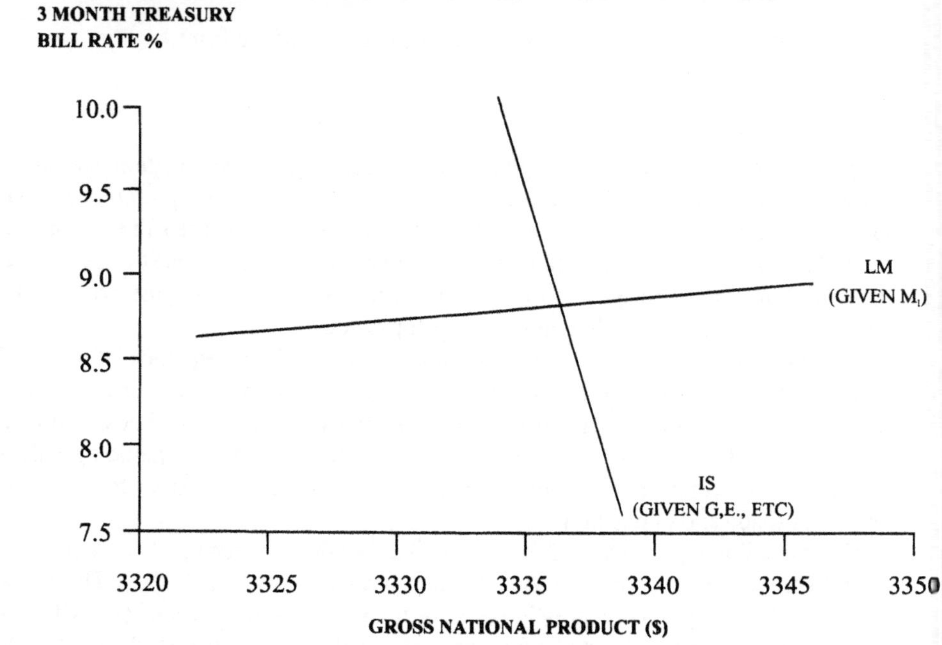

Consumer spending

$$C_t = \underset{(2.77)}{-0.011}\ \frac{r_t}{r_{r-1}} + \underset{(80.55)}{0.371}\ \frac{Y_t - T_t}{Y_t} + \underset{(80.55)}{0.278}\ \frac{Y_{t-1} - T_{t-1}}{Y_{t-1}} + \underset{(80.55)}{0.185}\ \frac{Y_{t-2} - T_{t-2}}{Y_{t-1}} + \underset{(80.55)}{0.093}\ \frac{Y_{t-3} - T_{t-3}}{Y_{t-3}}$$

$$AR(1) = 0.816,\ R^2 = 0.808,\ DW = 1.82$$

Gross capital formation

$$I_t = -\underset{(2.32)}{0.359} - \underset{(0.31)}{0.00235}\ \frac{r_t}{r_{t-1}} - \underset{(0.31)}{0.00176}\ \frac{r_{t-1}}{r_{t-2}} - \underset{(0.31)}{0.00118}\ \frac{r_{t-2}}{r_{t-3}}$$

$$\underset{(0.31)}{-0.000588}\ \frac{r_{t-3}}{r_{t-4}} + \underset{(3.23)}{0.193}\ \frac{Y_t}{Y_{t-1}} + \underset{(3.23)}{0.145}\ + \frac{Y_{t-1}}{Y_{t-2}} + \underset{(3.23)}{0.097}\ \frac{Y_{t-2}}{Y_{t-3}} + \underset{(3.23)}{0.048}\ \frac{Y_{t-3}}{Y_{t-4}}$$

$$R^2 = 0.319,\ DW = 1.38$$

Imports

$$(IM)_t = \underset{(7.28)}{0.390} + \underset{(1.91)}{0.106}\frac{Y_t}{Y_{t-1}} + \underset{(1.91)}{0.080}\frac{Y_{t-1}}{Y_{t-2}} + \underset{(1.91)}{0.053}\frac{Y_{t-2}}{Y_{t-3}} + \underset{(1.91)}{0.027}\frac{Y_{t-3}}{Y_{t-4}}$$

$$R^2 = 0.939,\ DW = 2.74$$

Taxes

$$T_t = \underset{(2.53)}{14.208} + \underset{(109.40)}{0.291} Y_t$$

$$R^2 = 0.998,\ DW = 1.17$$

Liquidity preference

$$r_t = \underset{(1.76)}{-8.199} + \underset{(3.33)}{2.638}\frac{Y_t}{M_{1t}}$$

$$AR(1) = 0.657,\ R^2 = 0.775,\ DW = 1.33$$

GNP definition

$$Y_t = C_t + I_t + X_t - (IM)_t + G_t$$

The liquidity preference equation is written as r_t is a function of M_1 – velocity. Instead of introducing the savings function directly, we have consumption functions, which when subtracted from [Y (GNP current value) less taxes] provide a derived estimate of savings. Also, domestic investment is estimated using gross rather than net investment values. The system is open, by virtue of an import equation, but exports are treated as though they are exogenous.

This is an interesting model, from which an ISLM diagram can be constructed very easily. It is defective, however, in the following respects:

(a) Investment is weakly related to interest rate; the coefficients are not *significant*

(b) There is serial correlation remaining in some of the estimated equations.

(c) Exports are not truly exogenous.

(d) The system is not homogeneous in prices and incomes.

It has some redeeming features. It is partially open. Lag structures have been estimated where appropriate. It has explicit taxation. An ISLM diagram is implied by this system.

A nice pedagogical feature is that by replacing the liquidity preference equation by a trend version of the quantity equation $\frac{Y_t}{M_{1t}} = 3.441 + 0.139t$.

We can examine contrasts between two main schools of thought in macroeconomics.[5] An essential difference between the Keynesian and Monetarist schools of thought is the dependence of velocity (Y/M_1) in the former on interest rate but lack of such independence in the latter.

This small system, specified and estimated directly is a good teaching device that can be used by students at all levels—beginning undergraduates to advanced post graduates. For the former, it is good for teaching the elements of simulation, forecasting, and standard multiplier analysis, all exemplified in an ISLM diagram. It is not as rich in policy choice or scenario specification as the large system from which a core, of ISLM dimensions, can be derived. For the latter, it serves as a good vehicle for learning about stochastic simulation, extension to a more general economy, and possibly for respecifying in a better nonlinear form. It is, however, just a pedagogical device that is realistic.

10.2 CONCLUSION

In this essay, the stress has been on realism. The ISLM construct is enduring and very useful, especially as a pedagogical device. It is relatively easy to explain and use; software is readily available to solve small systems and interpret the results in terms of the ISLM diagram.

Originally, the concept was introduced by J.R. Hicks without numerical parameter values and without regard to the correspondence between observation and theory. The purely theoretical contribution is large and readily available, but it is much better to present this device in meaningful numerical values for parameters, exogenous variables, and endogenous variables. Systems that are carefully fitted to observed data and capable of generating realistic values are far better for teaching purposes and "quick" analysis in carefully constructed research environments.

ENDNOTES

[1] Oskar Lange, "The Rate of Interest and the Optimum Propensity to Consume," *Economica*, N.S. 5 (February 1938), 12-32. J.R. Hicks, "Mr Keynes and the 'Classics,' A Suggested Interpretation," *Econometrica*, 5 (April 1937), 147-159.

[2] See R. Jeffrey Green. Bert G. Hickman. E. Philip Howrey, Saul H. Hymans. and Michael R. Donihue. "The IS-LM Cores of Three Econometric Models," *Comparative Performance of US Econometric Models*, ed. L.R. Klein (New York, Oxford University Press, 1991), 89-124.

[3] See the reference in fn. 2, above.

[4] J.R. Hicks. *A Contribution to the Theory of the Trade Circle* (Oxford. Clarendon Press, 1950), 145-54.

[5] Students using the ISLM model constructed in this way. will be able to see how monetarists'' strong reliance on a stable trend in M_1, velocity had to cope with the hard facts of life when institutional change, in the form of financial innovation, changed monetary behavior.

INDEX

GPSR Compliance

The European Union's (EU) General Product Safety Regulation (GPSR) is a set of rules that requires consumer products to be safe and our obligations to ensure this.

If you have any concerns about our products, you can contact us on ProductSafety@springernature.com

In case Publisher is established outside the EU, the EU authorized representative is:

Springer Nature Customer Service Center GmbH
Europaplatz 3
69115 Heidelberg, Germany

Batch number: 10761599

Printed by Printforce, the Netherlands